Environment and Agriculture in a Developing Economy

Environment and Agriculture in a Developing Economy

Problems and Prospects for Bangladesh

Mohammad Alauddin

School of Economics, The University of Queensland, Australia

Mosharaff Hossain

Former Professor of Economics, University of Dhaka, Bangladesh

Edward Elgar
Cheltenham, UK • Northampton, MA, USA

Published by
Edward Elgar Publishing Limited
Glensanda House
Montpellier Parade
Cheltenham
Glos GL50 1UA
UK

Edward Elgar Publishing, Inc.
136 West Street
Suite 202
Northampton
Massachusetts 01060
USA

A catalogue record for this book
is available from the British Library

Library of Congress Cataloguing in Publication Data
Alauddin, Mohammad, 1951–
    Environment and agriculture in a developing economy: problems and prospects for Bangladesh / Mohammad Alauddin and Mosharaff Hossain.
        p.cm
    1. Agriculture—Environmental aspects—Bangladesh. 2. Economic development—Environmental aspects—Bangladesh. 3. Agriculture—Economic aspects—Bangladesh. 4. Land use, Rural—Bangladesh—Management. 5. Agrobiodiversity conservation—Bangladesh. I. Hossain, Mosharaff. II. Title.

S589.76.B36 A43 2001
338.1'095492—dc21

                                                                        2001023721

ISBN 1 84064 043 X
Printed and bound in Great Britain by MPG Books Ltd, Bodmin, Cornwall

This book is dedicated to the memory of Bangabandhu Sheikh Mujibur Rahman without whose indomitable courage, total commitment to the cause of Bangladesh and life-long sacrifice, the people of Bangladesh would not have succeeded in realising their dream of an independent homeland.

Contents

Tables

Figures

Preface

This book examines the process of agricultural development in Bangladesh over a period of nearly five decades. It applies new points of view in economic thought about development and the environment and uses case study materials. It outlines and examines the major issues and challenges that face Bangladesh agriculture. This volume also examines the prospects for Bangladesh's sustaining agricultural production, taking into account the complex socio-economic, natural and environmental issues that surround Bangladesh agriculture. Particular issues such as sustainable resource use in agriculture are critically examined. This book emphasizes the importance of distributional aspects of environmental change and development in relation to employment and poverty. The agricultural economy of Bangladesh provides a useful case study of peasant agriculture under conditions of grinding poverty, intense pressure on land, a fragile environment, a narrow resource–base and a complex set of socio-economic and natural factors. Many of the issues that arise in Bangladesh in connection with the agriculture–environment nexus are not unique to it. Parallels exist elsewhere in the developing world and such similarities are noted. This is the first comprehensive study of its kind on Bangladesh agriculture.

The authors owe a special debt to Mr Akhter Hamid for his generous assistance at every stage of the process of writing, including drawing of complex diagrams. Research assistance by Dr Nilufar Jahan, Mr Abu Taher Mollik, Mr Abul Hossain, Miss Farhanaz Alauddin and Mr Nirmal Saha is also acknowledged. Dr Dorothy Jauncey deserves special thanks for copy-editing. We also wish to thank Ms Kay Dancey for excellent production of maps. The usual disclaimer applies.

A major part of the work relating to this volume was completed at The University of Queensland and at the Australia South Asia Research Centre (ASARC), Research School of Pacific and Asian Studies, Australian National University. We wish to express our thanks to these institutions for the use of facilities.

In relation to his contribution, Mohammad Alauddin would like to express his profound gratitude to Professor Clem Tisdell and Dr Richard Shand for support and encouragement. Mohammad Alauddin would further like to express his gratitude to Professors Anthony Chisholm, Gordon Conway, John Foster, Geoffrey Harcourt, John W. Mellor, W. Brian Reddaway, Vernon W. Ruttan,

S.K. Saha, and Dr Mustafa K. Mujeri for their encouragement for research in this area.

We are grateful to Edward Elgar Publishing Ltd. especially to Mr Edward Elgar for accepting our manuscript and extending the deadline for its completion. Thanks are also due to Alison Edwards, Alex Minton, Emma Meldrum and Julie Leppard for assistance at various stages.

Mohammad Alauddin would like to thank Mrs Amy Lindley, Mrs Marie Keynes, Mrs Barbara Dempsey, Mr Robert Harrison and Ms Margaret Cowan for useful assistance at various stages of this research.

Mohammad Alauddin wishes to thank his wife Ruba, and daughters Farzana and Farhanaz for their patience, encouragement and understanding that contributed significantly toward the completion of the book. Mosharaff Hossain wishes to thank his wife Inari and sons Zafar and Raza and daughters-in-law Kashfia and Zakia for their support and understanding.

1. Bangladesh's Economy, Agriculture and the Environment: Perspectives and Issues

1.1 INTRODUCTION

The old land of Bangladesh emerged as a new nation state more than a quarter of a century ago. Few countries on this planet started their journey at greater disadvantage than Bangladesh. At its birth Bangladesh was beset with problems inherited from decades of underdevelopment. Bangladesh's quarter century union with Pakistan embodied all the hallmarks of internal colonization: years of neglect, regional dualism and consistent attacks on the cultural rights of the *Bangalees* (R. Jahan, 1972). Significant and widening economic disparities between the Eastern and Western wings of Pakistan epitomized (united) Pakistan's growth and development (Sobhan, 1993; Bose, 1970; PPC, 1970). Prior to that, Bangladesh suffered 200 years of British colonial exploitation. Furthermore, the circumstances under which Bangladesh was born created a new set of problems in the form of, *inter alia,* rehabilitation of the inadequate and badly damaged physical infrastructure and ten million refugees (N. Islam, 1974; Khan, 1972). These issues, however, were ephemeral (Robinson, 1973) compared to the longer term development problem of Bangladesh extricating itself from a low-level equilibrium trap reflecting, among other things, grinding poverty, mass illiteracy, widespread deprivation of the basic necessities of life, low level of industrial development, poor health and sanitation.

During the years immediately following independence, Bangladesh was labelled as a *test case* for development implying that the Bangladesh case represented 'the world's most difficult problem of economic development. ... If the problem of Bangladesh can be solved, there can be reasonable confidence that less difficult problems of development can also be solved' (Faaland and Parkinson, 1976, p. 5).

Since these early days of independence, Bangladesh has experienced significant political, social, environmental and economic changes (Alauddin and Hasan, 1999). While these changes have not been an unmixed blessing, Bangladesh's economic and social progress since independence has been

1

significant (Tisdell, 1999). Above all, Bangladesh's belief in its capacity to do better is firm (Shand, 1996).

In the light of this background, the present volume examines the agricultural development–environment nexus. This chapter provides an analytical overview of the issues considered and the plan and design of this volume.

1.2 GROWTH AND CHANGE IN THE BANGLADESH ECONOMY: AN ANALYTICAL OVERVIEW

Over the last few decades, the economy of Bangladesh has undergone significant structural changes. Agriculture's share in gross domestic product (GDP) has declined from around 50 per cent in the early 1970s to just over 30 per cent in recent years (BBS, 1998b), but it still provides employment to about 60 per cent of the labour force (World Bank, 1997). Bangladesh has had considerable success in reducing its rate of population growth from over 2.5 per cent until the late 1970s to 1.6 per cent during the 1990–95 period (Tisdell, 1999, p. 19). This compares favourably with the performance of India and Pakistan in respect of population control (Tisdell, 1999). Bangladesh, however, remains an aid-dependent economy with aid disbursements as a percentage of GDP being higher than 6 per cent.

Significant changes have taken place in the occupational structure and composition of the labour force with an increasing number of women being employed in the formal sector, notably the ready-made garment industry (Majumder and Zohir, 1994). There have been noticeable changes in the structure of foreign trade with a discernible trend away from Bangladesh's traditional dependence on jute-based items. Ready-made garments constitute the single most important foreign exchange earner. In recent years garment exports have accounted for around two-thirds of Bangladesh's total export earnings (Alauddin, 1997; Shand and Alauddin, 1997). Manufactured goods account for nearly 90 per cent of Bangladesh's merchandise exports in recent years compared to 60 per cent in the late 1970s (Alauddin, 1999a). Despite a momentous decline in the share of primary exports, there has been a substantial growth of processed primary goods through the exports of frozen fish and shrimps and leather products especially footwear. However, 'the changing composition of Bangladesh's exports could be interpreted more as a process of two groups of items (shrimp and ready-made garments) replacing two others (raw jute and jute manufactures respectively) rather than heralding a process of real export diversification' (Alauddin, 1997, p. 105). Bangladesh's export trade rests not only on a narrow base but also represents an increasing degree of both market concentration and export commodity concentration (M.I. Hossain *et al.*, 1997).[1]

While the growth and changes in Bangladesh have been central to supporting a growing population they have not resulted in a significant rise in the living standards of the mass of population. Bangladesh is characterized by significant manifestations of, *inter alia,* mass poverty, illiteracy, malnutrition, deprivation and poor sanitation. Thus, Bangladesh still remains quite low in the development ladder both in terms of per capita income and human development index (UNDP, 1999).

Several measures (see Chapter 11 for further detail) of human development based primarily on the conceptual underpinnings of the human development index suggest that the countries of the South Asian region, especially Bangladesh, perform poorly relative to East and Southeast Asian countries where demographic transition took root several decades ago. South Asia is yet to come anywhere near that stage (Chakravarty, 1990; A. Sen, 2000), the recent East and Southeast Asian economic crises notwithstanding.

One of the disappointing aspects of Bangladesh's development process is that the manufacturing sector has not been a significant contributor to GDP. Bangladesh is the least industrialized of all the four major countries in South Asia. The decline in the relative share of the agricultural sector has not been matched by any significant increase in the relative share of the manufacturing sector. As of 1994, manufacturing contributed only 10 per cent (18 per cent by industry) to GDP compared to 30 per cent by agriculture and a very high 52 per cent by the services sector. One should exercise some caution in this disproportionately large share of the services sector (Lewis, 1966)[2].

Bangladesh's GDP has grown at a sluggish pace over the last decade and a half. During the 1991–96 period real GDP growth rate averaged 4.3 per cent per annum which is lower than the annual average growth rate of 4.8 per cent achieved during the 1980s. 'The 4 per cent syndrome has persisted for almost 15 years regardless of the political regimes. In recent years, however, there are more promising signs. From 1966 to 1998, growth has consistently topped 5 per cent, averaging 5.6 per cent' (Shand, 1999a, p. 36).

1.3 BANGLADESH AGRICULTURE: AN OVERVIEW

Consistent with the changes mentioned above, Bangladesh's agricultural sector has also undergone significant transformation in the last few decades.

In the first place, a productivity-based production spearheaded by the seed-fertilizer-irrigation technology popularly known as the 'green revolution', has replaced area-based production. This has led to significant changes in the physical environment (Brandon, 1998). Major environmental changes have occurred in rural Bangladesh in recent decades due mainly (but not exclusively) to the green revolution in agriculture and associated population increases. According to Alauddin and Tisdell (1998, p. 114) the green revolution technologies involve:

- The introduction of high yielding but environmentally sensitive crop varieties
- Greater irrigation and water control for crops
- Increased use of chemical fertilizers and pesticides
- Greater mechanization of agriculture
- A rise in the incidence of multiple cropping and in general intensification of agriculture.

Significant environmental change has accompanied each of the above factors (Ahmad and Hasanuzzaman, 1998). The introduction of high-yielding varieties (HYVs) of rice have crowded out traditional varieties many of which have been lost because of their displacement, thereby reducing biological diversity. The need for water supplies, especially in the dry season, has led to the construction of dams and barrages with adverse consequences for fishing and navigation. Underground water supplies have also been affected, for example, 'excessive' pumping of water from underground sources has had undesirable effects on available supplies (Alauddin and Tisdell, 1998). In some areas, salinization and arsenic contamination of soil or water has become a serious problem (Jahan, 1998). The use of artificial fertilizer has resulted in acidification of some soils and loss of organic matter (Jahan, 1998; A. Islam, 1993; BBS, 1999a) especially when combined with multiple cropping and use of mechanical equipment (Mahtab and Karim, 1992). The use of pesticides has caused the loss of useful insects as well as pests. In some areas, for example, Chittagong Hill Tracts, forest loss has increased, so adding to soil erosion. One could easily add to this catalogue of adverse environmental changes in rural areas. These changes have all to some degree involved a loss of natural resources.

Secondly, significant changes have taken place in the policy area (Raisuddin Ahmed, 1998) from a highly regulated agricultural input market in the 1960s and early 1970s to a completely deregulated one, two decades later. This has led to a greater penetration of market forces. One manifestation of this process is that private property rights have been extended and/or are being more rigorously enforced and common or community access to natural resources has decreased and/or the natural supply of such resources, for example, fish, has declined (Asaduzzaman and Toufique, 1997). Consequently, there may be less opportunities for the landless or functionally landless to use natural resources, for example, to collect fodder for their animals from communal land or to obtain free water supplies. A vicious environmental cycle seems to have emerged in parts of India and in Bangladesh, especially the west of Bangladesh where natural gas supplies are yet to be available[3]. Demand for bricks has increased for housing and road building, placing increased strain on natural fuel supplies used in the baking of bricks. At the same time, heightened demands on remaining natural areas, for example woodland, have made it more difficult to maintain supplies of fuel from such areas. Furthermore, inland fisheries have not only suffered from over-harvesting but also from unfavourable external effects from the development of agriculture and associated capital works.

New agricultural technologies and the concomitant growth of the market system and its overall impact on the economy have encouraged greater specialization in production, a reduction in the degree of subsistence farming and an increase in road building to enable marketing to take place at reduced cost. Consequently, social relationships have come to be guided increasingly by market-oriented self-interest rather than by custom or social exchange (Alauddin and Tisdell, 1991).

These changes have had a significant impact on Bangladesh agriculture in terms of increased physical production of crop output especially food-grains and socio-economic and environmental changes. This volume concentrates on the changes and their ramifications for Bangladesh agriculture over a period of nearly five decades. The process of Bangladesh's agricultural development is critically analysed in terms of productivity growth, property rights, environmental and ecological sustainability, poverty, and income distribution. Gender issues in development are given particular emphasis.

1.4 OUTLINE OF ISSUES CONSIDERED IN THIS VOLUME

The economy of Bangladesh is overwhelmingly agricultural and it is this sector that manifests significant incidence of poverty. The agricultural economy of Bangladesh provides a useful case study of peasant agriculture under conditions of grinding poverty, a dwindling supply of arable land per capita and a complex set of socio-economic and natural factors. While many of these problems including environmental issues typify many less developed countries (LDCs) throughout the Third World, few countries face a greater challenge of development than Bangladesh. An intense pressure on land and a fragile environment, narrow resource-base and a declining stock of natural resources complicate the problems even further.

Against this background, the present volume critically investigates the process of agricultural development in terms of its achievements, predicaments and prospects, concentrating primarily on Bangladesh but also considering comparative scenarios from other LDCs wherever applicable and appropriate.

Chapter 2 highlights the physical environment that characterizes Bangladesh agriculture. This chapter provides a comprehensive picture of land use and cropping patterns as well as soil types and broad agro-ecological zones

(Bramer, 1997). These provide an aid to understanding the physiographic and environmental complexities that surround Bangladesh agriculture.

Chapter 3 investigates the changes that have taken place in Bangladesh agriculture and analyses the impact of technological changes on crop output growth (Abdullah and Shahabuddin, 1997). Aggregate time series data are employed to examine growth in cereals and non-cereals and the implications thereof.

Chapter 4 examines the extent to which growth in crop production has led to increased availability of food in terms of dietary balance and nutritional standards. The question of overall food supply and self-sufficiency is critically examined using trends in per capita availability of cereal and non-cereal food items. Trends in import dependency are also examined. Earlier studies indicated that the potential gains from the green revolution appear to have been swallowed up in supporting a larger population rather than in improving living standards for the masses. To what extent does this phenomenon still persist? Or has this trend been reversed?

Chapters 5–7 analyse the performances of the non - crop sub - sectors – livestock, forestry and fisheries in some detail (Alam, 1997). These chapters employ available information for obtaining a broad picture in these sub-sectors over the years. It is argued that performances of these sub-sectors are as critical for the determination of the living conditions of the rural people as that of the crop sub-sector. This is because animal husbandry, fishing and tree growing are as much a part of the farming system of Bangladesh as crop production. Poultry, goats and cattle are bred and reared by the same peasant households who cultivate the fields and grow rice and other crops. While the planners try to plan for a better future for the rural people, they have to design programmes in such a way that both the crop and the non-crop sub-sectors can be developed simultaneously until industrial development leads to a complete or at least significant transformation of labour absorption patterns.

Chapter 8 examines agrarian relations and property rights issues. It proceeds first of all with an analysis of these in a historical context. Land distribution patterns are analysed employing various agricultural census data. Some implications are also discussed.

Chapter 9 explores the linkages between agricultural growth and environmental changes. In the first place it provides an overview of the current state and trends in Bangladesh's rural environment. Earlier studies (Alauddin and Tisdell, 1991) found that since the introduction of the green revolution there has been a comparative crowding out of non-cereals.

Chapter 9 further investigates the linkage between agricultural growth, resource use and the environment with special emphasis on land and water, two fundamental resources used in agriculture. Both of these resources are under considerable strain due to various factors including, *inter alia*, intensive agricultural practices, widespread deforestation in upstream areas, soil erosion, siltation, inadequate recharge of aquifers, dumping of effluents in the river system, loss of tree cover and inappropriate government policies. These factors have affected both the quantity and quality of water. Trends in the use of ground and surface water are analysed. This is followed by an analysis of environmental implications of agricultural resource use. Implications of these for sustainable livelihoods are critically examined (Alauddin and Tisdell, 1998).

Chapter 10 examines the role of research and extension in agricultural development of Bangladesh. This chapter portrays a brief history of agricultural research and extension in Bangladesh and presents a critical appraisal of their current state of play. The role of international research organizations is also analysed (Alauddin and Tisdell, 1986). This is followed by an analysis of the contribution of agricultural research to productivity growth.

Chapter 11 examines the relationship between agricultural growth and rural poverty in Bangladesh. Trends and the nature of rural poverty are discussed with particular emphasis on gender dimensions of rural poverty. The environment–poverty nexus is also explored. Farm-level evidence is employed in analysing such issues. The present study takes a broader view of poverty and deprivation (Bernstein, 1992; A. Sen, 2000).

Chapter 12 presents concluding overview and comments.

1.5 THE DESIGN OF THE VOLUME

This volume explores the environment–agriculture relationship focusing primarily on Bangladesh. The study takes stock of achievement to date and identifies the challenges and prospects that lie ahead for Bangladesh agriculture. Factors both intrinsic to the agricultural sector and affecting key ancillary activities are also considered. Using a blend of primary and secondary data, the study focuses on:

- Growth and change in the crop sector
- Ancillary activities within the agricultural complex
- Environment–poverty nexus and gender issues
- Environmental implications of Bangladesh's agricultural development process

The study proceeds first by defining and identifying the broad parameters of the physical environment within which Bangladesh agriculture operates. Chapters 2–4 address the growth and changes that have taken place in the crop sector of Bangladesh and the question of overall food supply, especially food self-sufficiency. After a through investigation in Chapters 5–7 of the issues confronting the ancillary sectors – livestock, forestry and fisheries –

within the agricultural complex, property rights, the nexus between property rights and agrarian development are taken up for discussion in Chapter 8. Environmental consequences of agricultural development are discussed in Chapter 9. Issues relating to agricultural research and extension are addressed in Chapter 10. Agrarian change and rural poverty with especial emphasis on gender and environmental issues are analysed in Chapter 11. Chapter 12 pieces together the findings, identifies the challenges that lie ahead and assesses the prospects for Bangladesh agriculture.

1.6 CONCLUDING COMMENTS

Within the framework of this study, the relationship embracing poverty, gender issues and the environment is examined in the context of agricultural performance in Bangladesh. The study takes particular note of the process of a changing policy environment over a period of several decades. The study also notes Bangladesh's achievement to date and identifies some challenges that lie ahead. It is argued that past development processes have failed fully to appreciate the inextricable linkage between agricultural development and the environment. Many of the issues that arise in Bangladesh in the context of the poverty–gender–environment nexus are not unique to it. Parallels abound elsewhere in the developing world especially in other South Asian countries.

NOTES

1   According to I. Hossain *et al.* (1997, pp. 166–77), the Gini–Hirschman indices for Bangladesh's export trade in terms of both its commodity composition as well as market destination show a trend toward increasing degree of concentration over time. For example, the value of the index for net exports increased from 0.324 in 1991–92 to 0.386 in 1995–96. The concentration index for exports to all countries increased from 0.12 to 0.32 between 1979–80 and 1994–95. The value of the index for exports to Bangladesh's 15 major trading partners increased from 0.04 to 0.25 over the same period.

2   According to Lewis (1966, pp. 181–2) '... it is important to get the right balance between commodities and services, since if the service sector is too large, the demand for commodities will exceed the supply, and inflation and a balance of payments deficit will result'.

3   The fuel situation in these areas is likely to improve in the future following the installation of gap pipeline via the road/rail bridge over the Jamuna river.

2. The Physical Environment of Bangladesh Agriculture: Soil, Land and Physical Constraints

2.1 INTRODUCTION

Bangladesh is a delta formed by the confluence of three mighty rivers: Ganges, Brahmaputra and Meghna. Floods and other natural disasters periodically ravage the country (BBS, 1999a; Mosharaff Hossain *et al.*, 1987). The development of agricultural production depends critically on three physical factors: land, soil and water. This chapter highlights the physical environment that characterizes Bangladesh agriculture. It provides a picture of the soil types and broad agro-ecological zones, land use and cropping patterns, all of which provide an aid to understanding the physiographic and environmental complexities that surround Bangladesh agriculture.

2.2 CLIMATE AND PHYSIOGRAPHY

2.2.1 Climatic Zones

Following Rashid (1977) and BBS (1999a), Bangladesh can be divided into seven climatic zones as follows:

Zone 1: Northern part of the Northern Zone comprising most of the (greater) Dinajpur and (greater) Rangpur regions is characterized by extremes – very dry summer and very wet monsoon seasons. The mean summer temperature is in the low 30°C and there is a mean winter temperature of 10°C.
Zone 2: North-Western Zone comprising remaining parts of greater Rangpur and Dinajpur regions, most of (greater) Bogra, Pabna, and Kushtia districts with extremes less than in Zone 1 and with lower rainfall.
Zone 3: Western Dry Zone comprising Rajshahi and parts of adjacent districts. This is the driest part of the country with a mean annual rainfall below 1500 mm.

Zone 4: South-Western Zone comprising parts of (greater) Dhaka, Jessore, Kushtia, and Faridpur districts. The climatic pattern of this zone is similar to Zone 2 except for a higher mean annual rainfall, ranging between 1500 and 1800 mm.

Zone 5: South-Central Zone comprising most of (greater) Mymensingh, Faridpur, Dhaka and Comilla districts and parts of (greater) Jessore, Khulna and Barisal districts. It is characterized by milder temperatures and an annual rainfall of above 1900 mm.

Zone 6: North-Eastern Zone comprising (greater) Sylhet and northern parts of (greater) Mymensingh districts. It receives the highest annual rainfall ranging between 4000 and 5000 mm. Winter months receive some rain and are subject to early morning fog.

Zone 7: South-Eastern Zone comprising coastal districts, all of the Chattagong and Chittagong Hill Tracts regions and a small part of the north-western part of the (greater) Mymensingh district. It enjoys weather patterns similar to Zone 6 and the annual rainfall ranges between 2500 and 3500 mm.

Bangladesh has a humid sub-tropical monsoon climate with three distinct crop seasons:

Kharif 1: Lasting from the end of March to May is the hot spring or pre-monsoon season with moderate humidity. The temperature and evaporation rates are at their highest in this season. Rainfall occurs with occasional heavy thunderstorms and sometimes damaging hailstorms and cyclones may take place.

Kharif 2: The second *kharif* season or the hot monsoon season, covering the period from May to September, is characterised by high humidity and low solar radiation. More than 80 per cent of the total annual rainfall occurs in this period.

Rabi Season: Lasting from mid-October to early March is a cool, dry winter season. In this season, there is a negligible amount of rainfall, low humidity and high solar radiation.

2.2.2 Topographical Features

Hill, terrace and flood plain areas characterize the topography of Bangladesh. According to Bramer (1997, p. 4), the Northern and Eastern Hills comprise about 12 per cent, the terrace areas (the Madhupur and Barind Tracts) which are actually uplifted fault blocks, not river or marine terraces, comprise 8 per cent while the remaining 80 per cent consists of floodplains. The location of the main physiographic units in Bangladesh is set out in Figure 2.1, with respective areas (km^2) in parentheses.

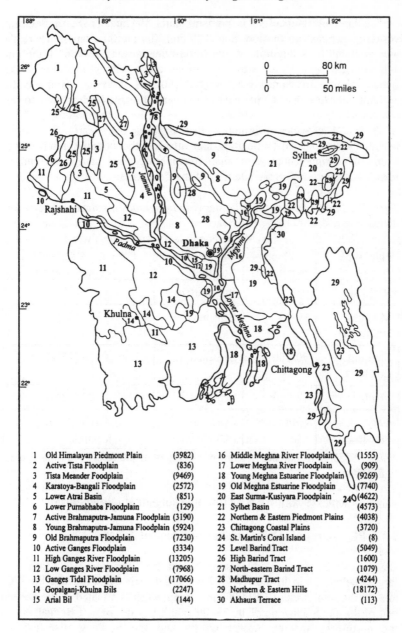

1	Old Himalayan Piedmont Plain	(3982)
2	Active Tista Floodplain	(836)
3	Tista Meander Foodplain	(9469)
4	Karatoya-Bangali Floodplain	(2572)
5	Lower Atrai Basin	(851)
6	Lower Purnabhaba Floodplain	(129)
7	Active Brahmaputra-Jamuna Floodplain	(3190)
8	Young Brahmaputra-Jamuna Floodplain	(5924)
9	Old Brahmaputra Floodplain	(7230)
10	Active Ganges Floodplain	(3334)
11	High Ganges River Floodplain	(13205)
12	Low Ganges River Floodplain	(7968)
13	Ganges Tidal Floodplain	(17066)
14	Gopalganj-Khulna Bils	(2247)
15	Arial Bil	(144)
16	Middle Meghna River Floodplain	(1555)
17	Lower Meghna River Floodplain	(909)
18	Young Meghna Estuarine Floodplain	(9269)
19	Old Meghna Estuarine Floodplain	(7740)
20	East Surma-Kusiyara Floodplain	(4622)
21	Sylhet Basin	(4573)
22	Northern & Eastern Piedmont Plains	(4038)
23	Chittagong Coastal Plains	(3720)
24	St. Martin's Coral Island	(8)
25	Level Barind Tract	(5049)
26	High Barind Tract	(1600)
27	North-eastern Barind Tract	(1079)
28	Madhupur Tract	(4244)
29	Northern & Eastern Hills	(18172)
30	Akhaura Terrace	(113)

Sources: Adapted from Bramer (1997, p.7) and BBS (1999a, p.78)

Figure 2.1 Physiographic units of Bangladesh

The land in Bangladesh is predominantly flat and prone to flooding, which may range up to more than 180 cm. The elevated lands, where the annual flooding is intermittent and floodwater ranges between 30 cm and 180 cm, are suitable for growing various crops with primary irrigation. Lands where floodwater rises above 180 cm become unsuitable for agriculture. More than 12 per cent of the net cultivable land belongs to this category.

Table 2.1 provides information that suggests that nearly six million hectares are subjected to flooding annually and the flooding depth ranges from 30 centimetres to more than two metres. Five land types can be identified depending on the intensity of the flood depth.

Table 2.1 Land type and flooding depth in Bangladesh: nature, intensity and extent

Land type	Flood depth (cm)	Nature of flooding	Net cultivable land (in million hectares)
Highland	0-30	Intermittent	3.514 (37%)
Medium Highland	30-90	Seasonal	3.288 (34%)
Medium Lowland	90-160	Seasonal	1.558 (16%)
Lowland	180-300	Seasonal	1.124 (12%)
Very lowland	>300	Seasonal/ perennial	0.078 (8%)

Notes: Figures in parentheses are percentages of the total land area subject to flooding.

Sources: MPO (1986); Bramer (1997); Mosharaff Hossain (1991).

2.2.3 Physiographic Units and Agro-ecological Zones

Bangladesh enjoys a unique geographical position, being in effect, the largest deltaic plain in the world. Rivers and their estuaries take up 8200 km² of the total area of 140 000 km². Bangladesh is situated at the eastern end of the Indo-Gangetic plain. To the south lies the Bay of Bengal and to the north-east are the Assam ranges and the Shillong plateau. The Himalayas lie in the northwestern corner of the country. Tertiary folds branch off from the Himalayas and run to the south through southern Sylhet along the eastern border into Chittagong and Chittagong Hill Tracts. With the above exceptions, the country is largely a flat alluvial plain with mainly floodplain soils.

For the purposes of understanding the kind of agricultural activities undertaken in the country, Bangladesh can be divided into three major physiographic units: hills, terraces and floodplains. These three categories may be further classified into eight units: the hill areas (high hill ranges and low hill ranges), terrace areas (Madhupur Tract and Barind Tract), active floodplains, meander floodplains, estuarine floodplains, tidal floodplains, piedmont alluvial plains and basins. The physiographic units, their topographical features and associated risks are set out in Table 2.2

Table 2.2 Physiographic units, topographical features and associated risk

Physiographic units: The Hills
High hill ranges   *Location:* Chittagong Hill Tracts, Greater Chittagong and Sylhet districts.   *Features:* Underlain by sandstones, siltstones and shales of Tertiary and Quaternary ages. Rocks folded, faulted, and uplifted and then deeply dissected by rivers and streams. Steep to very steep slopes.   *Associated risk:* Severe to very severe risk of erosion (sheet gully and landslide) loss of organic matter and nutrients, dry-season droughts.
Low hill ranges   *Location:* Comilla, Brahmanbaria, Netrokona, Jamalpur.   *Features:* Gentle to very steep slopes.   *Associated risk:* Moderate to severe risk of erosion (sheet gully and landslide) loss of organic matter and nutrients, dry-season droughts, localized soil mining, flash flood and sedimentation in valleys.
Physiographic units: the terraces
Madhupur Tract   *Location:* Parts of greater Dhaka, Mymensingh districts.   *Features:* Underlain by unconsolidated clay of Tertiary age. Broken into several fault blocks, surface lying several metres above the floodplain. More dissected and more complex relief patterns than Barind Tracts.   *Associated risk:* Loss of organic matter, nutrient depletion sheet erosion, severe dry season droughts, seasonal shallow to deep flooding valleys.
Barind Tract   *Location:* Parts of greater Rajshahi, Dinajpur, Rangpur and Bogra regions   *Features:* Underlain by unconsolidated clay of Tertiary age. Broken into several fault blocks, surface lying several metres above the floodplain. Less dissected and less complex relief patterns than the Madhupur Tracts   *Associated risk:* Loss of organic matter, nutrient depletion, sheet erosion, severe dry season droughts, seasonal shallow flooding in depressions of valleys.

Physiographic units: the floodplains
Active floodplains
Location: Parts of greater Mymensingh, Faridpur, Dhaka, Pabna, Rajshahi, Rangpur, Barisal, Noakhali, Chittagong districts. *Features:* Comprising the youngest alluvial land within and alongside main rivers subject to alternative deposition of new sediments and erosion by shifting channels within the main river course. Temporary alluvial formations known as chars have an irregular relief with stratified sandy and silty deposits. *Associated risk:* Bank erosion, on-rush/rapid floodwater rise, burial by sediments.
Meander floodplains
Location: Relatively older parts of the Teesta, Atrai, Brahmaputra-Jamuna, Karatoya-Bangali, Ganges, Surma-Kusiyara and middle Meghna floodplains. *Features:* Stable landscapes with complex patterns of curved ridges, basins and cut-off channels, crossed by a few active river channels (mainly distributary channels of the main rivers). *Associated risk:* Seasonal inundation to variable depths, dry-season, droughts, loss of organic matter, nutrient depletion, sheet erosion.
Estuarine floodplains
Location: Parts of the Old Meghna estuarine floodplain having a network of small, man-made canals. *Features:* Smooth and almost level relief. Differing elevation between adjoining ridges and depressions; have deep silty deposits, divided into stable old part no longer receiving new alluvial sediments and the young part adjoining the Meghna estuary. *Associated risk:* Bank erosion, loss of organic matter, nutrient depletion, dry-season salinity and droughts, tidal inundation, storm surges.
Tidal floodplains
Location: Ganges tidal floodplain comprising primarily the greater Khulna and Barisal districts. *Features:* Having an almost level, alluvial clay landscape crossed by numerous, often interconnecting tidal rivers and creeks; slight difference in elevation between riverbanks and basin centres. *Associated risk:* Dry season salinity and droughts, seasonal inundation, lack of suitable irrigation water in the south, organic matter and nutrient depletion, increased acidification, storm surges, excessive logging and lopping in the mangrove forest, localized sheet and bank erosion.

Piedmont alluvial plains

Location: Comprising primarily the greater Dinajpur district.

Features: Comprising gently sloping land at the foothills where alluvial and alluvial sediments are deposited by rivers and streams subject to flash floods; irregular relief with small local differences in elevation between ridge tops and neighbouring depressions. Latter unit contains predominantly loamy sediments with high sand content. Elsewhere piedmont sediments are predominantly silty, but they are almost sandy nearer to the hills and river channels.

Associated risk: Frequent flash flood, burial by sediments, loss of organic matter, nutrient depletion.

Basins

Location: Greater Sylhet, Mymensingh, Comilla, Faridpur, Barisal, Jessore Comilla and Khulna districts.

Features: Depressed and low-lying areas with poorly drained muddy and peat soils.

Associated risk: Seasonally deeply flooded clay basins, flash floods in pre-*kharif* early monsoon season, nutrient deficiency, heavy consistency, late draining, localized almost perennial wetness; deeply-flooded peat basins, low bearing capacity, localized waterlogging, dry-season salinity.

Sources: Based on Mosharaff Hossain (1991); BBS (1999a); Bramer (1997); SRDI (1995)

The hills

The hill areas comprise the high hill and low hill ranges. These hills are steeply or very steeply sloped and are subject to severe topsoil erosion owing to run-off. These areas also suffer from serious shortage of soil moisture in the dry season. The hill areas occur in the northern and eastern borders of the country in Khagrachhari, Rangamati, Bandarban, Chittagong, Cox's Bazar, Patia, Sylhet, Maulavi Bazar and Habiganj. The hill soils are under the general soil type – the brown hill soils. The natural vegetative cover for this region includes trees, shrubs and poor grasses, while the plantation crops consist of timber, rubber, tea and horticultural fruits. In the valleys, however, some rice crops are cultivated. The steep slopes of the hill areas are a major constraint to agricultural development. The topsoil is eroded by severe rain and occasional landslides; the soil is shallow and underlain by hard rocks, which affects plant rooting. The condition is further aggravated by the low moisture level in the dry season. The valleys are vulnerable to flash floods, which are responsible for crop damage almost every year.

The hilly regions can be developed by controlled clearing of forests for agriculture. However, the natural vegetation on very steep slopes should be left undisturbed. On gently to moderately steeply sloping sites, tree crops such as improved varieties of timber, rubber, tea and coffee can be grown as well as fruit trees and grasses. In the valleys, two rotations of high-yielding varieties of transplanted rice crops would be possible if irrigation from groundwater sources could be provided. Development efforts have to be concentrated on hilly lands because the valleys are small in area (Mosharaff Hossain, 1991).

The terraces

The terraces in Bangladesh consist of the Madhupur and the Barind tracts and the Akhaura terrace. Generally, the terraces are broadly level to dissected lands with either good or bad drainage systems. The soil composition ranges from friable brown loam to compact grey heavy clay. There is an acute shortage of soil moisture in the dry season. The Madhupur tract covers some areas of Narayanganj, Dhaka, Gazipur, Narsingdi, Tangail and Mymensingh. The Barind tract extends in the north Bengal region from the districts of Rangpur, Gaibandha, Dinajpur, Nawabganj, Naogaon and Bogra to Joypurhat, Natore and parts of Sirajganj. The Akhaura terrace comprises the Akhaura part in Brahmanbaria district. The soils of the terraces fall under the general soil types, deep red-brown terrace soils, shallow red-brown terrace soils, brown mottled terrace soils, deep grey terrace soils and shallow grey terrace soils.

Cultivation of *Rabi* (winter or dry season) crops in these areas is restricted due to shortage of soil moisture. On the well-drained sites of the Madhupur tracts, trees such as jackfruit and sal are mainly grown. On the poorly-drained sites in the Barind tract, single transplanted *Aman* (monsoon) or *Aus* (early monsoon) crops, followed by transplanted *Aman* are the major crop types.

The main constraint on agricultural production in the terrace soils is the severe shortage of soil moisture during the dry season and consequently, *Rabi* crops cannot be grown without adequate irrigation. The *Aus* crop is also badly affected, particularly during the sowing and primary stages of growth. Jute of low quality fibre is widely grown in these lands.

Development strategies include the use of extensive irrigation facilities from deep tube wells. On well-drained soils, improved winter crops of vegetables and perennials can be grown and on poorly-drained sites, two transplanted high-yielding varieties of rice crops including *b*oro can be cultivated.

The basins and peat areas

The Sylhet basin areas include a vast depressed area on the western part of the Surma-Kusiyara floodplain called the Haor. The Haor areas are deeply flooded by the monsoon rains and the water does not drain out until late in the dry season. Such areas occur in the districts of Habiganj, Sunamganj, Kishoreganj, Netrokona and Brahmanbaria and their general soil type is acid basin clay. *Kharif* (monsoon) paddy cannot be grown and the presence of water late in the dry season restricts cultivation of dry land *Rabi* crops.

The main constraint on agricultural development is the very deep flooding coupled with pre-monsoon flash floods. At the same time, the very firm clay soils and late draining of floodwater restricts cultivation of winter crops. Development strategies for the *haor* areas include cultivation of early maturing HYV *boro* in the dry season with the supply of irrigation water from surface water sources by means of low-lift pumps.

The peat areas are in the low-lying areas of the Gopalgang-Khulna *beel*. Thick peat and muck deposits are found in the wet basins which are deeply flooded by fresh water in the monsoon season and may be flooded by saline water in some places. These soils are highly soggy and have very low bearing capacity with irreversible shrinkage of the material on drying.

The peat areas are located in different parts of Madaripur, Gopalganj, Khulna, Bagerhat, Jessore, Narail, Pirojpur and Barisal. The peat soils are almost unsuitable for agricultural purposes and are a major constraint on agricultural development. The development of these lands for agricultural purposes is not economically viable. With traditional management, local *boro* paddy may be cultivated on the margins of the *beels*.

The floodplains

River *charlands* are found mainly along the active river systems. The soils are coarse in texture, ranging from sand to silt. The river *charlands* are subject to inundation and burial by fresh alluvium. River erosion occurs almost every year. These *charlands* are found in parts of Jamalpur, Tangail, Manikganj, Munshiganj, Goalunda, Faridpur, Madaripur, Sariatpur, Bogra, Sirajganj, Kurigram, Gaibandha, Rajshahi, Pabna, Nawabganj and Natore. Non-calcareous alluvium and, in some places, calcareous alluvium are the general soil types which occur in the river *charlands*. The availability of residual moisture determines cultivation of *Rabi* crops such as sweet potatoes, groundnuts and pulses.

The sudden on-rush of water caused by severe floods is the main constraint on cultivation of rice and other crops. Floodwater often sweeps away standing crops. Additionally, the nature of the land itself is also unstable and liable to erosion.

Embankments and other flood control measures would enable the cultivators to grow good harvests of *Aus*/jute crops followed by improved varieties of *Rabi* crops like wheat, mustard, pulses, groundnut, vegetables and sweet potatoes. These can be grown on residual moisture without extra irrigation. Limited use of irrigation facilities such as low-lift pumps and shallow tube wells would widen the options for the cultivation of various types of agricultural crops.

Coastal *charlands*, the vast tracts of land within the mainland of the coastal districts as well as the offshore islands, are vulnerable to severe cyclonic storm surges, tidal flooding and severe river erosion. Salinity develops on the topsoil in the dry season. The coastal *charlands* occur in the districts of Pirojpur, Barguna, Patuakhali, Bhola, Lakshmipur, Noakhali, Feni, Chittagong, Patia and Cox's Bazar. The coastal *charlands* contain partly calcareous alluvium in the general soil type. A single crop of transplanted *Aman* can be grown in the monsoon season. *Aus* is also grown by a dibbling method which keeps the emerging seedlings out of contact with the surface salt crust.

Dry season increases in the salinity of the land and severe storm surges, coupled with the hazards of river erosion, limit the scope of agricultural development. It is difficult to find salt-free irrigation water for dry land *Rabi* crops and *boro* paddy. Wet paddy and dry land *Rabi* crops may be grown, if all possible measures are taken for flood control and drainage, and if dry season irrigation facilities are improved. Possible sources of salt-free irrigation water need to be explored.

The river floodplains, which include the piedmont plains, are classified as shallow flooded areas and deeply flooded areas. The shallow flooded areas generally occupy the higher sites in the landscape and are inundated to a depth ranging from a few centimetres to less than one metre during the monsoon. The soil is usually friable loam and the land remains dry during the winter season. Areas flooded only to a shallow depth of the river floodplains are found in the districts of Khagrachhari, Rangamati, Chittagong, Cox's Bazar, Sylhet, Maulavi Bazar, Habiganj, Sunamganj, Kishoreganj, Netrokona, Mymensingh, Tangail, Jamalpur, Sherpur, Dhaka, Narayanganj, Narsingdi, Munshiganj, Faridpur, Goalunda, Madaripur, Gopalganj, Sariatpur, Panchargarh, Thakurgaon, Dinajpur, Bogra, Joypurhat, Natore, Rajshahi, Nawabganj, Naogaon, Pabna, Sirajganj, Nilphamari, Lalmonirhat, Rangpur, Kurigram, Gaibandha, Meherpur, Kushtia, Chuadanga, Jhenaidah, Magura, Narial, Jessore, Satkhira, Khulna, Bagerhat, Pirojpur, Jhalokati, Barguna, Patuakhali, Barisal, Bhola, Comilla, Lakshimpur, Noakhali and Feni. Generally, the following cropping patterns are followed: (a) *Aus*/jute followed by *Rabi* crops, (b) *Aus*/jute followed by transplanted *Aman,* followed by *Rabi* crops, and (c) *Aus*/jute followed by transplanted *Aman* and *Rabi* crops. Besides *Kharif* season paddy, *boro* paddy may be grown, with irrigation facilities on clay soils.

The deeply flooded areas occupy the lower sites in the landscape and are inundated to a depth of one metre to three and a half metres during the monsoon season. These areas are present in Sylhet, Maulavi Bazar,

Habiganj, Sunamganj, Kishoreganj, Netrakona, Mymensingh, Tangail, Jamalpur, Sherpur, Dhaka, Manikganj, Narayanganj, Narsingdi, Munshiganj, Faridpur, Goalunda, Gopalganj, Madaripur, Sariatpur, Brahmanbaria, Comilla, Chandpur, Lakshmipur, Noakhali, Feni, Natore, Nawabganj, Noagaon, Sirajganj, Pabna, Kushtia, Magura, Narial, Jessore, Khulna, Bagerhat, Pirojpur and Barisal. The cropping patterns followed in the deeply flooded areas are: (a) mixed *Aus* and broadcast *Aman* followed by either *Rabi* crops or dry season fallow, (b) broadcast *Aman* followed by *khesari* (a kind of pulse) and (c) broadcast *Aman*-fallow in the *Rabi* season. The pattern to be followed is dependent on the length of time needed for draining floodwater and the residual moisture status of the soil.

The general soil types that fall within this physiography are grey floodplain soils, calcareous grey floodplain soils, non-calcareous brown floodplain soils, black terai soils and grey piedmont soils.

The shallow flooded areas have clay-type soils and the available soil moisture is inadequate. Consequently, it is difficult to grow a wide range of *Rabi* crops without irrigation. In the deeply flooded areas, the main constraint to agricultural development is the deep flooding during the monsoon. The water remains standing and drains slowly during the dry season, although it does allow enough time for planting of *Rabi* crops. The soils in general have a heavy consistency.

The Sunderbans consist of the mangrove forests of Khulna and Chakaria in Cox's Bazar. These are tidally flooded lands with mangrove forests. Flooding with brackish water takes place all the year round. This is found to occur in and around Chakaria and Khulna Sunderbans and in some parts of Satkhira, Khulna, Bagerhat, Cox's Bazar and Patia. The general soil type of this area is acid sulphate soils.

The major disadvantage of these soils is that the land is subjected to regular flooding by tidal waves. The salinity is frequently strong and the soils stay wet throughout almost all the year, developing extreme acidity when drained.

2.3 PROBLEM SOILS OF BANGLADESH

The surveys conducted by the Soil Resources Development Institute (SRDI) during the 1960s and early 1970s have so far identified about 500 soil series. The soils range from the recently deposited, stratified alluvium of active floodplains or nearly perennially wet, strongly gleyed and poorly-developed hydromorphic soils of floodplain basin depressions, to the well-drained, strongly and deeply oxidized well-developed soils of upland terrace areas and hills. Some of the soils were found to be lacking in a balanced nutrient status while others had limits in physical soil characteristics. Table 2.3 sets out information on general soil types, their locations of significant occurrences and diagnostic properties.

Table 2.3 General soil types, their locations of significant occurrences and diagnostic properties

FLOODPLAIN SOILS: 113 895 km^2 (including area of miscellaneous land types), 79.1 per cent of total country area
Non-calcareous alluvium (5622 km^2, 3.9 per cent of total country area) **Location of significant occurrences:** Brahmanbaria, Chandpur, Chittagong, Chittagong Hill Tracts, Comilla, Cox's Bazar, Sunamganj, Sylhet, Dhaka, Jamalpur, Kishoreganj, Manikganj, Narayanganj, Narshinghdi, Netrokona, Sherpur, Tangail, Gaibandha, Kurigram, Lalmonirhat, Bogra, Dinajpur, Naogaon, Rajshahi, Panchagarh, Pabna, Rangpur, Sirajganj, Nilphamari, Barisal, Bhola, Patuakhali, Barguna. **Diagnostic properties:** Raw or stratified alluvium with no lime content and not extremely acid (actually or potentially) within 125 cm from surface; neutral to moderately alkaline in reaction; saline in the coastal tidal areas
Calcareous alluvium (5918 km^2, 4.1 per cent of total country area) **Location of significant occurrences:** Chandpur, Chittagong, Cox's Bazar, Feni, Lakshmipur, Noakhali, Dhaka, Faridpur, Gopalganj, Madaripur, Manikganj, Munshihanj, Rajbari, Shariatpur, Bagerhat, Khulna, Magura, Kushtia, Narail Satkhira, Chapai Nawabganj, Natore, Pabna, Rajshahi **Diagnostic properties:** Similar to characteristics of those of the non-calcareous. Raw or stratified alluvium, calcareous throughout or in some layer within 125 cm from the surface; saline in the coastal tidal areas
Acid sulphate soils (2266 km^2, 1.6 per cent of total country area) **Location of significant occurrences:** Cox's Bazar, Bagerhat, Khulna, Satkhira **Diagnostic properties:** Poorly or very poorly drained grey or dark grey soils, with or without a developed subsoil and containing sufficient sulphur compounds they are actually or potentially extremely acid (pH <3.5) within 125 cm from the surface. Mainly saline
Peat (1300 km^2, 0.9 per cent of total country area) **Location of significant occurrences:** Barisal, Pirojpur, Habiganj, Moulvi Bazar, Sylhet **Diagnostic properties:** Very poorly drained soils in which organic matter (peat or muck) comprises more than half the top 80cm

Non-calcareous grey floodplain soils (33 872 km², 23.5 per cent of total country area)
Location of significant occurrences: Barguna, Barisal, Jhalokathi, Patuakhali, Patualkahi, Pirojpur, Brahmanbaria, Chandpur, Chittagong, Comilla, Cox's Bazar, Feni, Habiganj, Khagrachhari, Lakshmipur, Moulvi Bazar, Noakhali, Sunamganj, Sylhet, Dhaka, Gazipur, Jamalpur, Kishoreganj, Manikganj, Munshiganj, Mymensingh, Narayanganj, Narshingdi, Netrokona, Sherpur, Tangail, Bagerhat, Bogra, Dinajpur, Gaibandha, Kurigram, Joypurhat, Lalmonirhat, Naogaon, Nilphamari, Panchagarh, Rangpur, Sirajganj, Thakurgaon
Diagnostic properties: Seasonally flooded soils with a developed subsoil; prismatic and/or blocky structured sandy loams to silty clay loams on young floodplain ridges and silty clay loams to clays in basins, not calcareous within 125 cm from top; when not submerged, topsoil is generally slightly to strongly acid in reaction; lower layers are between slightly acid and moderately alkaline

Calcareous grey floodplain soils (1708 km², 1.2 per cent of total country area)
Location of significant occurrences: Chandpur, Chittagong, Feni, Lakshmipur, Noakhali, Barisal Barguna, Bhola, Patuakhali, Pirojpur, Bagerhat, Khulna, Narail, Satkhira
Diagnostic properties: Structured, grey silt loams to silty clays, calcareous in some or all layers within 125 cm from the surface. Saline in the dry season in the coastal tidal areas

Grey piedmont soils (2153 km², 1.5 per cent of total country area)
Location of significant occurrences: Bandarban, Brahmanbaria, Chittagong, Chittagong Hill Tracts, Comilla, Cox's Bazar, Feni, Khagrachhari, Mymensingh, Netrokona, Sherpur, Habiganj, Moulvi Bazar, Sunamganj, Sunamganj, Sylhet
Diagnostic properties: Imperfectly to poorly drained soils, in piedmont alluvium, similar to non-calcareous grey floodplain soils, but generally more strongly mottled and medium to strongly acid in the subsoil; often affected by flash floods from the hills and liable to burial by fresh sandy deposits

Acid basin clay soils (3490 km², 2.4 per cent of total country area)
Location of significant occurrences: Brahmanbaria, Comilla, Habiganj, Moulvi Bazar, Sunamganj, Sylhet, Dhaka, Gazipur, Jamalpur, Kishoreganj, Mymensingh, Narshingdi, Netrakona, Sherpur, Tangail, Bogra, Chapai Nawabganj, Naogaon, Natore, Pabna, Rajshahi, Sirajganj
Diagnostic properties: Very strongly acid ($3.5 < pH < 5$) to 50 cm or more and calcareous within 125 cm from the top, grey to dark heavy plastic clay; seasonally heavily flooded with heavy consistency

Non-calcareous dark grey floodplain soils (15 997 km², 11.1 per cent of total country area)
Location of significant occurrences: Barisal, Patuakhali, Pirojpur, Brahmanbaria, Chandpur, Comilla, Feni, Habiganj, Lakshmipur, Moulvi Bazar, Sunamganj, Sylhet, Dhaka, Gazipur, Madhupur, Gopalganj, Jamalpur, Kishoreganj, Manikganj, Munshiganj, Mymensing, Narayanganj, Narshingdi, Netrakona, Shariatpur, Sherpur, Tangail, Bagerhat, Chuadanga, Jessore, Jhenaidah, Khulna, Kushtia, Magura, Meherpur, Narail Satkhira, Bogra, Dinajpur, Gaibandha, Kurigram, Naogaon, Natore, Nilphamari, Pabna, Panchagarh, Rajshahi, Rangpur, Sirajganj, Thakurgaon
Diagnostic properties: Structured dark grey loamy soils; seasonally flooded soils similar to non-calcareous grey floodplain soils; Slightly acid to somewhat alkaline in reaction

Calcareous dark grey floodplain soils (14 347 km², 10.1 per cent of total country area)
Location of significant occurrences: Dhaka, Faridpur, Gopalganj, Madaripur, Manikganj, Munshiganj, Rajbari, Shariatpur, Bagerhat, Chuadanga, Jhenaidah, Khulna, Kushtia, Magura, Meherpur, Narail Satkhira, Barisal, Jhalokathi, Pirojpur, Naogaon, Natore, Chapai Nawabganj, Pabna, Rajshahi
Diagnostic properties: Similar to non-calcareous dark grey floodplain soils but contains lime in some layers within the top 125 cm; clays highly cracking when dry, drought prone and become saline in the dry season in the tidal floodplain

Calcareous brown floodplain soils (4785 km², 3.3 per cent of total country area)
Location of significant occurrences: Chandpur, Feni, Lakshmipur, Noakhali, Dhaka, Faridpur, Gopalganj, Madaripur, Manikganj, Munshiganj, Rajbari, Shariatpur, Bagerhat, Chuadanga, Jhenaidah, Khulna, Kushtia, Magura, Meherpur, Narail Satkhira, Naogaon, Natore, Chapai Nawabganj, Rajshahi
Diagnostic properties: Calcareous, brown silt loams to light silty clays, occurring in the Ganges river floodplain and locally in the young and old Meghna floodplains. Locally they are leached of lime up to a depth of 100 cm from the surface

Non-calcareous brown floodplain soils (3395 km², 2.4 per cent of total country area)

Location of significant occurrences: Chittagong, Chittagong Hill Tracts, Khagrachhari, Jamalpur, Narshingdi, Mymensingh, Netrakona, Sherpur, Chuadanga, Jhenaidah, Jessore, Satkhira, Bogra, Gaibandha, Kurigram, Chapai Nawabganj, Lalmonirhat, Nilphamari, Panchagarah, Rangpur, Thakurgaon

Diagnostic properties: Moderately well to imperfectly drained soils with a yellow-brown or olive-brown subsoil; non calcareous within 125 cm from the surface; topsoil and upper subsoil generally are medium or strongly acid with lower layers less acid or neutral

Brown piedmont soils (440 km², 0.3 per cent of total country area)

Location of significant occurrences: Chittagong, Bandarban, Khagrachhari, Chittagong Hill Tracts, Mymensingh, Netrakona, Sherpur, Habiganj, Moulvi Bazar, Sylhet

Diagnostic properties: Brown sandy loams to clay loams, strongly acid.

Dark terai soils (834 km², 0.6 per cent of total country area)

Location of significant occurrences: Dinajpur, Panchagarh, Thakurgaon

Diagnostic properties: Topsoils are strongly to very strongly acidic; but the subsoils are only slightly acidic in reaction. Imperfectly to poorly drained soils with a black or a very dark brown topsoil more than 25 cm thick

HILL SOILS: 18 079 km² (including area of miscellaneous land types), 12.6 per cent of the total country area

Brown hill soils (15 420 km², 10.7 per cent of total country area)

Location of significant occurrences: Bandarban, Chittagong Hill Tracts, Comilla, Cox's Bazar, Feni, Mymensingh, Netrakona, Sherpur, Habiganj, Khagrachhari, Moulvi Bazar, Sunamganj, Sylhet

Diagnostic properties: Brown sandy loams to clay loams, slightly to strongly acid, occasionally shallow over shaly/sandstone bedrocks on very steep high hills

TERRACE SOILS: 12 025 km² (including area of miscellaneous land types), 8.3 per cent of the total country area

Shallow red-brown terrace soils (730 km², 0.5 per cent of total country area)

Location of significant occurrences: Dhaka, Gazipur Jamalpur, Mymensingh, Naogaon, Tangail

Diagnostic properties: Brown or red brown, usually strongly acid but very shallow soils contain lime nodules at triangular depths; moderately well to imperfectly drained soils.

Deep red-brown terrace soils (1906 km², 1.3 per cent of total country area) **Location of significant occurrences:** Brahmanbaria, Dhaka, Gazipur Jamalpur, Mymensingh, Narshingdi, Tangail, Bogra, Dinajpur, Gaibandha, Rangpur **Diagnostic properties:** Moderately well to well drained soils; strongly to very strongly acid throughout; red to yellow-brown subsoil overlying a strongly red mottled previous sub-stratum.
Brown mottled terrace soils (345 km², 0.3 per cent of total country area) **Location of significant occurrences:** Dhaka, Gazipur Jamalpur, Mymensingh, Tangail, Bogra, Dinajpur, Gaibandha, Rangpur **Diagnostic properties:** Brown mottled with specks of grey, pale brown and red, slightly acid, structured friable clay loams to clays integrating into a mixed red black and pale brown.
Shallow grey terrace soils (2671 km², 1.8 per cent of total country area) **Location of significant occurrences:** Dhaka, Gazipur Jamalpur, Mymensingh, Tangail, Bogra, Chapai Nawabganj, Dinajpur, Joypurhat, Naogaon, Rajshahi, Rangpur, Sirajganj **Diagnostic properties:** Poorly drained similar to deep grey terrace soils in the topsoil and upper subsoil; slightly acid to strong acid; friable somewhat porous silt loams to silty clays integrated into a weakly mottled grey, compact and little altered Madhupur clay substratum at a shallow depth.
Deep grey terrace soils (3544 km², 2.4 per cent of total country area) **Location of significant occurrences:** Dhaka, Gazipur Jamalpur, Tangail, Bogra, Chapai Nawabganj, Dinajpur, Joypurhat, Naogaon, Rajshahi, Rangpur **Diagnostic properties:** Poorly drained, grey porous silty soils; mainly medium to strongly acid throughout.
Grey valley soils (1150 km², 0.8 per cent of total country area) **Location of significant occurrences:** Dhaka, Gazipur Jamalpur, Tangail, Bogra, Chapai Nawabganj, Dinajpur, Joypurhat, Naogaon, Rajshahi, Rangpur **Diagnostic properties:** Poorly drained, deep grey porous silty soils; medium to strongly acid

Sources: Based on information from Mosharaff Hossain (1991); BBS 1998b, 1999a); Bramer (1997); SRDI (1995).

Recently-formed *charlands* are found to occur in the recent alluvium of the Tista, the Brahmaputra and the Jamuna. They are generally sandy hazards of the rapid rise in the floodwater level. These areas and soils are vulnerable to severe river erosion and are often buried under fresh sediments. The same conditions prevail in the recently formed estuarine alluvial soils of the Ganges and the young Meghna, except that some portions of the Meghna estuarine and coastal areas also have saline soils.

Soils with low bearing capacity are organic soils with poor physical and chemical properties. They occur in the districts of Gopalgani, Madaripur, Khulna, Narail and Barisal. The improvement of drainage will cause irreversible shrinkage of the peat layer and this in turn will cause surface cracking, subsidence of land and deeper flooding. These soils are nutrient-deficient, tidal floodplain soils with extreme acidity, severe aluminium toxicity, and moderate to strong salinity. The peat soils are used as salt beds.

There are potential acid sulphate soils under the tidal mangrove vegetation and such soils are found in the districts of Satkhira, Khulna, Bagerhat and Cox's Bazar. Soils with potential zinc deficiency problems are usually observed in the calcareous soils of the Ganges river floodplain, which includes the districts of Nawabganj, Rajshahi, Natore, Pabna, Rajbari, Faridpur and Manikgani. However, some locally non-calcareous soils of the irrigation project areas as DND (Dhaka Narayanganj Demra) and Chandpur also have the problem of zinc deficiency.

Soils with potential problems of sulphur deficiency occur mainly in the Old Brahmaputra floodplain with ridged and piedmont alluvial plains. They are also seen to occur in a scattered form in other areas of the country. The districts affected by this problem are Sherpur, Jamalpur, Mymensingh, Netrokona and parts of Thakurgaon and Dinajpur.

Saline soils are the saline tidal floodplain soils that are mainly clays and are found in Satkhira, Khulna, Bagerhat, Barguna, Patuakhali, Bhola and Noakhali districts. Locally, they occur in buried peat layers towards the west and loams in other areas. Alkaline soils (both saline and non-saline) are found in small patches mainly in Kushtia, Meherpur, Magura, Jhenaidah and Jessore districts.

Soils with heavy consistency are in the areas which are deeply flooded seasonally, with parts of them remaining wet through the year. These soils are heavy clays and are strongly acidic in nature. They occur in Sunmganj, Kishoreganj and parts of Comilla district.

Soils with erosion problems are hill soils with moderate to severe erosion problems. They are mainly loamy soils on the slopes of steep low hills of unconsolidated sediments. Their nutrient status is low and these soils remain very dry especially on the southern and western slopes. Hill soils with very severe erosion problems are observed in shallow, brown loamy soils on very steep high hills of consolidated shale, sandstone and so on. These soils occur in Khagrachhari, Rangamati, Chittagong, Bandarban, Cox's Bazar, Habiganj, Moulavibazar and Sylhet.

Soils depleted of organic matter, or the red-brown terrace soils form deep and shallow red-brown loamy clays in the Madhupur and Akhaura terrace areas and are also found locally in the Barind tract soils. These not only have low organic matter, but also suffer from nutrient deficiency and problems of phosphate fixation and remain dry in the dry season. The shallow soils create problems of root penetration and the risk of erosion increases because of the impervious clay layer at a shallow depth and the irregular or rolling topography. These problem soils occur in Tangail, Dhaka and in small parts of Rangpur and Brahmanbaria districts.

Mixed red-brown terrace soils, brown mottled terrace soils and grey terrace soils constitute problem soils and are generally well drained or moderately well drained. However, imperfectly to poorly-drained mottled brown to grey soils occur in the lower interiors of the northern part of the Barind tract and locally in the Madhupur tract. They are acid or strongly acid in reaction. These soils are loams to clays with low organic matter and nutrient content, and also have problems of phosphate fixation. These problem soils are found in Tangail, Gazipur, Dhaka and parts of Bogra districts.

Level grey terrace soils are poorly-drained silty soils over clay substratum. These occur on level terraces in the Barind tract and locally in the Madhupur tract and locally on the older parts of the north-eastern piedmont alluvial plain. The topsoils become degraded because of puddling for transplanted rice cultivation. They have very low nutrient and organic matter contents. These soils also occur in Noagaon, Jaipurhat, Bogra, Gaibandha, Dinajpur, Sherpur, Mymemsingh and Netrokona.

Closely dissected grey terrace soils mainly have problems similar to those of level grey terrace soils but they occur on the terraced slopes of western edges on the Barind tract, where narrow valleys dissect it. They are found in some parts of Noagaon, Jaipurhat, Dinajpur and Bogra districts.

Soils with problems related to effective rooting depth and drainage are brown soils of the low hills of Dupi Tila and Dihing formations. These soils have a thick iron-manganese indurated concretionary layer on hard iron pan at rooting depth. These problem soils are found to occur in various parts of Sylhet, Chittagong, Khagrachhari, the Chittagong Hill Tracts and Bandarban districts.

Soils with problems related to extreme acidity of tea garden soils are the brown soils of low hills. The extreme acidity is caused by the continuous application of ammonium sulphate fertilizer for the growth of the tea plants. The soils with this problem occur in Habiganj and Moulavibazar.

2.4 WATER RESOURCES IN BANGLADESH

The availability of water for crops is one of the most important determining factors for increasing agricultural production. The major sources of water in Bangladesh of rainfall, stream-flow and groundwater are closely related. Stream-flow increases partly because of the snow in the Himalayas, but mainly because of rainfall in the catchment areas of the three major river networks. The rainwater and stream-flow overspills are absorbed into the groundwater stocks. Traditionally, water management in Bangladesh for agriculture, fisheries, domestic use and cottage industries has relied on rainwater and stream-flow. Modern methods of low-lift pumps, deep tube wells and irrigation canals have led to the utilization of surface and groundwater for agriculture during the dry season. The main constraint on the growth of agricultural production through irrigation during the dry period is the scarcity of surface and groundwater when it is needed the most.

The dry season availability of surface water depends on the water from the main rivers and regional rivers. The areas covered by the main rivers, including the Ganges, the Brahmaputra and the Meghna river systems and the smaller rivers, have been grouped into five regions: north-west, north-east, south-east, south central and south-west. The main component of the available regional water is the inflow from the main rivers that come from India and the stream-flow generated within the catchment area. The flat topography and land scarcity limit the scope of storing surface water.

As mentioned before, the two main sources of water in Bangladesh are the rains, which usually arrive in May and last until September, and the river water originating in the mountains of India and Nepal and the monsoon catchment areas of India and Bangladesh. Bangladesh is one huge drainage area through which three large river networks of India and Nepal discharge water into the Bay of Bengal. It also has very heavy seasonal precipitation. Most of the water that passes through Bangladesh, however, comes from across the boundaries. Violent pre-monsoon storms and heavy downpours of rain often precede the monsoon season.

After the rainy season, in October and November, the climate is characterized by warm and humid atmospheric conditions which frequently cause severe cyclones and thunderstorms. The period from December to March is cool, dry and sunny. There may be some winter rain but this accounts for less than 5 per cent of the annual rainfall. The very hot pre-monsoon weather causes the north-western storms.

The monsoon season begins in May-June with strong winds and heavy squalls coming from the south-east. Except for the Sylhet region where the highest rainfall occurs in June, July is the wettest month in Bangladesh. The annual rainfall within Bangladesh varies greatly with time and location. The mean annual rainfall is 2320 mm. The highest annual rainfall is in northern Sylhet with 5690 mm and the lowest in western Chapai Nawabganj with 1110 mm.

2.5 PRESENT CROPPING PATTERNS

In Bangladesh, the local complexities of land type, soil type, fragmentation of land and land tenure systems are responsible for the wide array of cropping patterns. Table 2.4 provides a very generalized cropping pattern for the country as a whole.

Table 2.4 A generalized cropping pattern for Bangladesh

Crop	Followed by	Followed by
Rice/jute	Fallow	*Rabi* crops
Rice/jute	Rice	Fallow
Rice/jute	Rice	*Rabi* crops
Fallow	Rice	Fallow
Mixed Rice	*Rabi* crops	
Rice (B. *Aman*)	Fallow	
Rice (*Boro*)	Fallow	
Rice (*Boro*)	Rice (T. *Aman*)	
Mixed *Aus* rice and other *Kharif* crops		
Jhum (shifting) cultivation		

Note: T. *Aman* and B. *Aman* are respectively transplanted and broadcast *Aman* crops of rice.

Source: Adapted from Mosharaff Hossain (1991, p. 12).

    The cropping patterns described in Table 2.4 are highly generalized and in reality, there are local differences. Most of the cropping patterns are based on rice or have rice in common with other crops. In Bangladesh, there are more than sixty variations of cropping patterns, depending on the local agro-ecological conditions. Mosharaff Hossain (1991) provides details of these and we do not wish to repeat them here.

Table 2.5   A generalized cropping pattern for the main regions of Bangladesh

Crop	Followed by	Followed by
Aus	T. *Aman*	*Rabi* crops
Aus	T. *Aman*	Fallow
Aus/jute	T. *Aman*	*Rabi* crops
Aus/jute	T. *Aman*	Fallow
Mixed Aus/B. Aman	*Rabi* crops	
Aus	*Rabi* crops	
T. *Aman*	Fallow	
B. *Aman*	Fallow	
Boro	Fallow	

Note: T. *Aman* and B. *Aman* are respectively transplanted and broadcast *Aman* crops of rice.

Source: Adapted from Mosharaff Hossain (1991, p. 12).

Based on the Reconnaissance Soil Survey Reports, the cropping patterns that are followed (with slight variations in the four main regions of Bangladesh) are set out in Table 2.5.

In the Dhaka region (consisting of Dhaka, Tangail, Jamalpur and Mymensingh) *Aus*-T.*Aman*-fallow is the main cropping pattern followed by *Boro*–fallow and mixed *Aus* and B.*Aman-Rabi* crops. In some parts, deep-water *Aman* is also grown. Sugarcane is grown widely and the cultivation of groundnut and betel-vine is common. Clusters of *gazari* forests and jackfruit trees are grown in the Dhaka district.

In the Chittagong region (consisting of Comilla, Sylhet, Noakhali) the main cropping pattern is *Aus*-T.*Aman*-fallow but it is followed by *Boro*-fallow and *Aus*/jute-T.*Aman-Rabi* crops. Broadcast *Aman* is also cultivated in some parts. Betel nut grows well in this region. There are tea gardens both in Sylhet and Chittagong districts and mangrove forests in the coastal areas. Apart from these, there are teak forests in the hilly region.

Rajshahi, Pabna, Bogra, Rangpur and Dinajpur make up the Rajshahi region. Here the main cropping pattern is T.*Aman*-fallow closely followed by *Aus*-T.*Aman*-fallow and jute substituting *Aus*. *Aus* followed by *Rabi* crops is also widely practised. Millet is also grown in small quantities. Tobacco and betel-vine are cultivated in this region and sugarcane is grown. There are large mango orchards and some guava orchards in Rajshahi and most of the country's supply of mangoes comes from here.

The Khulna region is made up of Kushtia, Jessore, Faridpur, Barisal and Khulna. T.*Aman*-fallow is the main cropping pattern used here as in the Rajshahi region. This is followed by mixed *Aus*, B.*Aman-Rabi* crops, and *Aus-Rabi* crops. Betel-vines are grown in the interior while coconut plantations are seen near the coastal belt. Closer to the sea grow the mangrove thickets for which the saline soils are suitable.

To sum up, in all the regions of Bangladesh, the most common cropping pattern is T.*Aman*-fallow after which comes *Aus*-T.*Aman*-fallow, mixed *Aus* and B.*Aman-Rabi* and *Boro* or B.*Aman*-fallow. Jute replaces *Aus* in some parts and sugarcane is found to be grown in all the regions except Chittagong.

Rice is the main food crop grown in Bangladesh. Broadcast, transplanted and deep-water *Aman* together form the main rice crop. *Aus* is the second largest crop. *Boro* rice is also grown all over the country but mainly in the Dhaka and Chittagong regions. Some transplanted *Aus* is grown in the Chittagong and Khulna regions, while transplanted deep-water *Aman* is cultivated in all the regions except Chittagong.

The *Rabi* crops include wheat, potato, vegetables and others. The *Rabi* season with bright sunlight and less moisture in the air is well suited for the cultivation of crops, particularly where irrigation water is available. The *Rabi* crops are grown all over the country with wheat and potatoes growing in large quantities in the Rajshahi region. Also millet and sesame are grown in small quantities.

Two other K*harif* crops, jute and sugarcane, are also cultivated throughout the country, with sugarcane especially abundant in the Rajshahi and Khulna divisions. Ginger and tobacco are cultivated in the Rajshahi region, while tea and rubber plantations are seen in the Sylhet and Chittagong regions. *Gazari* and jackfruit trees are seen in the Dhaka region while mango, coconut and guava orchards are found in Rajshahi and Khulna regions. Mangrove forests occur in the coastal areas of both Khulna and Chittagong regions.

In the light of the preceding discussion, cropping patterns consistent with the agro-climatic conditions and specific to agro-ecological zones are illustrated in Figure 2.2. Figures 2.3 and 2.4 illustrate a crop calendar of Bangladesh.

As is clear, crop production dominates Bangladesh agriculture. Furthermore, Bangladesh agriculture is a virtual rice monoculture. As of 1996–97, food-grains (rice and wheat taken together) account for nearly four-fifths of the gross cropped area. Jute accounts for about 3.5 per cent while pulses account for 5.5 per cent. Other major crops are sugarcane, oilseeds, fruits, vegetables and spices.

2.6 LAND UTILIZATION

Bangladesh represents one of the classic examples of an extremely unfavourable land–man ratio. Apart from some coastal areas that present special difficulties, almost all available arable land is under cultivation. Bangladesh virtually reached its extensive margin of cultivation by the late 1960s. Table 2.6 sets out information on land utilization in Bangladesh for 1984–85 and 1996–97. Some discernible patterns emerge as follows:

- The percentage of land not available for cultivation has increased from 20 per cent in 1984–85 to nearly 27 per cent in 1996–97.
- Forest area has increased marginally.
- Cultivable waste has nearly doubled.
- Net cropped area has declined from 8.64 million hectares in 1984–85 (nearly 60 per cent of the total) to 7.85 million hectares in 1996–97 (53 per cent of the total), as has net cultivable area.
- The increase in total land area may have been due to siltation in the riverbeds through soil erosion and landslides in the (Indian) upstream of the (Bangladesh) river system.

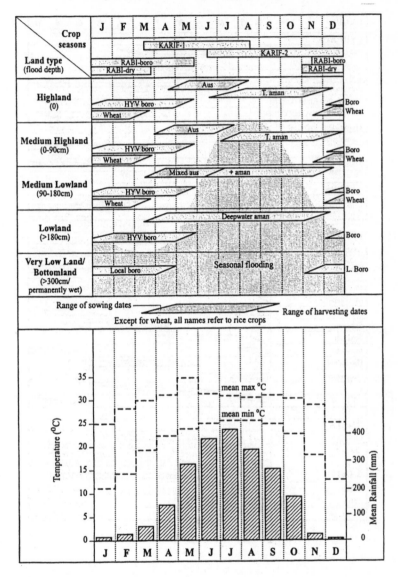

Figure 2.2 Cropping patterns in relation to climate and seasonal flooding

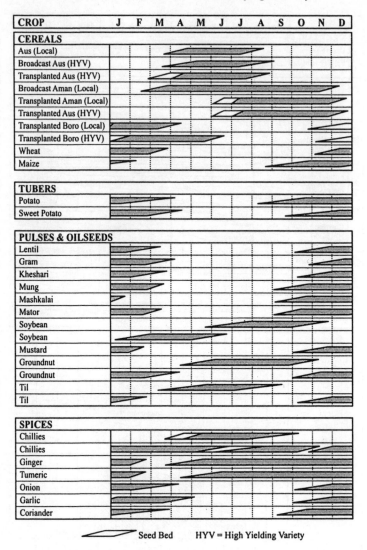

Figure 2.3 *Crop calendar of Bangladesh*

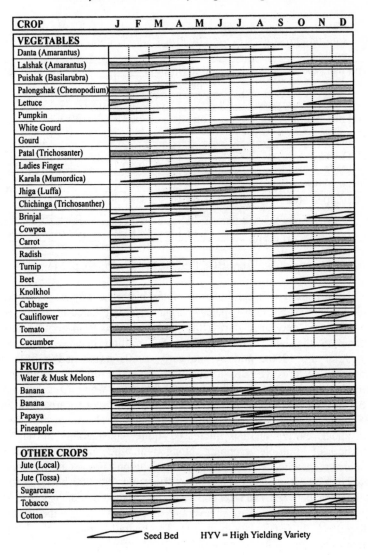

CROP	J	F	M	A	M	J	J	A	S	O	N	D
VEGETABLES												
Danta (Amarantus)												
Lalshak (Amarantus)												
Puishak (Basilarubra)												
Palongshak (Chenopodium)												
Lettuce												
Pumpkin												
White Gourd												
Gourd												
Patal (Trichosanter)												
Ladies Finger												
Karala (Mumordica)												
Jhiga (Luffa)												
Chichinga (Trichosanther)												
Brinjal												
Cowpea												
Carrot												
Radish												
Turnip												
Beet												
Knolkhol												
Cabbage												
Cauliflower												
Tomato												
Cucumber												
FRUITS												
Water & Musk Melons												
Banana												
Banana												
Papaya												
Pineapple												
OTHER CROPS												
Jute (Local)												
Jute (Tossa)												
Sugarcane												
Tobacco												
Cotton												

Seed Bed   HYV = High Yielding Variety

Figure 2.4 Crop calendar of Bangladesh

Table 2.6 Land utilization in Bangladesh: 1984–85 and 1996–97

Land use type	Area (million hectares)		Percentage of total	
	1984–85	1996–97	1984–85	1996–97
Land not available for cultivation	2.91	4.02	20.1	27.0
Forest	2.14	2.15	14.8	14.4
Cultivable waste	0.29	0.50	2.0	3.4
Current fallow	0.49	0.39	3.4	2.6
Net cropped area	8.64	7.85	59.7	52.6
Net cultivable area	9.42	8.74	65.1	58.6
Total land area	14.48	14.91	100.0	100.0

Sources: Based on data from BBS (1988a, p. 157; 1999b, p. 51).

The above pattern is a continuation of the historical process at work. As Alauddin and Tisdell (1991, p. 297) argue: 'Net cultivated area, that is the area cultivated only once during the year, increased from about 8 million hectares in the late 1940s to about 8.4 million hectares on average throughout the 1950s, and by the early 1960s it reached a little over 8.5million hectares (EPBS, 1969, p. 41)... The upward trend in net cultivated area continued until the end of the 1960s when it reached a peak of 8.8 million hectares.' Since the 1970s, the net cropped area has, albeit with minor fluctuations registered a steady decline. However, the effective area under cultivation has increased quite considerably through the incidence of multiple cropping along with the introduction of new technology spearheaded by the green revolution. For example, the area triple-cropped (annually) expanded from around 480 000 hectares to 649 000 hectares between 1965–69 and 1980–84 (Alauddin and Tisdell 1991, p. 50). This area increased to an average of 968 000 during the triennium ending 1996–97 (BBS, 1999b, p. 51). The overall impact of the land use pattern over time is the increased intensity of cropping, from an average of around 130 per cent during the 1950s to around 140 per cent during the 1960s. This had increased to more than 170 per cent three decades later in the 1990s. This process of intensification has led to a substantial increase in the overall annual yield per cultivated hectare. However, this process has also exposed the fragility of the environment, to be further investigated in Chapter 12 (see also Alauddin and Tisdell, 1998).

2.7 CONCLUDING COMMENTS

The physical environment surrounding Bangladesh agriculture is quite complex and is critically influenced by topography and soils, water and land resources. The cropping patterns prevalent in Bangladesh today have been developed over decades or even longer, and are based on the complex ecosystem. Through intensification and other factors, some of which are transboundary in nature, these resources have been under considerable strain (Alauddin and Tisdell, 1998; N. Jahan, 1998). Some of these have manifested themselves in the form of a dwindling supply of arable land. With urbanization likely to increase much further than the current level of 20 per cent (Alauddin and Tisdell, 1998) and land required for human settlement, the land area available for crop production is likely to fall even further. The only recourse to increase an effective supply of land is through increased intensification far beyond the current level. This is likely to put further strain on the physical environment. Chapter 9 takes up these issues for further analysis.

3. Growth and Change in the Crop Sector

3.1 INTRODUCTION

The production performance of the agricultural sector, particularly the crop sector, has an important bearing on the rate and structure of poverty and malnutrition, the trade balance and the government fiscal position and consequently upon the rate of growth of the economy as a whole (Mosharaff Hossain, 1991, p. 24). Crop production dominates Bangladesh agriculture. Since the early 1970s, the crop sub-sector has maintained a constant share of over 75 per cent of total agricultural value added while the remainder is made up of the combined shares of livestock, forestry and fisheries (Shahabuddin and Rahman, 1998, p. 6). Even though a large number of crops are grown in Bangladesh, crops such as rice, wheat, jute, pulses and oilseeds account for the bulk of the cropped area. Food-grain production is central to the agricultural economy of Bangladesh. Rice and wheat together occupy about 80 per cent of the gross cropped area (including the area under multiple cropping) (BBS, 1998a, pp. 120–45). Bangladesh agriculture primarily involves rice monoculture, which accounts for nearly three-quarters of the gross cropped area in recent years.

Over the last five decades, agriculture in Bangladesh has undergone significant transformation. The changes have manifested themselves in the form of increasing intensification of agriculture following a gradual decline in net cultivated area, cropping pattern and output mix. The motive force underpinning such changes is the technological innovation known as the green revolution.

This chapter investigates growth and change in the crop sector of Bangladesh over the last five decades, encompassing the period 1947–48 to 1996–97. The entire period covers two broad sub-periods: pre- and post-green revolution phases (1947–48 to 1966–67 and 1967–68 to 1996–97). The post-green revolution phase can be further sub-divided into two phases: early-green revolution phase: 1967–68 to 1981–82 and policy rationalization phase: 1982–83 to 1996–97. Earlier studies (see for example, Alauddin and Tisdell, 1991) of the green revolution found evidence of a comparative crowding out of the non-cereal crops in Bangladesh and elsewhere in the developing world, such as in India. This chapter also investigates the extent to which this phenomenon still persists.

- For the entire period, 21 crops consisting of eight cereals (six rice crops and two wheat crops) and thirteen non–cereal crops, categorized into four broad commodity groups, are considered: cereals, cash crops, oilseeds and pulses
- A more detailed and comprehensive analysis is made for the post-green revolution period. For this period, the analysis is extended to 36 crops and to seven broad commodity groups: cereals, cash crops, pulses, oilseeds, vegetables, fruits and spices.

The initial choice of the number of crops and number of commodity groups and the subsequent extension of this choice is due entirely to availability of data. This chapter also examines the growth in total factor productivity over the 1948–92 period. It provides a rigorous analysis of the sources of growth in the crop sector of Bangladesh.

3.2 TECHNOLOGICAL CHANGE IN BANGLADESH AGRICULTURE: AN OVERVIEW

By way of necessary background, this section provides a broad overview of technological change in agriculture in Bangladesh. Government policies and priorities for agricultural development, which have varied over the years, have critically influenced the process of technological change over the last five decades. A brief review of these policies and priorities in relation to technological change in agriculture in Bangladesh is required in order to encapsulate the chronological nature of the process. Following Alauddin and Tisdell (1991, pp. 6–7) and Faaland and Parkinson (1976, pp. 128–9) the main policies adopted during the 1950s and 1960s can be summarized as follows:

- The most important objective of the development plans of the 1950s and 1960s was to reduce the growing dependence on imported food, exacerbated by growing population pressure on the one hand and the static nature of food-grain production on the other.
- To deal with the situation, a two-pronged strategy was formulated (1) to facilitate large-scale efforts and investment in installing irrigation and drainage structures and even to control the flow of the rivers themselves; (2) ensure the allocation of exchange for large and growing quantities of food-grain imports financed through industrialization, import-saving and export-earning development and also by foreign assistance.

- Government efforts in advancing food-grain production technology in the 1950s and 1960s emphasized large-scale irrigation projects of a lumpy and indivisible nature. Technologies such as the use of chemical fertilizers, small-scale irrigation and biological innovations did not feature prominently in the government's agricultural development strategy (see also Haq, 1963, pp. 157–8 and Papanek, 1967, pp. 165–6).
- Toward the latter part of the 1960s, partly because of growing food-grain imports and partly because Bangladesh had reached the limit of extensive margin of bringing in additional land under cultivation, a new strategy for increasing food production was called for. This led to the promotion of new agricultural technology known as the green revolution, designed to intensify agriculture.

One needs to note, however, that:

> the government's efforts to increase agricultural productivity before the liberation of the country did not bear any fruit because of the willingness of the United States' government to meet the entire amount of food-grain deficit under the PL-480 programme. Food aid during the 1960s not only meant that the government was absolved of the responsibility to spend the scarce development resources for agricultural development and carry out institutional reforms but it also meant that additional funds could be obtained by the government by selling PL-480 grains to the domestic consumers so long as the country remained on food aids. (Mosharaff Hossain, 1991, p. 2)

The green revolution in Bangladesh was introduced in several phases. It began with the increased distribution of chemical fertilizers. This was followed by the introduction of more modern irrigation techniques, such as shallow and deep tube wells (STWs and DTWs) and low-lift pumps (LLPs) in the early 1960s. However, it was not until the late 1960s when the high-yielding varieties (HYVs) of rice and wheat were introduced, that the use of irrigation and fertilizers assumed any real significance.

The introduction of HYVs (biological innovations) in Bangladesh involved several phases of technology transfer. Following Hayami and Ruttan (1985, pp. 260–62), these can be distinguished as:

- *Material transfer:* Characterized by simple transfer or import of new materials, such as seeds, plants, animals, machines and associated techniques. Systematic local adaptation features very little if at all in this phase. The local adaptation of technology transferred results, primarily from the trial and errors by farmers, among others (see, for example, Biggs and Clay, 1981).
- *Design transfer:* Characterized by transfer of certain designs and corresponds to an early stage of the evolution of publicly supported

agricultural research, in that experiment stations conduct primarily simple tests and demonstrations.

• *Capacity transfer*: Characterized by transfer of scientific knowledge and capacity, which enables the production of locally adaptable technology, based on the prototype that exists abroad. A salient feature in the process of the capacity transfer is the migration of agricultural scientists.

In the late 1960s, IR-5, IR-8 and IR-20 varieties of rice were introduced, initially through the direct import of seeds, and in the late 1960s and early 1970s, HYVs of wheat were introduced. Subsequently, however, the Bangladesh agricultural research system adapted and indigenously developed different strains of rice and wheat that were multiplied and released to farmers for expanded production (Alauddin and Tisdell, 1986; 1991; see also Alauddin, 1981; Pray and Anderson, 1985).

The above changes are certainly significant. However, they should be seen as part of a continuing process of agricultural intensification as correctly observed by Jones (1984, p. 198) in the context of agrarian change in a Bangladesh village. This is also consistent with an earlier observation by Farmer (1977, p. 13):

> Contrary to a popular misapprehension, rice-growing in South Asia was not sunk in the primitive cultivation of low-yielding indigenous varieties until, suddenly, new high-yielding varieties (HYVs) became available. Rice-breeding like plant breeding in general, is a continuum. A long process of selection was undertaken by farmers through the ages, and the modern period of rice-breeding has a respectably long history, stretching back in India to the early years of this century. ... HYVs, then, are no revolutionary phenomenon. There is, however, a technical sense in which high-yielding varieties did suddenly become available.

In Bangladesh, the introduction of the irrigated HYVs did not mark the only change that took place three decades ago, nor is the present situation static (Jones, 1984). The changes that have taken place over this period must be seen in a dynamic context. For example, more than 30 varieties of rice were developed by the Bangladesh agricultural research system (Dey *et al.*, 1996, p. 185). This process typifies a combination of design and capacity transfer.

Since the introduction of the green revolution technologies, agriculture in Bangladesh has experienced significant changes both on the input and output sides. Some selected indicators are set out in Table 3.1. Changes in different variables between two end-points in time, spanning nearly three decades, are compared. The salient features of the period between the late 1960s (three year average of 1967–68 to 1969–70) and the first half of the 1990s (three year average of 1994–95 to 1996–97) are as follows:

Table 3.1 Selected indicators of technical change in Bangladesh agriculture, 1967–69[a] to 1994–96[b]

Indicator	1967-69[a]	1994-96[b]	Index (1967–69=100)
Gross cropped area (000 hectares)	12 871	13 610	105.7
Net cropped area (000 hectares)	8 786	7 799	88.8
Area under rice crop (000 hectares)	9 987	10 022	100.4
Rice area as % of gross cropped area	77.6	73.6	94.8
Area under HYV rice (000 hectares)	162	5 007***	3 090.7
HYV area as % of total rice area	1.6	50.3**	3 143.8
Area under wheat crop (000 hectares)	105	692	659.4
Area under HYV wheat (000 hectares)	6.4	692	10 812.5
HYV area as % of total wheat area	6.1	100	1 639.3
Total irrigated area (000 hectares)	1 060*	3 606	340.2
Irrigated area as % of gross cropped area	8.0*	26.5	331.3
Irrigated food-grain area as % of total irrigated area	85.8*	91.5	106.6
Irrigation by methods: modern (%)[c]	31.5*	88.7	281.6
traditional (%)[d]	68.5*	11.3	18.0
Total fertilizer used (000 m/tons nutrient)	113.1	1 017**	899.2
Fertilizer use (nutrient kg/net hectare)	12.9	130.4	991.9
Cropping intensity (%)	146.5	174.5	119.1

Food-grain production: rice	11 669	17 801	152.5
wheat	97	1 356	1 398.4
total	11 766	19 157	162.8
Food-grain yield (kg/gross ha): rice	1 169	1 776	151.9
wheat	924	1 959	212.0
total	1 166	1 788	153.3
Food-grain yield (kg/net ha)[e]: rice	1 713	3 099	180.9
total	1 708	3 120	182.7

NOTES

* 1969–70 only.
** Average of 1992–93, 1993–94 and 1994–95.
a Average of 1967–68, 1968–69 and 1969–70.
b Average of 1994–95, 1995–96 and 1996–97.
c Irrigation by shallow and deep tube wells, low-lift pumps, and large-scale canals.
d Irrigation by all other methods including swing baskets, *doon* etc.
e Adjusted for multiple cropping (inflated by intensity of cropping).

Sources: Based on data from Alauddin and Tisdell (1991, p. 26) and BBS (1998b, pp. 124–7; 1999b, pp. 51, 54–5); Shahabuddin and Rahman (1998, p. 219); GOB (1998, pp. 36–7, 107).

- While there is a 5.7 per cent increase in gross cropped area (including multiple cropping), the net cropped area decreased by more than 11 per cent. This resulted in a greater intensity of cropping by 19 per cent (from 146.5 per cent in 1967–69 to 174.5 per cent in 1994–96).
- The gross area under rice crops decreased marginally but the relative share of rice to total cropped area decreased by 5.2 per cent. The area under wheat cultivation registered a spectacular six-fold boost. Overall, the combined area under food-grains (rice and wheat) increased by nearly 7 per cent.
- The area under HYV rice increased significantly from 1.6 per cent of the gross rice area at the onset of the green revolution to more than 50 per cent three decades later.
- The total irrigated area more than trebled from 1.06 million hectares to more than 3.3 million hectares over the period under consideration. A quarter of the gross cropped area is under irrigation. One noteworthy feature of this process is that the share of areas irrigated by modern methods (STWs, DTWs, LLPs and large-scale canal irrigation) rose from less than a third of the total to nearly 89 per cent. Furthermore, the bulk (more than 90 per cent) of the irrigated area is under food-grain production.
- The use of chemical fertilizers increased more than eight-fold from 8.8 kilograms per hectare in 1967–69 to 75 kilograms per hectare in the 1990s.
- Overall, food-grain production increased by nearly 63 per cent, with rice registering a moderate increase of 52 per cent while wheat output rose dramatically by nearly 1300 per cent.

3.3 PERFORMANCE OF THE CROP SECTOR: AN ANALYSIS OF THE AGGREGATE TIME SERIES DATA

One of the principal objectives of this chapter is to compare growth rates of various crops and commodity groups, between and within sub-periods. The conventional way is to fit exponential trend lines to each segment of a time series. Alternatively, growth rates over, say, two sub-periods can be estimated by fitting a single equation involving a dummy variable. Thus estimating a single trend equation using a dummy variable is equivalent to estimating two individual trend equations. If there are three sub-periods, as is the case here, then one needs to use two dummy variables. Furthermore, one might *a priori* expect the intercepts to differ between sub-periods. Thus, it is possible to have differential intercepts as well as differential slopes (Gujarati, 1995, pp. 512–13). Given that the 50-year time is divided into three sub-periods, there are two trend breaks: 1967–68 and 1981–82. Considering these possibilities, the following functional form is postulated:

$$\ln Y = \alpha_1 + \beta_1 T + \beta_2 D_1 + \beta_3 D_2 + \alpha_2 D_3 + \alpha_3 D_4 + \varepsilon \qquad (3.1)$$

Where

- T is 1 for 1947–48 etc.
- D_1 assumes value of T for the sub-period 1967–68 to 1981–82 (Years 21–35) and 0 otherwise
- D_2 assumes value of T for the sub-period 1982–83 to 1996–97 (Years 36–50) and 0 otherwise
- D_3 assumes value of 1 for the sub-period 1967–68 to 1981–82 (Years 21–35) and 0 otherwise.
- D_4 assumes value of 1 for the sub-period 1982–83 to 1996–97 (Years 36–50) and 0 otherwise

For the post-green revolution period (1967–68 to 1996–97), the postulated equation is as follows:

$$\ln Y = \alpha_1 + \beta_1 T + \beta_2 D_1 + \alpha_2 D_2 + \varepsilon \qquad (3.2)$$

Where

- T is 1 for 1967–68 etc.
- D_1 assumes value of T for the sub-period 1982–83 to 1996–97 (Years 16–30) and 0 otherwise
- D_2 assumes value of 1 for the sub-period 1982–83 to 1996–97 (Years 16–30) and 0 otherwise

To facilitate aggregation, output is measured in value terms using 1981–83 (average for the years 1981–82, 1982–83 and 1983–84) harvest prices of agricultural commodities. The average prices have been derived using respective production figures as weights. The growth rates have been estimated using index numbers of the relevant variables with the average of the triennium ending 1977–78 as the base.

3.3.1 Crop Output Growth: 1947–48 to 1996–97

The 21 crops comprising four broad commodity groups and for the entire period of the time series are set out in Table 3.2. Growth rates are estimated employing equation (3.1). A model like (3.1) or (3.2) is particularly useful in situations where the explanatory variable is time, (T), since in that case the model describes the constant relative (= slope) or constant percentage (100 x slope) rate of growth (Gujarati, 1995, p. 170). The slope coefficient gives the instantaneous (at a point of time) rate of growth and not the compound (over a period) rate of growth. Taking the anti-log of the slope coefficient gives the compound rate of growth (Gujarati, 1995, p. 171).

Table 3.2 Crops included for analysis for crop output growth during various sub-periods: Bangladesh, 1947–96

Commodity group	Crops included (1947–96)	Crops included (1967–96)
Cereals	Six crops of rice: *Aus* local, *Aman* local, *boro* local, *Aus* HYV, *Aman* HYV, *Boro* HYV, wheat local, wheat HYV	Six crops of rice: *Aus* local, *Aman* local, *boro* local, *Aus* HYV, *Aman* HYV, *boro* HYV, wheat local, wheat HYV
Cash crops	Jute, sugarcane, tobacco and tea	Jute, sugarcane, tobacco and tea
Oilseeds	Rape and mustard, sesame seeds, linseeds, groundnut (*Rabi* and *Kharif*) and coconut	Rape and mustard, sesame seeds, linseeds, groundnut (*Rabi* and *Kharif*) and coconut
Pulses	Lentils, gram, *mashkalai* and *moong*	Lentils, gram, *mashkalai*, *khesari*, pea and *moong*
Vegetables	Data not available	Mango, banana, pineapple and jackfruit
Fruits	Data not available	Potato, sweet potato, tomato, cabbage and cauliflower
Spices	Data not available	Chilli, onion, garlic and turmeric

Table 3.3 sets out the instantaneous growth rates of various crops and commodity groups for the three sub-periods. It can be clearly seen that:

- Various crops/commodity groups have experienced differential rates of growth both between and within sub-periods. Growth rates in all the sub-

Table 3.3 Estimated growth rates in output and yield of major crops for different periods: Bangladesh, 1947–96
Equation estimated: $lnY = \alpha_1 + \beta_1 T + \beta_2 D_1 + \beta_3 D_2 + \alpha_2 D_3 + \alpha_3 D_4 + \varepsilon$

Crop Output	Intercept			Growth rate (% per annum)			Diagnostics		
	1947–66 α_1	1967–81 $\alpha_1+\alpha_2$	1982–96 $\alpha_1+\alpha_3$	1947–66 β_1	1967–91 $\beta_1+\beta_2$	1982–96 $\beta_1+\beta_3$	Adj-R^2	D-W Statistic	Log of likelihood function
Cereals	3.956	4.039	4.042	2.304	2.123	2.267	0.951	1.931	60.978
t-value	72.070	0.483*	0.341*	4.713	-0.245*	-0.051*			
Rice	3.967	4.114	3.995	2.308	1.850	2.312	0.945	1.928	60.928
t-value	72.660	0.858*	0.110*	4.733	-0.623*	0.061*			
Wheat	1.693	-1.357	5.455	5.697	20.208	1.353	0.989	1.815	19.601
t-value	6.298	-4.596	4.179	2.989	4.680	-1.597			
Jute	4.605	5.221	5.350	1.526	-1.721	-1.973	0.115	1.967	15.440
t-value	43.160	1.770	1.715	1.399	-2.165	-2.055			
Cash crops	4.314	4.874	4.888	1.991	-0.712	-0.399	0.429	1.978	38.986
t-value	63.240	2.456	1.699	3.662	-2.842	-2.538			
Oilseeds	4.157	4.859	3.890	2.541	-0.682	3.219	0.776	1.972	14.155
t-value	37.990	1.903	-0.525*	2.881	-2.103	0.399*			
Pulses	5.052	5.074	4.249	-2.696	-1.534	2.651	0.806	2.001	20.321
t-value	47.280	0.065*	-1.549	-3.150	0.788*	3.682			
Non-cereals	4.340	4.861	4.603	1.769	-0.679	0.601	0.666	1.915	43.769
t-value	59.900	2.239	0.768*	3.073	-2.482	-1.213*			
All crops	4.020	4.171	4.107	1.979	1.456	1.556	0.955	2.023	68.057
t-value	77.310	0.947*	0.374*	4.880	-0.760*	-0.216*			

Yield per gross cropped hectare

Crop	Intercept			Growth rate (% per annum)			Adj-R^2	D-W Statistic	Diagnostics Log of likelihood function
	1947–66 α_1	1967–81 $\alpha_1+\alpha_2$	1982–96 $\alpha_1+\alpha_3$	1947–66 β_1	1967–91 $\beta_1+\beta_2$	1982–96 $\beta_1+\beta_3$			
Cereals	6.739	6.700	6.435	1.332	1.368	2.208	0.937	2.042	72.505
t-value	161.200	-0.297	-1.561	4.025	0.065*	1.593			
Rice	6.741	6.320	6.343	1.341	1.211	1.447	0.934	2.037	72.303
t-value	161.600	-0.007*	-2.400	4.062	-0.231*	1.916			
Wheat	6.202	5.056	8.037	1.636	7.142	-1.072	0.954	1.886	38.238
t-value	51.130	-3.335	3.376	1.785	3.859	-1.899			
Jute	1.220	0.823	0.800	0.106	0.911	1.104	0.438	2.008	43.413
t-value	15.190	-1.583	-1.147*	0.168*	0.748*	0.960*			
Cash crops	8.740	8.461	8.383	0.461	1.138	1.373	0.655	2.011	58.979
t-value	124.900	-1.350	-1.195	0.858*	0.746*	1.063*			
Oilseeds	7.771	8.309	7.524	2.184	-0.340	2.217	0.173	2.008	-17.609
t-value	44.270	0.878*	-0.270*	1.521	-1.004*	-0.023*			
Pulses	7.823	8.228	7.377	0.083	-1.407	1.183	0.511	1.993	82.255
t-value	287.200	4.419	-3.278	0.375*	-3.904	2.905			
Non-cereals	8.402	8.393	8.338	1.265	0.691	0.699	0.378	1.960	56.977
t-value	172.200	-0.059*	-0.268*	3.224	0.847*	-0.845*			
All crops	10.050	9.674	9.836	1.496	2.809	1.881	0.780	1.888	39.514
t-value	130.300	-1.508	-0.584*	2.436	1.247*	0.374*			

Yield per net-cropped hectare

Crop	Intercept			Growth rate (% per annum)			Diagnostics		
	1947–66 α_1	1967–81 $\alpha_1 + \alpha_2$	1982–96 $\alpha_1 + \alpha_3$	1947–66 β_1	1967–91 $\beta_1 + \beta_2$	1982–96 $\beta_1 + \beta_3$	Adj-R^2	D-W Statistic	Log of likelihood function
Cereals	6.974	6.967	6.467	1.596	1.764	3.309	0.960	2.063	65.234
t-value	106.400	-0.039*	-1.862	3.193	0.200*	2.217			
Rice	6.975	7.003	6.375	1.608	1.621	3.495	0.958	2.057	65.103
t-value	106.800	0.144*	-2.203	3.225	0.160*	2.400			
All crops	10.290	9.931	9.890	1.751	3.226	2.938	0.874	1.860	37.093
t-value	120.300	-1.321	-1.003*	2.585	1.274*	1.053*			

Note: 1947 refers to financial year beginning July 1947 etc. The *t*-values for the estimated intercepts and slopes actually relate to those of the corresponding dummy variables. Critical values of *t*-statistic with 40 degrees of freedom and on tails test are: 1.303 (10% level of significance), 1.684 (5% level of significance) and 2.423 (1% level of significance). An * implies that the estimated coefficient is not statistically significant.

Sources: BBS (1976, pp. 1–7, 12–29, 66–91, 104–29, 144–76, 198–205, 218–27, 258–77; 1979, pp. 160–71, 182–4, 190–92, 192–207, 368; 1980, pp. 25–37; 1982, pp. 230–49; 1984a, pp. 31–42; 1984b, pp. 244–83; 1985a, pp. 24–58, 157–9, 203–36, 383–401, 485–6, 792–806; 1985b, pp. 258–328; 1985c, pp. 426–35; 1986a, pp. 39–66; 1986d; 25–48; 1988a, pp. 154–98; 1996, pp. 147–50, 571; 1998b, pp. 124–7, 140–4; 1999b, pp. 51, 54–9); EPBS (1969, pp.40–1); GOB (1998, p.36–7, 107); Shahabuddin and Rahman (1998, p. 219); World Bank (1982, Tables 2.5, 2.20).

periods for cereals are closer to those of rice. All crops except pulses experienced positive rates of growth in sub-period 1.

- In the second sub-period, non-cereals as a whole experienced a negative rate of growth, as did jute, cash crops as a group and pulses. Overall, the crop output increased at a slower rate in the second sub-period compared to the first although the choice of sub-periods may have influenced the pattern of output growth. In the early 1970s, agricultural output suffered due to the dislocation caused by the War of Liberation, and the effects of severe droughts and floods. It was not until 1975–76 that crop output regained the pre-independence level of the late 1960s, at a time which marks the beginning of our second sub-period. Furthermore, the drought in the late 1970s had a slowing effect on the growth rate.
- Wheat output increased by more than 20 per cent during the second sub–period.
- During the third sub–period, crop output increased at a faster rate, although some of the estimated coefficients are not statistically significant. One notable improvement occurred in the case of pulses, which registered a significantly positive rate of growth during the last segment of the time series. Wheat output growth slowed quite considerably in the third sub-period. Overall, output-composition exhibits a pattern away from non-cereals.
- This analysis identifies two types of yields per hectare: yield per gross cropped hectare (i.e., including multiple cropping) and yield per net cropped hectare (i.e., yield per gross cropped hectare deflated by the index of cropping intensity). Crop output growth in the latter sub-periods has resulted primarily from higher growth in yield. This phenomenon features even more prominently in the case of yield per net hectare.

3.3.2 Crop Output Growth in the Period of the New Agricultural Technology: 1967–68 to 1996–97

Table 3.2 also sets out the extended commodity group, Pulses, and the three additional commodity groups: Fruits, Vegetables and Spices.

Let us now turn to the rate of growth of output and yield by major commodity groups following the green revolution. Table 3.4 sets out estimated growth rates for the relevant crops. The following patterns in crop output growth seem to emerge:

- Output of non-cereal crops increased at a faster rate in the third sub-period than in the second. Spices growth has decelerated quite considerably. There are some improvements in the growth of fruits. Pulses have registered the fastest growth rates among the non-cereals due primarily to area-based increase of *khesari*, a nutritionally inferior variety of pulses.

- Growth in yield per gross cropped hectare for pulses has changed from negative to positive between the two sub-periods. Spices yields have declined quite considerably. Yields of non-cereal crops have, in general declined. Gross yield of all crops taken together has shown signs of a decline, as has net yield per hectare.

3.4 TOTAL FACTOR PRODUCTIVITY GROWTH

This section investigates growth in total factor productivity (TFP) in agriculture in Bangladesh focusing on the crop sector. Previous studies (such as Pray and Anderson, 1985; Dey and Evenson, 1991), while substantial, concentrate on a limited number of crops and a limited number of inputs. Furthermore, these studies either pre-date or cover only the initial years of the structural reform process.

This section draws on an earlier study by Jahan and Alauddin (1996b). Applying the Tornqvist–Theil (T–T) index of total factor productivity growth, Jahan and Alauddin (1996b) extended the previous studies by incorporating a larger number of crops and inputs, as well as the time series to assess the impact of recent policy changes. They identified phases when TFP growth exhibits upward and downward trends. Based on Jahan and Alauddin (1996b), Jahan (1998) carried out further analysis of the process of productivity growth in Bangladesh. Jahan and Alauddin (1996b) and Jahan (1998) provide a detailed survey of literature, discussion on methodological issues and data sources and their limitations that we do not wish to repeat here. The remainder of this section reports some of the findings of the two above-named studies.

Here we employ the TFP index proposed by Christensen and Jorgenson (1969; 1970). Equation (3.3) below expresses the T–T index in logarithmic form as follows:

$$\left(\frac{TFP_t}{TFP_{t-1}}\right) = \frac{1}{2}\sum_{i=1}^{n}(R_{it} + R_{it-1})\ln\left(\frac{Y_{it}}{Y_{it-1}}\right) - \frac{1}{2}\sum_{i=1}^{n}(S_{jt} + S_{jt-1})\ln\left(\frac{X_{jt}}{X_{jt-1}}\right)$$

(3.3)

Where
R_{it} = output revenue shares
Y_{it} = output indices
S_{jt} = input cost shares
x_{jt} = input indices

The above index has been compiled by Christensen and Jorgenson (1969; 1970) as a discrete approximation to the Divisia index (further details are provided in Jahan, 1998).

Table 3.4 Estimated growth rates of output and yield of various crops included in the extended commodity groups: Bangladesh, 1967–96

Equation estimated: $\ln Y = \alpha_1 + \beta_1 T + \beta_2 D_1 + \alpha_2 D_2 + \varepsilon$

Crop	Intercept		Growth rate (% per annum)		Diagnostics		
Output	1967–81 α_1	1982–96 $\alpha_1 + \alpha_2$	1967–81 β_1	1982–96 $\beta_1 + \beta_2$	Adjusted R^2	D-W Statistic	Log of likelihood function
Pulses	5.282	3.857	-2.281	3.510	0.861	1.968	14.172
t-value	16.280	-2.620	-2.028	-3.822			
Vegetables	4.273	4.131	1.197	1.723	0.837	1.809	39.101
t-value	20.340	0.542*	1.679	-0.413*			
Fruits	5.004	4.542	-1.417	-0.019	0.954	2.411	63.993
t-value	29.290	-1.763	-2.571	1.876			
Spices	1.876	3.852	8.050	2.419	0.921	1.574	45.409
t-value	1.588*	-1.767	2.495	1.756			
Non-cereals	4.591	4.341	0.193	1.084	0.726	1.939	45.055
t-value	16.990	-0.584*	0.217*	0.733*			
All crops	4.220	4.238	1.676	1.770	0.924	2.007	48.583
t-value	25.840	0.067*	3.040	0.125*			

Yield per gross cropped hectare

Crop	Intercept		Growth rate (% per annum)		Diagnostics		
	1967–81 α_1	1982–96 $\alpha_1+\alpha_2$	1967–81 β_1	1982–96 $\beta_1+\beta_2$	Adjusted R^2	D-W Statistic	Log of likelihood function
Pulses	8.165	7.693	−1.681	0.045	0.585	2.031	52.947
T-value	88.280	−3.060	−5.260	4.007			
Vegetables	9.214	8.887	0.178	1.208	0.865	1.782	59.473
T-value	76.620	−1.675	0.440*	1.863			
Fruits	11.254	10.321	−3.086	−0.369	0.984	2.371	69.812
t-value	127.800	−6.541	−10.46	6.723			
Spices	6.943	8.766	6.741	1.548	0.919	1.751	44.954
t-value	6.678	1.698	2.311	−1.708			
Non-cereals	8.832	8.869	0.250	0.065	0.108	1.899	41.144
t-value	46.470	0.118*	0.387*	−0.210*			
All crops	9.655	10.093	2.181	0.766	0.622	1.845	33.013
t-value	31.630	0.884*	2.129	−1.008*			

Yield per net-cropped hectare

All crops	9.818	10.165	2.90	1.782	0.804	1.810	31.236
t-value	28.160	0.616*	2.492	−0.700*			

Note: 1967 indicates financial year beginning July 1967 etc. The *t*-values for the estimated intercepts and slopes actually relate to those of the corresponding dummy variables. Critical values of *t*-statistic with 25 degrees of freedom and one-tail test are: 1.316 (10% level of significance), 1.708 (5% level of significance) and 2.485 (1% level of significance). An * implies that the estimated coefficient is not statistically significant.

Sources: Based on data from sources mentioned in Tables 3.1 and 3.3.

Table 3.5 specifies the crops and factor inputs used to estimate total factor productivity for the period encompassing 1948–49 to 1992–93. It considers 25 crops comprising several commodity groups. The total area under these crops accounts for more than 95 per cent of gross cropped area in Bangladesh. The input side includes (a) costs on primary inputs such as land and human labour, (b) costs on inputs from the manufacturing complex such as irrigation, chemical fertilizers, pesticides, and (c) costs on organic matters such as cow and other animal dung. Farmgate prices of crop outputs are used to obtain an aggregate value of output and to derive revenue shares.

Table 3.5 Crops and factor inputs included in the analysis of total factor productivity (TFP) growth in the Bangladesh crop sector

Crops	Factor inputs
Aus local rice, *Aman* local rice, *boro* local rice, *Aus* HYV rice, *Aman* HYV rice, *boro* HYV rice, wheat local, wheat HYV, jute, sugarcane, tobacco, rape and mustard, sesame seeds, linseeds, groundnut (*Rabi* and *Kharif*), lentils, gram, *mashkalai, khesari*, pea and *moong*, potato and sweet potato	Gross cropped area (including area under multiple cropping); labour (male and female); seeds (of all crops included in TFP estimates); fertilizers (urea, triple superphosphate, muriate of potash); irrigation (LLPs, DTWs, STWs and traditional and canal irrigation) draught animal power; cow and other animal dung; all types of pesticides

Sources: Based on Jahan and Alauddin (1996b, pp. 5–6) and Jahan (1998, pp. 70–71).

Employing Equation (3.1) and the methodology summarized in Table 3.5, the TFP indices as derived by Jahan (1998) are set out in Table 3.6 which also sets out growth rates in TFP for different phases during the time series under consideration (see also Figure 3.1).

Table 3.6 clearly shows that TFP increased at a rate of 1.85 per cent per annum during the pre-green revolution phase (1948–67). During the second phase, the growth rate rose to 2.05 per cent per annum during the early green revolution phase (1968–81). The policy rationalization phase (1982–93) is characterized by a statistically significant negative rate of growth of nearly 2.8 per cent.

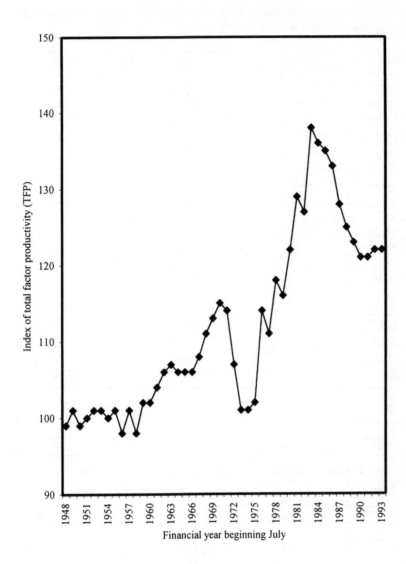

Figure 3.1 Total factor productivity growth in Bangladesh agriculture, 1948–93

Table 3.6 Estimated growth rates in total factor productivity indices in the Bangladesh crop sector, 1948–92

Year	Output	Input	Total Factor Productivity
1948	100	100	99
1949	102	100	101
1950	100	101	99
1951	101	101	100
1952	103	101	101
1953	103	101	101
1954	102	102	100
1955	104	102	101
1956	101	102	98
1957	103	102	101
1958	102	103	98
1959	106	103	102
1960	106	104	102
1961	109	104	104
1962	111	105	106
1963	113	105	107
1964	115	108	106
1965	116	109	106
1966	117	110	106
1967	120	110	108
1968	124	110	111
1969	127	112	113
1970	129	112	115
1971	127	111	114
1972	117	109	107
1973	110	109	101
1974	113	111	101
1975	114	111	102
1976	128	112	114
1977	127	114	111
1978	137	116	118
1979	140	120	116
1980	153	125	122
1981	167	128	129
1982	166	129	127
1983	181	130	138
1984	178	130	136
1985	178	131	135

Year	Output	Input	Total Factor Productivity
1986	175	131	133
1987	170	132	128
1988	166	132	125
1989	165	133	123
1990	161	133	121
1991	163	134	121
1992	164	134	122
1993	165	134	122
Growth rates (%) in total factor productivity			
1948–93	1.56 (significant at 0.1 per cent level)		
1948–68	1.85 (significant at 0.1 per cent level)		
1969–81	2.05 (significant at 2.5 per cent level)		
1982–93	–2.77 (significant at 2.5 per cent level)		

Notes: 1948 indicates financial year beginning July.

Sources: Based on a large number of sources cited in Jahan and Alauddin (1996b) and Jahan (1998, p. 74).

The slow growth rate in TFP in the pre-green revolution is due primarily to the predominance of traditional technology coupled with low responding varieties of rice. During this phase, elements of green revolution technology such as mechanized irrigation and chemical fertilizers were introduced. This may have caused TFP to increase somewhat in the period immediately preceding the introduction of the HYVs.

The subsequent introduction of seed–fertilizer–irrigation technology led to an increase in TFP in the late 1960s. However, TFP declined in the early 1970s for a number of reasons including dislocation caused by the War of Liberation and successive natural calamities such as flood and drought (Mahabub Hossain, 1984). At the end of the 1970s, research, extension and introduction of more suitable minor irrigation facilities, that is STWs, were conducive to faster growth in output and hence total factor productivity.

During the 1982–93 period, TFP has experienced a declining trend. This declining trend may have occurred when, with liberalization in agricultural inputs, unexpected demand shocks lead to under- or over-utilization of capacity or when sudden changes in factor prices such as the irrigation equipment price shocks or diesel price shocks of 1983, 1984, 1985, 1986 and 1989 result in short-run relative factor usage, which is inappropriate for the long run. Besides, consecutive natural calamities such as floods compounded the situation in 1984, 1985, 1987 and 1988.

The results of the present study indicate not only a slowing down of TFP growth in the Bangladesh crop sector but also are a sign of retrogression.

Several factors may be at work. These include, *inter alia,* faster growth rate in inputs (irrigation, chemicals and so on) compared to output. Furthermore, the adverse environmental implications of intensive agriculture may have affected agricultural production at the margin (see for example, Alauddin and Tisdell, 1995). The results from Bangladesh seem consistent with those in other developing countries, such as India, Pakistan and the Philippines, where TFP growth has slowed down considerably or is on the decline (Evenson and Pray, 1991).

3.5 CONCLUDING COMMENTS

The agricultural sector of Bangladesh has undergone massive transformation over a period of nearly five decades. The most important manifestation of this process is the intensification of agriculture. The process of change has been a continuous phenomenon and in the last five decades, the most important episode was the introduction of new technology known as the green revolution in the latter part of the 1960s. The green revolution has made a significant contribution to the growth of crops in Bangladesh. The output of food-grains in the 1990s is 2.5 times that of the 1950s. Since the green revolution, overall food-grain output has increased by more than 60 per cent through a moderate rise in rice output and spectacular growth in wheat output. However, the Bangladesh crop sector remains a virtual rice monoculture. The period under consideration has witnessed a trend away from non-cereals with no noticeable increase in the output of non-cereal crops. If anything, outputs of some of these crops might have remained static or in some cases may have fallen. In terms of growth in total factor productivity, the process exhibits a phenomenon of a slow-down, if not retrogression. Recent evidence supports a deceleration hypothesis in agriculture in Bangladesh in the early 1990s (Shahabuddin and Rahman, 1998). This means that the greater use of modern input, such as chemical fertilizers and pesticides, underpins crop output growth in agriculture in Bangladesh. The late 1990s, however, has witnessed a significant recovery in agricultural growth (H.Z. Rahman, 2000).

The above process of crop output growth has significant implications for balance between food supply and demand. Furthermore, the process has engendered spillover effects, which have ramifications for the environment and the sustainability of the livelihoods of the rural masses. Subsequent chapters, especially Chapter 9, discuss these issues in greater depth.

4. Overall Food Supply and Self-sufficiency: Some Observations

4.1 INTRODUCTION

As discussed in earlier chapters, especially in Chapter 3, Bangladesh's food-grain production has substantially increased since the introduction of the green revolution technologies. However, there seems to be a commodity bias in favour of cereals. Earlier evidence on Bangladesh agriculture clearly suggested that the green revolution might have been primarily a cereal revolution rather than a broad-based crop revolution (Alauddin and Tisdell, 1991; see also Mellor, 1994). This was consistent with the earlier evidence from elsewhere in the developing world, which seemed to suggest a process typifying a phenomenon of a trend away from non-cereals and a trend in favour of cereals (see, for example, Staub and Blasé, 1974, pp. 584–5; Sawant, 1983, pp. 479–91). Redclift (1984, p. 64) has argued that the narrowing of popular diets was one of the costs of the green revolution.

Against the above background, this chapter examines the extent to which crop production has led to increased availability of food in terms of dietary balance and nutritional standards. The question of overall food supply and self-sufficiency is critically examined using trends in per capita availability of cereal and non-cereal food items. Also examined is the trend in import dependency. Earlier studies (for example, Alauddin and Tisdell, 1991) indicated that the potential gains from the green revolution appear to have been swallowed up in supporting a larger population, rather than in improving living standards for the masses. To what extent does this phenomenon still persist or has this trend been reversed? Higher economic production does not necessarily imply an increase in economic welfare (Meier, 1984). To what extent has increased agricultural production led to increased welfare of the average Bangladeshi consumer? Is the average Bangladeshi diet more or less diversified? This chapter explores these questions based on more recent evidence from Bangladesh.

4.2 TRENDS IN FOOD-GRAIN PRODUCTION, IMPORT AND AVAILABILITY FOR CONSUMPTION

Table 4.1 sets out information on domestic production of rice and wheat (RICEP and WHEATP) used as a proxy for overall food-grain production (FOODP). Table 4.1 also sets out total quantities of food-grains imported (IMPORT), off-take of food-grain quantities from government stock (OFFTAKE) and the amount that the government procures internally (PROCURE). The quantity of food-grains actually available for consumption (AVLFOOD) is defined as FOODP (less 10 per cent for seed, feed and wastage) − PROCURE + OFFTAKE. Government stock formation and OFFTAKE subsume imported quantities.

In aggregate terms, domestic food production in the 1992–96 period has increased by 125 per cent compared to the 1950–54 level of production. At the same time, however, Bangladesh on average imported more than 8 per cent of the total quantity of available food-grains during 1992–96 compared to an import content of only 2 per cent during the first half of the 1950s.

Bangladesh, for generations, had been self-sufficient in food, but in the last few decades, it has become a net importer of food-grains. Furthermore, agricultural production in Bangladesh has displayed considerable variability because of climatic variability (BBS, 1999a). These fluctuations in domestic production require varying quantities of imports to meet the needs of a growing population. Considering food imports as a percentage of total amounts of food-grains available for consumption can highlight the import intensity of Bangladesh's food-grains. In the 32 years since the 1966 financial year, on 20 occasions the food import intensity of Bangladesh has exceeded 10 per cent of the total food-grains available for consumption (see Figure 4.1). In the last nine years of the time series, the intensity of food-grains imports has decreased somewhat, in that on seven occasions, Bangladesh imported less than 10 per cent of total food-grain requirements. While this may be an encouraging sign, one should exercise caution for two reasons.

- First, as Shahabuddin and Rahman (1998, pp. 96–9) have shown, a recent slow down of agricultural growth rates has led to an increasing divergence between the actual quantity of food-grain required and the amount available from domestic sources. Shahabuddin and Rahman (1998, p. 96) derive food-grain requirement assuming a per capita daily requirement of 465 grams. The widening 'food gap' between domestic supply and available food was earlier identified by Alauddin and Tisdell (1991, p. 259). Lower import intensity implies, in this situation, a lower per capita availability of food-grains for consumption.

Table 4.1 Domestic production, availability and import intensity of food-grains in Bangladesh, 1950–96

YEAR	RICEP	WHEATP	FOODP	IMPORT	OFFTAKE	PROCURE	AVLFOOD	IMPAVL
1950	7460.78	20.42	7481.20	144.28	193.05	66.04	6860.09	2.10
1951	7147.61	23.17	7170.78	94.49	254.01	19.31	6688.41	1.41
1952	7452.88	24.39	7477.27	289.57	243.85	15.24	6958.15	4.16
1953	8377.09	24.08	8401.17	202.19	111.77	26.42	7646.40	2.64
1954	7711.06	26.62	7737.68	50.80	81.28	127.01	6918.19	0.73
1955	6486.70	22.56	6509.26	172.73	50.80	0.00	5909.14	2.92
1956	8315.92	23.78	8339.70	599.47	124.97	0.00	7630.70	7.86
1957	7110.68	22.74	7133.43	684.82	98.56	33.53	6485.11	10.56
1958	7032.53	25.50	7058.03	473.48	169.68	33.53	6488.38	7.30
1959	8617.89	29.16	8647.05	621.82	194.07	200.16	7776.25	8.00
1960	9672.26	32.92	9705.18	709.20	204.23	24.39	8914.50	7.96
1961	9617.29	39.68	9656.97	414.55	259.09	26.42	8923.95	4.65
1962	8869.76	45.17	8914.93	1459.04	721.39	10.16	8734.67	16.70
1963	10623.80	34.94	10658.74	1018.08	451.13	4.06	10039.93	10.14
1964	10500.06	34.69	10534.75	350.54	753.91	13.21	10221.97	3.43
1965	10500.73	35.66	10536.39	937.81	961.18	94.49	10349.44	9.06
1966	9575.47	59.32	9634.79	1117.65	1101.39	3.05	9769.65	11.44
1967	11171.60	59.05	11230.65	1035.35	659.41	22.35	10744.65	9.64
1968	11344.07	93.70	11437.76	1136.96	1085.14	9.14	11369.98	10.00
1969	12005.62	104.96	12110.59	1571.82	1375.73	6.10	12269.16	12.81
1970	11143.91	111.64	11255.56	1164.39	1338.13	6.10	11462.03	10.16

YEAR	RICEP	WHEATP	FOODP	IMPORT	OFFTAKE	PROCURE	AVLFOOD	IMPAVL
1971	9931.69	115.01	10046.70	1715.09	1762.84	10.16	10794.71	15.89
1972	10066.19	90.96	10157.16	2870.33	2660.01	5.08	11796.37	24.33
1973	12010.22	110.93	12121.15	1692.73	1754.71	72.14	12591.61	13.44
1974	11384.10	116.72	11500.82	2599.05	1785.19	129.04	12006.89	21.65
1975	12902.93	221.67	13124.59	1468.19	1694.77	355.62	13151.29	11.16
1976	11859.24	264.99	12124.23	807.76	1473.27	324.12	12060.96	6.70
1977	12969.37	349.25	13318.63	1634.82	2029.04	581.18	13434.62	12.17
1978	12852.42	498.96	13351.38	1180.65	1814.66	360.70	13470.21	8.76
1979	12740.58	829.24	13569.82	2871.35	2440.54	269.25	14384.13	19.96
1980	13881.40	1110.06	14991.46	1078.03	1550.49	1032.00	14010.80	7.69
1981	13630.84	856.49	14487.33	1245.67	2068.67	303.00	14804.27	8.41
1982	14216.43	1095.38	15311.80	1870.54	1936.58	192.00	15525.20	12.05
1983	14508.92	1211.44	15720.36	2133.70	2042.25	270.00	15920.57	13.40
1984	14622.86	1462.63	16085.49	2616.32	2562.00	344.00	16694.94	15.67
1985	15041.49	1041.83	16083.31	1200.00	1541.00	349.00	15666.98	7.66
1986	15163.50	1091.50	16255.00	1768.00	2120.00	181.00	16568.50	10.67
1987	15414.00	1047.80	16461.80	2922.00	2503.00	375.00	16943.62	17.25
1988	15544.00	1021.95	16565.95	2138.00	2942.00	411.00	17440.36	12.26
1989	17617.00	890.00	18507.00	1534.00	2164.00	962.00	17858.30	8.59
1990	17852.00	1004.00	18856.00	1577.00	2372.00	783.00	18559.40	8.50

YEAR	RICEP	WHEATP	FOODP	IMPORT	OFFTAKE	PROCURE	AVLFOOD	IMPAVL
1991	18252.00	1065.05	19317.05	1564.00	2345.00	1035.00	18695.35	8.37
1992	18340.00	1175.63	19515.63	1183.00	1073.00	227.00	18410.07	6.43
1993	18042.00	1131.05	19173.05	958.00	1376.00	166.00	18465.75	5.19
1994	16833.00	1245.00	18078.00	2569.00	1573.00	278.00	17565.20	14.63
1995	17687.00	1369.13	19056.13	2434.00	1900.00	422.00	18628.52	13.07
1996	18883.00	1454.00	20337.00	732.00	1326.00	684.00	18945.30	3.86

Notes: 1950 refers to financial year beginning July 1950 etc. RICEP and WHEATP respectively refer to production of (cleaned) rice and wheat. IMPORTF indicates imported quantities of rice and wheat. OFFTAKE indicates off-take of food-grains from government stocks. PROCURE refers to internal procurement of food-grains. IMPAVL is imported food-grains as a percentage of AVLFOOD. AVLFOOD = [0.9 x (RICEP + WHEATP) + OFFTAKE − PROCURE.]. All of the variables above except IMPAVL are measured in thousands of tons.

Sources: Adapted from Alauddin and Tisdell (1991, pp. 257–8). Shahabuddin and Rahman (1998, p. 103); BBS (1996, pp. 147–50, 571; 1998b, pp. 140–4, 615; 1999b, pp. 54–9).

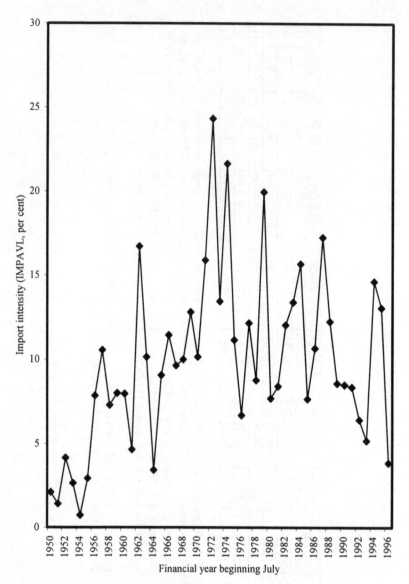

Figure 4.1   Import intensity of available food-grain for consumption (IMPAVL): Bangladesh, 1950–96

- Second, lower level of grain import does not necessarily imply a lower food import bill because Bangladesh is now becoming increasingly dependent on the import of lentils, edible oils and other food items like onions and chillies (see for example, BBS, 1998b, pp. 616–17). Import dependency on these non-cereal food items has risen significantly in recent years.

4.3 TRENDS IN PER CAPITA AVAILABILITY AND PRODUCTION OF CEREALS AND NON-CEREALS

This section analyses trends in the per capita availability of cereals and per capita production of selected non-cereal food commodities. Note that consistent and continuous time series data on consumption of the non-cereal food items are not readily available. Given that domestic supply and consumption for these commodities are likely to be highly correlated, one can use the production data as proxies for availability for consumption, especially in case of fruits and vegetables. Table 4.2 sets out relevant information on these variables. It can be clearly seen that per capita availability of cereals has not increased over the last three decades while per capita outputs of fruits and spices have registered a marked decline. They are half, or less than half of the levels of three decades ago. Per capita production of vegetables, having shown considerable annual fluctuations, has been stagnant since the early 1990s and regained the 1967–68 level only in 1996–97.

Per capita production of pulses has displayed considerable fluctuations over the years. After exhibiting a consistently declining trend for more than a decade to the early 1980s, per capita pulses production started to increase and since the early 1990s, has remained above the 1967–68 level. However, note that since the significant reversal of a trend toward production of pulses, in the mid-1980s, production levels of all nutritionally superior quality pulses especially lentils, *moong*, and gram have not increased significantly. In the 1990s, the increased production of pulses was underpinned by a significant increase in the production of a nutritionally inferior variety of pulses, namely *khesari*. Thus on a per capita basis, production of nutritionally superior pulses has declined.

After a steady decline for nearly two decades since the late 1960s (especially for a decade to the late 1980s), per capita fish production started to increase steadily, albeit from a very small base. However, it is yet to regain the late 1960s level.

Figure 4.2 highlights the changing situation in relation to the per capita availability/production of main food items over a period of three decades. Employing 1967–68 as the base year, the availability of each of the relevant commodity groups is illustrated. A massive decline in fruits and vegetables and spices can be observed. Availability of cereals per capita has shown very little tendency to increase. Both vegetables and fish have regained some lost ground

Table 4.2 Per capita availability/production of cereals (rice and wheat) and selected non-cereal food commodities in Bangladesh, 1967–96 (kg per head of population)

Year	Cereals	Pulses	Vegetables	Fruits	Spices	Fish
1967	168.55	3.68	23.90	27.35	5.08	12.31
1968	172.06	4.30	25.08	25.11	5.73	12.02
1969	177.24	4.13	25.85	23.37	5.46	11.70
1970	161.70	4.18	24.92	20.72	5.32	11.48
1971	148.95	3.88	21.41	19.07	4.71	11.23
1972	159.08	2.99	20.08	18.22	4.34	11.03
1973	163.62	2.72	18.51	17.20	3.92	10.66
1974	152.82	2.85	21.12	16.72	3.89	10.46
1975	162.98	2.73	21.82	16.47	3.83	10.20
1976	146.21	2.79	18.88	16.30	3.45	10.01
1977	168.30	2.98	20.33	16.72	3.63	8.06
1978	165.28	2.79	20.63	15.75	3.61	7.91
1979	163.95	2.44	20.21	15.14	3.40	7.36
1980	155.54	2.34	19.73	15.17	2.66	7.22
1981	162.72	2.25	21.26	15.28	3.21	7.54
1982	165.86	2.26	20.73	15.44	3.19	7.73
1983	166.29	3.77	20.55	14.27	4.13	7.88
1984	169.14	3.59	20.46	14.34	3.03	7.84
1985	155.45	3.32	19.71	14.11	2.93	7.88
1986	165.27	3.26	19.55	14.35	2.88	8.13
1987	163.74	3.28	21.38	14.01	3.37	7.99
1988	165.20	3.14	19.16	12.77	2.88	7.97
1989	168.01	3.07	19.53	13.23	3.10	8.04
1990	169.21	3.02	20.90	12.79	2.91	8.17
1991	167.24	4.64	22.06	12.53	2.88	8.52
1992	161.70	4.41	22.34	12.31	2.82	8.97
1993	158.67	4.55	22.37	12.11	2.79	9.37
1994	147.86	4.58	22.57	11.95	2.73	9.92
1995	153.74	4.32	22.41	11.78	2.59	10.23
1996	164.54	4.22	23.90	11.49	2.57	11.05

Note: 1967 refers to financial year beginning July 1967. Figures pertaining to cereals are the per capita quantities available for consumption while the remaining figures refer to quantities produced per capita.

Sources: Based on data from Alauddin and Tisdell (1991, p. 92); sources mentioned in Table 4.1; BBS (1997a, p. 252; 1988a, pp. 154–98); GOB (1998, p. 39) and sources mentioned in Table 3.3.

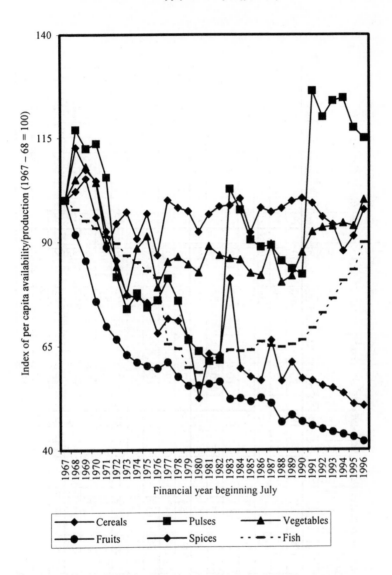

Figure 4.2   Trends in per capita availability of cereals and per capita production of selected non-cereal food items in Bangladesh, 1967–96

but are, at best, close to or below their respective late–1960s levels. The apparent increase in the per capita production of pulses masks the nutritional dimension.

Table 4.3 Real and relative price indices of cereal and selected non-cereal food commodities: Bangladesh, 1969–97 (1969–70 = 100)

Year	FOODCPI	Rice	Lentil	Potato	Chilli	Onion	Mustard oil	Fish	Beef	Chicken	Banana	Milk
1969	100	100	100	100	100	100	100	100	100	100	100	100
1972	187	105	120	95	53	68	140	111	116	117	114	86
1973	257	103	149	113	106	123	130	110	118	105	110	88
1974	508	106	88	75	242	69	137	67	81	66	72	75
1975	343	99	163	115	92	109	137	117	126	117	115	136
1976	323	91	131	88	134	67	124	144	133	136	112	147
1977	377	99	153	88	203	184	144	137	133	134	110	128
1978	430	95	155	80	103	76	126	153	154	143	109	120
1979	528	103	147	76	60	127	101	152	141	131	113	115
1980	545	86	180	89	149	106	127	159	152	142	120	126
1981	624	74	156	77	127	201	105	151	151	135	111	130
1982	633	100	166	59	68	135	102	159	145	138	105	127
1983	725	94	151	75	126	101	121	166	129	148	104	117
1984	817	96	129	67	137	108	113	169	156	166	114	125
1985	911	83	172	74	67	120	100	204	173	182	132	127
1986	1030	87	187	92	86	107	98	215	159	166	110	117
1987	1173	85	177	88	104	164	87	192	144	156	92	114
1988	1152	87	188	96	96	148	90	183	150	164	94	142

1989	1231	72	95	86	115	94	207	146	174	96	140
1990	1236	77	75	129	183	97	245	149	193	105	147
1991	1285	77	73	172	139	102	257	167	185	111	145
1992	1289	71	85	85	106	106	295	172	193	107	156
1993	1370	66	89	106	140	99	288	166	185	101	150
1994	1469	73	73	105	97	99	274	155	174	95	147
1995	1564	77	88	166	156	84	267	151	184	115	171
1996	1513	67	86	113	114	85	321	165	221	122	192
1997	1604	62	67	77	152	81	326	176	246	139	186

Notes: 1969 indicates financial year beginning July 1969 etc. FOODCPI is wholesale food price index. Columns represent real retail price indices derived by deflating the retail prices by FOODCPI.

Sources: Adapted from Alauddin and Tisdell (1991, pp. 96–7); BBS (1996, pp. 435–8; 1998b, pp. 465–76; 1999b, pp.13–27).

Thus, the commodity bias in Bangladesh agriculture still seems to persist. This seems to be consistent with the recent available evidence elsewhere in South Asia such as India (GOI, 1998).

4.4 MOVEMENTS IN RELATIVE PRICES OF SELECTED CEREALS AND NON-CEREALS

By now, it is widely recognized that relative to cereals, technological progress in Bangladesh agriculture has been much slower in the case of most non-cereal food crops. In the last three decades, non-cereal food prices have risen much faster than those for cereals. This is as a result of:

*   slower growth rates in non-cereals following slower pace of technological change;
*   rising aggregate demand from rising population growth.

Table 4.3 sets out information on relative price movements of essential food items such as rice, lentils, potatoes, chillies, onions, mustard oil, fish, bananas, beef, chicken and milk. These proxy for proxies for various cereal and non-cereal food sources.

In real terms, the rice price has displayed a consistent declining trend. Potatoes display a similar but somewhat less pronounced trend. Other non-cereal food items, while differing widely one from the other, have registered significant   price increases. The price movements in non-cereals can be summed up as follows:

*   Real prices of lentils, chicken and fish have registered the highest increases. Fish in 1997–98 is more than three times as expensive as the late-1960s level. Over the same period, both chicken and lentils have become more than twice as expensive;
*   Real prices of bananas and milk have registered steady increases;
*   Real prices of onions and chillies have been on the rise but with considerable fluctuations.

Overall, real price movements of non-cereals have shown a greater degree of instability than cereals and potatoes. These come into sharper focus when illustrated in terms of Figure 4.3 and Figure 4.4. Annual variability (coefficient of variation) of the wholesale price of food-grains has fallen over the years. For instance, during the 1980s, the coefficient of variation of wholesale rice price was estimated to be 21.9 per cent, which declined to 11.2 per cent during the 1990–95 period. A similar declining trend in the variability of monthly wholesale prices of rice can be observed (Shahabuddin and Rahman, 1998, pp. 113–4).

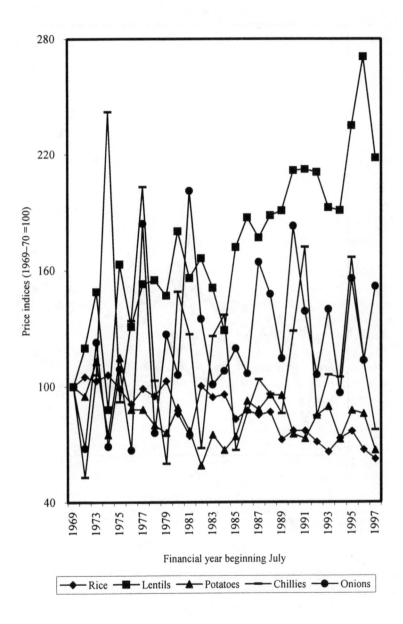

Figure 4.3 Relative price movements for rice, lentils, potatoes, chillies and onions in Bangladesh, 1969–97

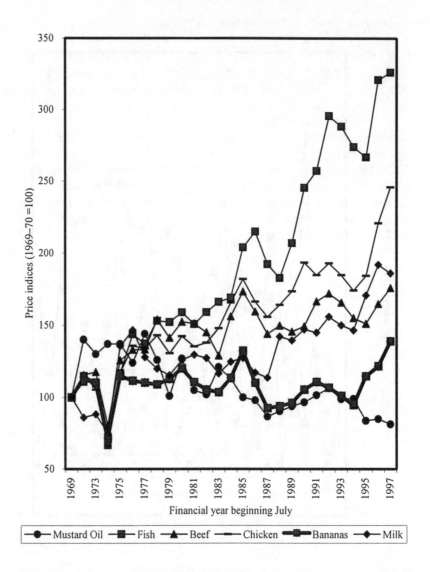

Figure 4.4   Relative price movements of mustard oil, fish, beef, chicken, bananas and milk in Bangladesh, 1969–97

4.5 SOME FURTHER OBSERVATIONS

In the light of the above, what implications do the changes in per capita production and real prices of the cereal and non-cereal commodities have for overall consumer welfare? Is the average consumer better or worse off than before? This section addresses these questions using basic tools of the theory of consumer behaviour (Samuelson, 1948; Tisdell, 1972).

A substantial fall in the real price of cereals on the one hand, and a substantial rise in the prices of non-cereal food items as a whole on the other, will lead to a shift in the average consumer's budget line as portrayed in Figure 4.5. The hypothetical consumer is able to buy a larger quantity of cereals and a smaller quantity of non-cereals. The new budget line is *A'B'* while the old one is *AB*. The initial equilibrium is at *E*. Where is the possible location of the new point of equilibrium likely to be?

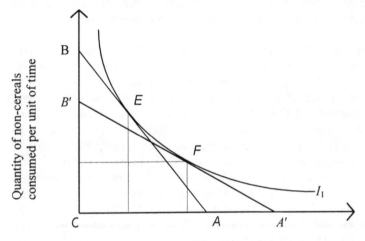

Quantity of cereals consumed per unit of time

Figure 4.5 Consumer's budget line under changing price conditions

NOTES: A hypothetical Bangladesh consumer appears to have moved from an initial equilibrium position at *E* to a new equilibrium at *F* on the same indifference curve I_1. This is probably the most optimistic scenario. In reality, the new equilibrium is likely to be on a lower indifference. To avoid clutter, Figure 4.5 does not portray this scenario.

To answer this question one needs to look at (a) the relative proportion of cereals in the family budget, and (b) sensitivity to changes in prices/income. Let us consider these in turn.

- According to the 1995–96 Bangladesh Household Expenditure Survey (BBS, 1998a), cereals constitute nearly 48 per cent of the monthly expenditure on major food items while non-cereals account for the remaining 52 per cent. Thus, one could reasonably assume that cereal and non-cereal food items have equal relative importance in rural Bangladesh. In the urban areas, non-cereals constitute more than two-thirds of the monthly food expenses. For Bangladesh as a whole, the relative share of non-cereals is 56 per cent of the monthly expenditure on food.

Given that (a) the elasticity of demand with respect both to price and income for cereals is lower than for non-cereal food items, and (b) Bangladesh is a semi-subsistence economy with cereals, especially rice, being the staple food, *a priori* the degree of sensitivity of price changes in cereals would be lower than that in non-cereals. The Bangladesh Household Expenditure Survey 1988–89 (BBS, 1991, p. 20; see also BBS, 1988b) estimates income elasticity of demand for rice for rural Bangladesh to be 0.43 compared to 0.70 for pulses and 0.95 for fish.

In the light of the above, it seems unlikely that increase in income, consequent upon a decrease in cereal price, could have *ceteris paribus* outweighed a fall in income, following increase in non-cereal price. Furthermore, quantities of both cereals and non-cereals consumed are limited by the quantities of these items available per capita. Available evidence presented in Table 4.2 indicates that non-cereal supply per capita has not increased. If anything, there is some evidence to the contrary. Furthermore, the average Bangladeshi is constrained by increased endowments of real income, which further constrains his/her entitlements (Khan, 1985) to a varied basket of food items. There does not seem to have been any significant increase in real agricultural wages (Alauddin and Tisdell, 1995). According to Shahabuddin and Rahman (1998, pp. 136–8), real agricultural wages have remained stagnant over the decade to 1994.

According to the Summary Report of the Household Expenditure Survey 1995–96 (BBS, 1997b, p. 18), there has been a gradual improvement in the per capita daily intake of calories and protein since 1983–84. However, per capita daily intake of calories registered a marginal decrease from 2266 in 1991–92 to 2244 in 1995–96. For protein, the increase in daily intake is consistently upwards. These improvements notwithstanding, cereals remain the most important source of protein contributing about 60 per cent of the average per capita daily protein and four-fifths of per capita daily calorie intake. Thus, the average Bangladeshi diet is probably less varied and probably less nutritious than three decades ago.

Therefore, the new equilibrium point is unlikely to be on a higher indifference curve than I_1. At best, the new equilibrium point would be at F to the right of E on the same indifference curve (Karmel and Polasek, 1970, pp.

353–5). At worst, the new equilibrium point would be an indifference curve slightly lower than I_1. In all probability, average consumer welfare per head might have declined marginally. This suggests that more and more people are able to survive in Bangladesh because of agricultural growth, but at a slightly lower level of equilibrium.

4.6 CONCLUDING COMMENTS

Although overall crop production has increased markedly in absolute terms, this is primarily due to an increase in the production of cereals – rice and wheat. However, increased food-grain production has not necessarily resulted in an overall qualitative improvement in dietary balance. There is also clear evidence that despite some decline in the import intensity of food-grains, import of non-cereals such as edible oils, chillies and lentils has strained Bangladesh's balance of payments. Thus, the supply of most non-cereal food items has not kept pace with rising aggregate demand because of population growth and, to a much lesser extent, growth in per capita income. Successive development plans since the 1950s have aimed to achieve food self-sufficiency, defined simply as making available a per capita annual quantity of 165–70 kilograms of food-grains. However, that goal, after eluding Bangladesh (see, for example, Mosharaff Hossain, 1991; 1994) for three decades seems to have been achieved.

However, the real significance of the technological change in Bangladesh agriculture lies not so much in raising the living standard of the average Bangladeshi, but in preventing mass starvation. In this context, it is worth recalling what Hayami and Ruttan (1985, pp. 360–61) rightly argue:

> In the absence of the new technology many developing countries would have moved closer to the Ricardian trap of stagnation and even greater stress over the distribution of income. The conclusion that should be drawn from this experience is not that growth has been 'immiserizing' but stagnation has.

In conclusion, one needs to express some caution regarding the continued viability of agricultural production to meet the requirements of the growing population of Bangladesh. These concerns stem from resource degradation, including land quality, groundwater availability and environmental externalities from intensification that may adversely affect future production. Chapter 9 provides a detailed analysis of the environmental changes resulting from agricultural development.

5. Ancillary Sectors within Agriculture: Livestock

5.1 INTRODUCTION

The preceding two chapters presented an analysis of growth and change in the Bangladesh crop sector and its implications for the broader issue of overall food self-sufficiency. This is the first of the three chapters (Chapters 5–7) that analyse the achievements and predicaments of the non-crop cluster of Bangladesh agriculture, namely livestock, fishery and forestry. While the primary focus of this chapter is on the livestock sector, it begins with a broad introduction as an aid to the understanding of the importance of non-crop agriculture in the Bangladesh economy in general and agriculture in particular. Subsequent sections take up an in-depth investigation of the issues that underlie the Bangladesh livestock sector.

5.2 THE NON-CROP CLUSTER IN BANGLADESH AGRICULTURE: A GENERAL OVERVIEW

Agricultural development in Bangladesh over the last few decades has been synonymous with the growth of the crop sector, especially the production of food-grains – primarily rice and wheat. However, performances of livestock, fishery and forestry sectors are as critically important for living conditions as those of the crop sector. This is because animal husbandry, fishing and tree growing are as much a part of the farming system of Bangladesh as crop production. Poultry, goats and cattle are bred and reared by the same peasant householders who cultivate the fields and grow rice and other crops.

The significance of these sub-sectors of agriculture, particularly of livestock, can be gauged from further evidence that animal power, which accounts for over 20 per cent of the input use in agriculture, is overwhelmingly the chief source of draught power in Bangladesh.

Despite the importance of livestock, forestry and fishery, their significance to agriculture and the national economy does not appear to have received due consideration. The fact that crops, livestock, forestry and fishery all together form a system where the various components are interdependent, seems to be inadequately realized by policy makers – the government and aid donors alike. While the introduction of new agricultural technology has, without doubt, helped expand food output to some extent, this achievement has been costly in as much as neglect or lack of proper attention has brought about a decline in the production of almost all non-food crops, the production of meat and inland fish and the depletion of rural forestry. Additionally, it has given rise to 'draught power constraint', which is reported to be threatening the process of agriculture in many parts of Bangladesh. These observations point to the need for a more conscious policy in these sub-sectors of the agricultural system, by adopting an integrated development strategy. This in turn, should derive from the understanding of the states of livestock, forestry and fishery, and the role they play in the agricultural system and the national economy.

In the case of fishing, traditionally there are fishing households, residing beside open water in inland and coastal areas, whose primary occupation is catching fish. Some of them also have small plots of land where crops are grown. Bodies of open water abound everywhere in the country. The irrigated *boro* rice and wheat cultivation became widespread in the last decade, resulting in the depletion of water resources in the canals, rivers, ponds and *beels*. Most of the peasants residing in the rural areas owned fishing nets and were able to catch fish for household consumption, prior to the depletion of water resources due to irrigation expansion. The rapid growth in population during the last few decades, and the extension of cultivation and increase in land use for non-agricultural purposes, have also considerably diminished the opportunities for catching fish by the rural people.

The farming system was such that the sons of the peasantry, reared in the age-old culture of self-sufficiency, learnt to grow crops, catch fish, plant trees and build thatched homes where they could reside. The girls learnt to look after the animals, perform most of the post-harvest operations, collect food and look after children and their menfolk. While this might not have been exactly an idyllic existence, livestock, fishery and tree plantation complemented crop production to help the peasants survive and operate the traditional farming system.

The non-crop agricultural sector contributes more than 8 per cent of gross domestic product (GDP). According to Alam (1997, p. 253), this sector generates about 15 per cent of the total foreign exchange earnings of Bangladesh and provides equivalent full-time employment to nearly a quarter of the rural labour force and part-time employment to a large number of rural people. Alam (1997, p. 253) argues that 'the utilization of labour is more productive and remunerative in the non-crop agricultural sector than in the crop sector'. One important facet of this process is that a higher percentage of women are engaged in non-crop sector employment.

Table 5.1 Crop, non-crop and overall agricultural value added and gross domestic product (GDP) of Bangladesh at constant 1984–85 market prices, 1972–97

Year	Relative share (%) of			Index of			
	Crop value added in GDP	Non-crop value added in GDP	Agricultural value added in GDP	Crop value added	Non-crop value added	Agricultural value added	GDP
1972	37.54	12.21	49.76	100.0	100.0	100.0	100.0
1973	37.37	10.95	48.33	109.1	98.3	106.4	109.6
1974	36.80	11.29	48.09	103.0	97.1	101.6	105.1
1975	38.59	10.81	49.33	114.2	97.6	110.1	111.1
1976	35.83	10.45	46.29	108.8	97.6	106.1	114.0
1977	36.13	10.48	46.61	117.5	104.8	114.4	122.1
1978	34.85	9.33	44.18	118.8	97.8	113.6	128.0
1979	34.61	9.28	43.89	118.9	98.0	113.8	129.0
1980	35.12	9.10	44.23	124.8	99.4	118.6	133.4
1981	34.34	9.42	43.76	123.5	104.1	118.7	135.0
1982	34.10	9.38	43.48	128.7	108.8	123.8	141.6
1983	33.90	8.83	42.73	134.8	108.0	128.2	149.3
1984	33.18	8.59	41.77	135.9	108.1	129.1	153.8
1985	32.88	8.47	41.35	140.5	111.3	133.4	160.5
1986	31.56	8.28	39.84	140.5	113.4	133.9	167.2

1987	30.13	8.30	38.43	138.0	116.9	132.9	172.0
1988	28.83	8.26	37.08	135.4	119.2	131.5	176.4
1989	30.32	7.94	38.26	151.9	122.3	144.6	188.1
1990	29.66	7.94	37.60	153.6	126.4	146.9	194.5
1991	28.93	7.94	36.86	156.2	131.7	150.2	202.7
1992	27.92	8.01	35.92	157.5	138.8	152.9	211.8
1993	26.35	8.23	34.58	154.9	148.8	153.4	220.7
1994	24.28	8.48	32.77	149.1	160.2	151.8	230.5
1995	23.69	8.56	32.24	153.2	170.1	157.3	242.8
1996	23.75	8.66	32.41	162.7	182.2	167.5	257.1
1997	22.81	8.79	31.66	164.9	196.5	172.7	271.4

Notes: 1997 means financial year beginning July. Figures for financial year 1997 are provisional.

Sources: Based on data from BBS (1993b, pp. 66–71; 1998b, pp. 489–91).

Enterprises in these sub-sectors have a higher nutritional and economic value. Depending upon land and climatic suitability, a farmer can *ceteris paribus* produce and earn more from livestock, forest and fisheries relative to crop production, provided that production, processing and the marketing system for these non-crop activities are properly organized. Furthermore, all animal protein for human consumption originates from fishery and livestock components of the agricultural sector (Abdullah *et al.*, 1996, p. 145; Shahabuddin and Rahman, 1998, p. 29). Essential materials such as timber, fuel wood, bamboo, wild fruits and honey originate from forests and trees which also provide sanctuary to wild life. This also underscores the importance of forestry for the environment and biodiversity.

A relative dearth of information, both in terms of quality and quantity, poses serious problems for a reliable estimate of the contribution of the non-crop sectors to the national accounts of Bangladesh. Available data on these sectors are not of comparable quantity and quality to those available on the crops (BBS, 1993b, pp. 14–15).

Table 5.1 sets out information on the relative share of non-crop agricultural sectors in GDP, and comparative trends in value added in crop and non-crop agricultural sectors, overall agricultural value added and GDP for more than two and half decades to the 1997–98 financial year. Table 5.1 also presents the relative importance in Bangladesh GDP of the agricultural sector and its two components: crop and non-crop.   Figure 5.1 graphically illustrates these phenomena. The trends in growth of value added in crop and non-crop agriculture, overall agricultural value added and GDP during 1972–97 are illustrated in Figure 5.2. The information contained in Table 5.1 and Figures 5.1 and 5.2 reveal the following characteristic features of the process of growth in Bangladesh agriculture and its contribution to the overall economy:

- As expected, there has been a progressive decline of the agricultural sector in Bangladesh GDP. The primary source of this decline is the steady decline of the relative importance of the crop sector.
- The contribution of the non-crop sector declined from just over 12 per cent to just below 8 per cent in 1991. Since then there has been a slow but steady increase in its share and by 1997 it edged close to 9 per cent of GDP.
- The growth in agricultural value added lagged behind that in GDP. While Bangladesh GDP has increased by more than 170 per cent between 1972–73 and 1997–98, agricultural value added increased by 72 per cent over the same period. This is primarily due to a slower growth in the crop sector value added by only 65 per cent. Only a relatively faster growth of 96 per cent in the non-crop value added partly compensated for the dismal performance of the crop sector value added. Thus, the vast sector of agriculture languished with very sluggish growth.

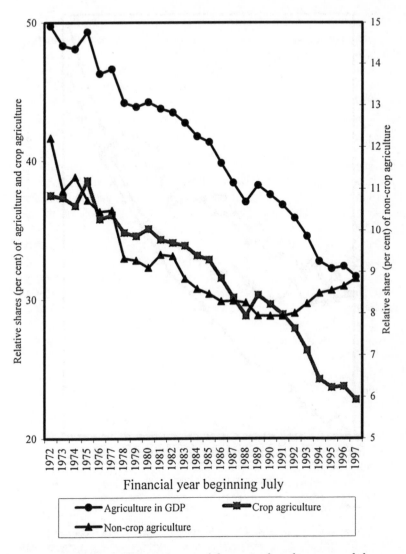

Figure 5.1 Trends in relative shares of the agricultural sector and the crop and non-crop agricultural sub-sectors in Bangladesh's gross domestic product (GDP) at constant 1984–85 market prices, 1972–97

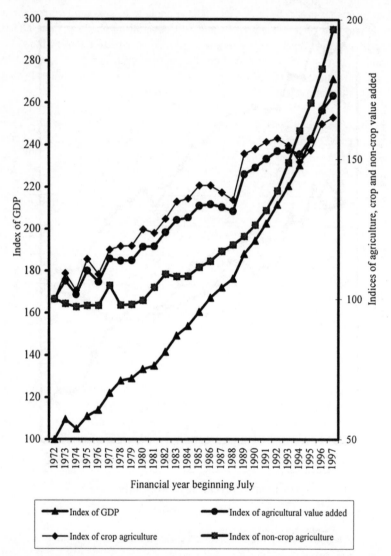

Figure 5.2 Trends in growth of crop and non-crop agricultural sectors in Bangladesh, agricultural value added and gross domestic product (GDP) at constant 1984–85 market prices, 1972–97 (1972–73 = 100)

Table 5.2 sets out the growth rates that have been estimated using a semi-logarithmic trend. As mentioned in Chapter 3, the coefficients of the time variable represent the instantaneous growth rate while taking the anti-log gives the compound growth rate (Gujarati, 1995, p. 171). Table 5.2 presents both these growth rates. The crop sector in Bangladesh agriculture grew at a compound rate of less than 2 per cent while overall agricultural value added grew by just over 2 per cent per annum over a 26 year period. During the same period, the non-crop sector within the agricultural complex grew at a compound annual rate of just over 2.5 per cent. Thus, overall agricultural value added grew at about half the rate of growth in GDP.

Table 5.2 Instantaneous and compound rates of growth in crop and non-crop sectors of Bangladesh agriculture and in gross domestic product (GDP) at 1984–85 constant market prices, 1972–97
Estimated equation: $\ln Y = \alpha + \beta T + \varepsilon$, $T = 1$ *for 1972–73 etc.*

Variable	Estimated growth rate (per cent)		Adjusted R^2
	Instantaneous	Compounded	
Value added in crop agriculture	1.87 (19.70)	1.89	0.939
Value added in non-crop agriculture	2.52 (11.36)	2.55	0.838
Value added in livestock	2.76 (12.18)	2.80	0.855
Value added in agriculture	2.03 (32.02)	2.05	0.976
Gross domestic product	3.84 (59.59)	3.91	0.993

Notes: Figures in parentheses refer to *t*-ratios. All the estimated coefficients of the time variable, *T,* are significant at the 0.01 per cent level.

Source: Based on information contained in Table 5.1.

5.3 GROWTH AND CHANGE IN THE LIVESTOCK SUB-SECTOR

Against the background of the preceding discussion, the remainder of this chapter concentrates on the livestock sector. Table 5.3 sets out the relevant information and Figure 5.3 illustrates the trends in the relative importance of the livestock sector in GDP, in overall agricultural value added and in non-crop sector value added. Its share in GDP has revolved around the 3 per cent mark for the last quarter of a century. It declined to less than 3 per cent for more than a decade to 1993–94, before rising again to just above 3 per cent in recent years. The relative share of livestock in non–crop agriculture, albeit with minor fluctuations, has shown a steady increase and by 1997–98 it contributed more than 36 per cent of non-crop agriculture value added. Similarly, livestock is gaining in importance in overall agricultural value added as has non-crop agriculture value added.

Table 5.3   Trends in livestock value added, its relative shares in gross domestic product (GDP), non-crop value added, agricultural value added and the relative importance of non-crop in agricultural value added in Bangladesh at constant 1984–85 market prices, 1972–97

Year	Relative share (%) of livestock in			Relative share of non-crop in agriculture	Index of livestock value added
	GDP	Non-crop agriculture	Agriculture		
1972	3.81	31.22	7.66	24.54	100.0
1973	3.54	32.29	7.32	22.67	101.7
1974	3.75	33.21	7.79	23.47	103.3
1975	3.61	33.60	7.31	21.76	105.0
1976	3.57	34.14	7.71	22.59	106.8
1977	3.48	33.23	7.47	22.49	111.5
1978	3.40	36.43	7.69	21.12	114.1
1979	3.45	37.16	7.86	21.14	116.7
1980	3.41	37.49	7.72	20.59	119.4
1981	3.46	36.73	7.91	21.52	122.5
1982	3.38	36.02	7.77	21.57	125.5
1983	2.89	32.71	6.76	20.67	113.1
1984	2.90	33.73	6.93	20.56	116.8
1985	2.86	33.74	6.91	20.48	120.3
1986	2.89	34.92	7.26	20.80	126.9
1987	2.84	34.20	7.39	21.60	128.1
1988	2.86	34.64	7.71	22.27	132.3
1989	2.77	34.93	7.25	20.76	136.8
1990	2.74	34.52	7.29	21.12	139.8
1991	2.73	34.34	7.39	21.53	144.9
1992	2.77	34.62	7.71	22.28	153.9
1993	2.88	35.04	8.34	23.80	166.9
1994	2.99	35.24	9.13	25.90	180.8
1995	3.07	35.86	9.51	26.53	195.3
1996	3.13	36.14	9.65	26.71	210.9
1997	3.20	36.19	10.11	27.93	227.8

Notes: 1997 means financial year beginning July. Figures for financial year 1997 are provisional.

Sources: Based on data from BBS (1993b, pp. 66–71; 1998b, pp. 489–91).

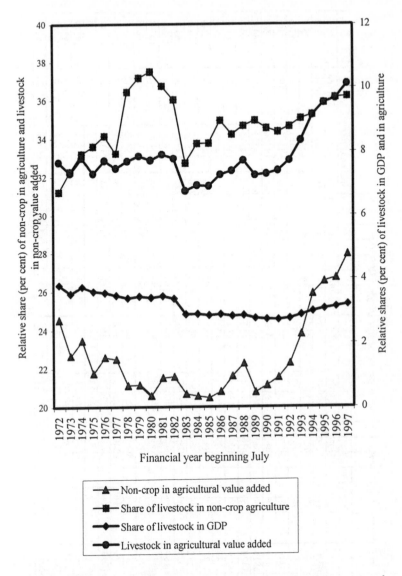

Figure 5.3 Trends in relative shares of livestock in gross domestic product, in agricultural value added and in non-crop agricultural value added in Bangladesh at constant 1984–85 market prices, 1972–97

Table 5.4 Trends in the growth of livestock population in Bangladesh, 1960–94

Year	Animal numbers (000)					Animal units (000)					
	Poultry	Sheep	Goat	Cattle	Buffalo	Poultry	Sheep	Goat	Cattle	Buffalo	Total
1960	20096	477	5660	18961	455	100	48	566	14221	596	15531
1961	21290	479	5794	19049	456	106	48	579	14287	597	15617
1962	22554	481	5932	19137	457	113	48	593	14353	598	15705
1963	23894	482	6073	19225	457	119	48	607	14419	599	15793
1964	25313	484	6217	19314	458	127	48	622	14486	600	15883
1965	26816	486	6365	19404	459	134	49	636	14553	601	15973
1966	28409	488	6516	19494	460	142	49	652	14620	602	16065
1967	30096	490	6671	19584	461	150	49	667	14688	604	16158
1968	31884	491	6829	19674	462	159	49	683	14756	605	16252
1969	33777	493	6992	19765	462	169	49	699	14824	606	16347
1970	35783	495	7158	19857	463	179	49	716	14893	607	16444
1971	37909	497	7328	19949	464	190	50	733	14962	608	16541
1972	40160	499	7502	20041	465	201	50	750	15031	609	16641
1973	42546	501	7680	20134	466	213	50	768	15100	610	16741
1974	45073	502	7862	20227	466	225	50	786	15170	611	16843
1975	47750	504	8049	20321	467	239	50	805	15240	612	16947
1976	50586	506	8240	20415	468	253	51	824	15311	613	17052
1977	53590	508	8436	20509	469	268	51	844	15382	614	17158
1978	56515	532	9130	20670	484	283	53	913	15503	634	17385
1979	59599	556	9882	20833	500	298	56	988	15624	655	17621
1980	62851	582	10695	20996	516	314	58	1069	15747	676	17865
1981	66281	609	11575	21161	532	331	61	1157	15871	697	18118
1982	69898	637	12527	21327	549	349	64	1253	15996	720	18381

1983	73713	667	13558	21495	567	369	67	1356	16121	743	18655
1984	77834	654	13205	21263	577	389	65	1320	15948	756	18479
1985	82185	641	12861	21034	588	411	64	1286	15776	770	18307
1986	86779	629	12525	20808	599	434	63	1253	15606	784	18140
1987	91631	617	12199	20584	610	458	62	1220	15438	799	17976
1988	96753	605	11881	20362	621	484	61	1188	15272	814	17817
1989	103644	870	22033	22470	690	518	87	2203	16853	904	20565
1990	109800	910	23480	22650	710	549	91	2348	16988	930	20906
1991	156000	950	25410	22830	730	780	95	2541	17123	956	21495
1992	122540	990	27490	23020	750	613	99	2749	17265	983	21708
1993	129950	1040	29750	23200	780	650	104	2975	17400	1022	22151
1994	147850	1090	32190	23390	800	739	109	3219	17543	1048	22658

Notes and sources: The basic data are for the years 1960, 1977, 1983–84, 1988–89 and 1990–91 to 1994–95. Data for the intervening years for the 1960–88 period have been derived applying the respective compound annual growth rates for the intercensal years. Data for 1989–90 are derived using the growth rates for 1990–91 contained in Shahabuddin and Rahman (1998, pp. 43–6). One animal unit = 200 kg of live animal weight. The conversions factors from animal numbers to animal units for cattle, buffalo, poultry, sheep, goat are respectively 0.75, 1.31, 0.05, 0.10 and 0.10 (Mosharaff Hossain, 1991, p. 52).

Table 5.3 presents information on the index of livestock value added which shows a steady increase over the years. In the 1990s, the growth was appreciably faster. Table 5.2 presents instantaneous and compound growth rates of the livestock sector, which respectively are 2.76 per cent and 2.80 per cent. These growth rates compare favourably with those of overall value added in agriculture, the non-crop sector and the crop sector.

Table 5.4 presents information on the growth trends in various animals and poultry birds, recorded in various censuses and surveys in terms of physical numbers and animal units. Figure 5.4 graphically illustrates the growth process. The growth in cattle, the mainstay of the livestock, experienced very slow progress. Over a period of 35 years, cattle population has increased from nearly 19 million to over 23 million head. Poultry numbers (including ducks) have experienced the fastest rate of growth from 20 million to nearly 148 million. Growth in buffalo numbers has remained sluggish. Growth in the numbers of goats and sheep remained steady until the late 1980s but in the 1990s, they experienced a surge in their numbers. Total animal units increased from 15.5 million to nearly 23 million, an overall change of approximately 46 per cent over a period of three and a half decades.

In order to examine the historical trends in the various components of the livestock sector, estimated instantaneous and compound rates of growth are set out in Table 5.5. Cattle population grew at a compound rate of only 0.54 per cent per annum over the period under consideration, while the buffalo population experienced a growth rate of 1.63 per cent per annum. Poultry numbers experienced the highest rate of growth (5.94 per cent) followed by goat (4.80 per cent) and sheep (nearly 2.20 per cent). Given the dismal performance of the cattle sector and given its overwhelming importance in the livestock complex, total animal units only increased by less than 1 per cent per annum over the same period.

Given the pattern of growth in the livestock sector of Bangladesh, it is important to consider the dynamics of change in the overall 'output mix'. A closer inspection of the last six columns in Table 5.4 shows that relative share of cattle in total animal units has progressively declined from more than 90 per cent up to the mid-1970s to less than 80 per cent by the early 1990s. Since the late 1980s, the combined relative importance of sheep, goats and poultry has increased significantly. In view of the overwhelming importance of the cattle population in the total livestock resources, its growth rate is the critical determinant of the overall growth rate. Given the information contained in Tables 5.4 and 5.5, the cattle-elasticity of animal resource growth over the period under consideration is estimated to be 1.79. This implies that growth rate in cattle has a more than proportional impact on the growth of livestock resources.

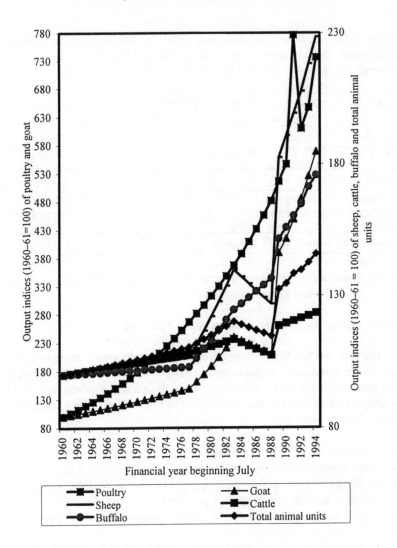

Figure 5.4 Trends in growth of livestock in Bangladesh, 1960–94

Table 5.5   Instantaneous and compound rates of growth in livestock population and total animal units in Bangladesh, 1960–95
Estimated equation: $\ln Y = \alpha + \beta T + \varepsilon$, T $=1$ *for 1960–61 etc.*

Animal type/unit	Estimated growth rate (%)		Adjusted R^2
	Instantaneous	Compounded	
Cattle	0.54 (14.86)	0.54	0.866
Poultry	5.77 (68.93)	5.94	0.993
Goat	4.69 (15.53)	4.80	0.876
Sheep	2.17 (10.42)	2.19	0.760
Buffalo	1.62 (12.37)	1.63	0.817
Total animal units	0.97 (14.36)	0.97	0.858

Notes: Figures in parentheses refer to *t*-ratios. All the estimated coefficients of the time variable, *T*, are significant at the 0.01 per cent level.

Source: Based on information contained in Table 5.4.

The statistics on fertility rate, death rate, slaughter rate, imports and so on, which determine livestock growth rates are very scanty. Furthermore, information on the death rate due to various endemic diseases is woefully inadequate. Following Alam (1997, p. 255) some factors can be identified: These include *inter alia,*

- low birth rates
- high mortality rates due to diseases and frequent natural disasters
- slaughter of good quality young cattle in large numbers during religious festivals such as Eid-ul-Azha (7 per cent)
- unplanned slaughter of cattle for meat throughout the year (16 per cent).

In this context, some earlier findings of an earlier study by Mosharaff Hossain (1991, pp. 54–55) are worth reporting:

- A survey of 500 farms in three villages in Mymensingh in 1981 shows that 47.6 per cent of the cattle were infected and 22.6 per cent of the diseased cattle died. Statistics on death rate due to slaughtering are also inadequate. As a Muslim-majority country, the slaughter rate of cattle is higher in Bangladesh than the neighbouring non-Muslim majority countries and a significant portion of the slaughtered cattle are cows, which in turn has adverse implications for the future livestock growth rate. A study shows that 23.6 per cent of the slaughtered bovines in the slaughtering houses of Dhaka and Chittagong and 40 per cent of the slaughtered bovines in 114 villages during Eid-ul-Azha, were cows.

- As many as 0.47 to 2.8 million bovines were lost in a single cyclone in November of 1970. During the War of Liberation in 1971, the occupation army of Pakistan slaughtered some 2.3 million bovines. Cyclones in 1988 and 1991 together caused the death of more than 130 thousand domestic animals (BBS, 1999a, p. 97)
- The floods of 1974, 1988, 1991 and 1998 are believed to have caused colossal damage to livestock population, even though quantitative estimates are not readily available. The flood of 1988 caused the deaths of 172 000 large animals and 410 000 poultry. The 1998 flood was the severest of all the floods in living memory.

5.4 SOME IMPLICATIONS WITH SPECIAL REFERENCE TO DRAUGHT POWER

The sluggish overall growth in the livestock sector, especially cattle population, has some significant implications. These can be summed up as follows:

- High density of livestock population notwithstanding, Bangladesh suffers from chronic shortages of milk, meat and eggs, the three important products originating from livestock. Alam (1997, p. 256) points out that milk, meat and eggs cater for only 12.82 per cent, 10.42 per cent and 24.28 per cent of minimum nutritional requirements.
- Egg production has increased significantly resulting in an increase in their per capita availability of 16 in 1987–88 to 20 in 1994–95. This has resulted from increased production in the commercial poultry sector.
- There is an acute shortage of animal power. Alam (1997, p. 256) estimates the extent of this shortage to be in the order of 40 per cent. The draught power shortage has a regional dimension, the problem varying in nature and extent in different regions, both according to the intensity of draught power distribution over the regions, and because of varying regional socio-economic conditions.
- Accepting a surplus draught power of 25 per cent over the requirement as the safe margin, Mosharaff Hossain (1991, p. 60) presents a dismal picture of the draught power situation in various districts of Bangladesh. Out of 20 districts only four, namely Chittagong, Jamalpur, Patuakhali and Rangpur are found to have sufficiently excess draught power. Four other districts, namely Tangail, Khulna, Bogra and Dinajpur are found

to have some surplus draught power but the surpluses are too small to meet the demand of deficit farmers of these areas according to the safe margin condition. The remaining 12 districts are faced with shortages of draught power ranging from moderate to acute.

Many areas of Bangladesh face acute shortages of draught power. While this will call for a higher stock of animals in these areas, some other factors require attention. The size of the rental market plays a very important role in channelling surplus power to the deficit farmers. According to Mosharaff Hossain (1991, pp. 60–61), smaller farmers own more draught animals than larger farmers, relative to their farm size. Also smaller farmers make fuller utilization of draught power than larger farmers, in as much as smaller farmers are prepared to make their surplus power readily available for renting out. This seems to suggest that, by putting more land at the disposal of smaller farmers, coupled with making provision of adequate credit facilities to smaller farmers, the stock of draught power as well as the size of the rental market can be enlarged. Along with these strategies, the minimization of dependence on nature, by way of providing infrastructural facilities for irrigation and drainage, will also help ease off draught power constraint because agricultural processes will thus be less interrupted.

Relevant to the above issue, are the questions of the existing technique of animal-drawn implements and the quality of draught animals. In some parts of Sylhet district, single animal (buffalo) ploughing has been in practice and this system is observed to be more efficient both technically and economically. However, since buffaloes constitute only about 2 per cent of the total number of draught animals, the expansion of this system with buffaloes is limited. It is yet to be seen whether bullocks can be used in this system. As regards the quality, the livestock and poultry population of Bangladesh, not to speak of bullocks alone, is generally inferior to that of North India and Pakistan. The quality of animals and poultry depends on several factors, the three most important being adequacy of feed, the state of health and genetic status of the species, to all of which we turn in the next section.

5.5 FEED, FODDER AND ANIMAL HEALTH

Improvement of the livestock and poultry population, and its future development for improved draught power and animal protein food, depend on the extent of the availability of feed and fodder and veterinary facilities to the animals and birds. The future development of these resources is also conditional upon the genetic character of the species. This section examines these.

5.5.1 Feed and Fodder Condition[1]

Table 5.6 presents an estimate of the major groups of feedstuff, expressed in terms of dry matter (DM), total digestible nutrients (TDN) and digestible crude protein (DCP). It also presents sources of type of feed and fodder. These estimates are based on 1981 Bangladesh statistics. In the absence of more recent information, these are indicative of a serious emerging problem.

Table 5.6 Nutrient components of feed and fodder supply

Type of food stuff	Dry matter (000 tons)	TDN (000 tons)	DCP (000 tons)
Green roughage (Stubble, regrowth, fallow, waste land and forest) 45% TDN, 4.0% DCP	18 850 (53)	8 483 (55)	754 (74)
Dry roughage (Straw, Hay etc) 38% TDN, 0.3% DCP	14 964 (42)	5 685 (37)	45 (4)
Concentrates (Industrial and farm by-products and harvest waste) 75% TDN, 12% DCP	1 852 (5)	1 390 (9)	222 (22)
Total feed shift	35 662 (100)	15 558 (100)	1 021 (100)

Note: Figures in parentheses are percentages of respective column totals.

Source: Adapted from Mosharaff Hossain (1991, p. 62).

Table 5.7 provides information on the total food requirements of livestock and poultry population for approximately 18 million units derived using the conversion factors mentioned in Table 5.4. These estimates relate to the 1983–84 figures of livestock animals. Assuming no loss and full utilization of feed and fodder, 89, 102 and 61 per cent of DM, TDN and DCP requirements respectively can be met from the current production of feed and fodder. However, full utilization of feed and fodder as animal diet is hardly achieved because a substantial part of total production is being used up as domestic fuel, industrial inputs etc. Therefore, it is likely that the supply is likely to fall far short of the actual requirement.

Table 5.7 Annual nutrient requirement of an animal population equivalent to approximately 18 million animal units

Species	DM (000 tons)	TDN (000 tons)	DCP (000 tons)	Total (000 tons)
Cattle	33 000	10 574	1 013	44 587
Buffalo	1 450	900	48	(78.2)
Goats and sheep	2 900	1 570	158	2 398
Poultry	2 775	2 220	444	(4.2)
				4 628
				(8.1)
				5 439
				(9.5)
Total	40 125 (70.3)	15 264 (26.7)	1 663 (2.9)	57 052 (100)

Note: The figure of 18 million is derived from the animal population according to 1983–84 Livestock Census (BBS, 1986b; see also Table 5.4 for conversion factors used). Figures in parentheses are percentages of the grand total of 57 052.

Source: Adapted from Mosharaff Hossain (1991, p. 62).

Improvement of livestock and poultry resources through dietary measures must acknowledge the above facts and look for potential availability of feed and fodder. This would entail an examination of the sources of the feed and fodder. Table 5.8 provides information relevant to the sources of different feedstuff. It can be seen that 87 per cent of the feedstuff comes from cultivated land and only 13 per cent originates from non-cultivated land like embankments, road sides, forest and low land. Although small in proportion, this green roughage of non-cultivated land is very important from the point of view of its higher quality in digestibility and protein content. These green grasses somewhat balance the diets of the ruminants that take a high proportion of dry straw, and also cater for much of the grazing and browse needs of goats and sheep.

As regards improvement of dietary conditions of livestock and poultry resources, it is worth noting some points:

Table 5.8 Source of type of feed and fodder (000 tons DM)

Source feedstuff	Crop residue regrowth weeds	Fallow land	Agricultural industrial farm by-product feed	Wasteland roadside, lowland and forest	Total
Green roughage	12 250	2 000	–	4 600	18 850 (53)
Dry roughage	14 960	–	–	–	14 960 (42)
Concentrate by-product	–	–	1 526	–	1 526 (4)
Concentrate harvest waste	326	–	–	–	326 (1)
Total	27 536 (77)	2 000 (6)	2 000 (6)	4 600 (13)	35 662 (100)

Note: Figures in parentheses are percentages of the overall total 35 662.

Source: Adapted from Mosharaff Hossain (1991, p. 63).

- First, although production of rice is increasing through increased use of fallow land and increased cropping intensity, the amount of straw and hay is not increasing proportionately. This is because more land is being cultivated for rice in the *boro* season. This crop is harvested at the beginning of the rainy season and in most cases, the straw decays and becomes unsuitable for animal diet. In *Aus* and *Aman* seasons, an increasing amount of land is being devoted for the cultivation of HYV rice which yields less straw per acre of land relative to local rice; moreover, straw from HYV rice is inferior to that of local rice, in that HYV straw is less digestible (BPC, 1985, p. ix–45). The spread of HYV rice has been accompanied by an expansion of the use of pests and insecticides that contaminate weeds and such other plants in the rice fields. The area under fodder crops has declined drastically during the last three decades. In the 1990s, the total area under fodder crops has been less than a third of that of the 1960s. Fodder output has fallen at a faster rate than its area under cultivation over the same period (BBS, 1976, pp. 284–93; 1997b, pp. 110–11).
- Second, expansion of irrigation facilities has increased the cultivation of rice and wheat at the cost of cultivation of pulses, oilseeds, sugarcane and cotton. Consequently, poultry and other birds are being increasingly deprived of crop residues.
- Third, there are some low lands called *haors* or *beels* in some parts of Sylhet, Mymensingh and Pabna districts. The grass and weeds grown in these lands usually provide sufficient food for several months for the livestock and birds of these areas. But some of this land has been brought under crop production, *haor* development schemes and fish cultivation projects, etc., which reduces the scope of the natural grazing of animals.

The above points are indicative of the fact that increasing demand for human food due to increasing population is limiting the scope of making more land available for the production of animal feedstuff. Increasing demand for human food is also constraining the amount of crop residues which used to be important sources of food for animals, poultry and other birds. This, however, does not imply that means of improving feedstuff are exhausted. Feedstuff like straw, hay and so on, constitutes 10 per cent of total dry matter (DM). These are usually an inferior type of food. Quality and digestibility of these foods can be substantially increased in two ways. First, straw and hay may be mixed with one or more of the following: urea, molasses, mineral salt, oil cake, dry ground fish, water hyacinth, green grasses and so on. This adds to the taste of the food as well as increasing digestibility and food quality. Secondly, straw and hay may be chemically processed before giving it to the animals as feed. It will be instructive to point out some of the results in this regard. It is observed that when processed with lime, the digestibility of straw increases by 9–17 per cent and intake by animals also increases by 10–13 per cent. In addition, if such processed straw is mixed with some urea or molasses, the overall quality further increases. Also, if processed with caustic soda or urea, digestibility and intake increases considerably. The processed feed may have side effects, which are required to be properly tested before farmers are advised to adopt the measures.

In addition to the improvement of straw and hay by chemical or other processes, efforts may be made to increase the availability of non-conventional feedstuff. At present, some farm and agro-industrial by-products, which can constitute a source of high quality food, are not properly preserved. Animal blood from slaughter houses, bones, fruit skin, by-products of sericulture, rubber seed, water hyacinth, leaves of jute, potato and some other plants, algae and so on, fall in this category. In many cases, these are not even properly removed and constitute a source of environmental pollution. These can be turned into animal and poultry food by proper methods, adequate measures of processing, and by preservation.

There is also scope for producing animal feed like grass and weeds in the forestland. In many countries, satisfactory results are obtained by growing grass as intercrops along with forest trees. In particular, such culture of grass in coconut, palm and rubber gardens has been satisfactory. Such intercrops also help increase soil fertility. Although land under *haors* and *beels* are decreasing, the available land is capable of yielding much more animal feedstuff. The present production of feedstuff from these areas is only by means of natural process and there does not exist any programme for the preservation and reservation of the products. The application of scientific methods to grow different grass, weeds, algae and so on, and the appropriate measures of preservation of these products can largely make up the shortage. Only 2 per cent of the farmers cultivate HYV fodder while the area under fodder cultivation is 0.08 hectare per farm (Alam, 1997, p. 261).

5.5.2 Disease Conditions

Next to feed and fodder restraints, disease restraints are critical to the improvement of livestock and poultry resources. Few studies exist in Bangladesh to quantify disease conditions of livestock and poultry and their economic impact.

Mosharaff Hossain (1991, p. 65) estimates a 30 per cent mortality rate for calves up to one year and a 10 per cent mortality thereafter. As regards poultry, Newcastle disease alone is reported to have caused the deaths of 40 to 60 per cent of poultry in one year. Apart from loss due to death, the loss due to debilitating effects resulting from various diseases is no less important.

The main diseases which are reported to be the causes of mortality and debility are authorax, septicaemic pasteurellosis, blackleg, brucellosis, mastitis, tuberculosis, colibacillosis, foot and mouth disease, rinderpest, virus diarrhoea, ephemeral fever, rabies, papillomatosis, parasitic disease, fasciliasis, roundworm infestation, tapeworm infestation, toxocariasis, schestosomiasis, hydatidosis, stephano-filariasis and infertility. Apart from these, milk fever disease in goats and yoke-gall in draught animals are widespread. Among the main diseases observed in poultry are Newcastle disease, pastenrallosis, lymphomatosis, fowlpox, eimeriasis, salmonellosis and duck-plague.

It is believed that a 30 per cent increase in livestock and poultry resources is possible only by making available sufficient veterinary facilities for the prevention and control of various contagious and infectious diseases. Furthermore, there is an unregulated spread of diseases originating from across the border, due to illegal import of livestock from India. Any measure to improve dietary conditions will also improve disease conditions.[2]

Current supply of vaccines and treatment of livestock diseases is far short of requirements. According to Alam (1997, p. 261) there is one veterinary doctor for about 168 000 head of livestock (about 50 000 large and small animals and about 118 000 poultry). Many of these veterinarians are constrained by lack of modern equipment and poor infrastructural facilities in remote areas. Only about 5 per cent of the households have ever visited a livestock extension officer. Seventy-four per cent of the rural areas do not have any livestock extension centre, artificial insemination centre or veterinary hospital within a 4 km radius. Over the five years to 1994–95, poultry vaccination has increased significantly while cattle vaccination has remained much the same.

5.5.3 Genetic Improvement

The genetic character of animals and birds is an important factor in determining their efficiency to convert feed into protein, power and other products. It is observed that the average milk yield per day is about 0.9 and 1.8 kg for indigenous cattle and buffaloes respectively. However, indigenous animals are found very resistant to disease and climatic stress. In comparison to the indigenous cows, Friesian cows (*Bos taurus*) have a milk yield of about 12 kg under conditions at the dairy farm at Savar near Dhaka. Milk yield of Friesian–local crossbreed cows (50:50) is about 7.0 kg per day. Under farm conditions, about 4.5 kg of milk yield can be expected from these cows. Indigenous cattle, with improved feeding and management, are capable of giving 2.5–3.0 kg of milk per day. It is important to note that the average lactation period for indigenous cattle is 300 days compared to 370 days for pure Friesian at Savar. Experiments of crossbreeding need to be made under farmers' conditions, especially in the milk pocket areas of Pabna, Faridpur, Tangail and Manikganj, around artificial insemination centres and at the central animal inspection station, Savar. In this connection, it is worth mentioning that crossbreeds require better feed and care than indigenous animals. Experience of the milk pocket areas shows a deficiency in this respect and there are cases of malnutrition, frequent outbreak of diseases, lack of proper protection during festivals, and slaughtering at times of drought, flood and other natural disasters. Artificial insemination has nearly doubled in the five years to 1994–95.

As regards power of bullocks for draught purposes, crossbreeds appear to be superior. Indigenous bullocks are smaller. Bodyweights of draught bullocks and cows are, on average, 200–250 and 150–170 kg respectively. Against this, draught bullocks of North India and Pakistan have on the average a weight of 500 kg. Under Savar Farm conditions, an average local animal and an average Friesian cross weigh 250 and 390 kg respectively. It is observed that the power of animals increases proportionately with their weight up to 500 kg. Obviously then, Friesian crossbreeds, because of their bigger size, are superior to local bullocks. However, these animals are only suitable for use on high-land areas.

By crossbreeding local animals with Hariana and Sahiwal (*Bos indicus*), these milk pocket animals have been developed over the past 100 years. These animals are 50 per cent bigger than local ones and their milk yield is 5 times that of local cattle. Having been acclimatized, they are suitable for draught and milk in other areas as well.

The number of livestock farms in the private sector proliferated during the first half of the 1990s. As of 1994–95 Bangladesh numbered nearly 27000 dairy farms, 17 000 goat farms and 8000 sheep farms. Poultry and duck farms, including poultry and duck rearing farms numbered more than 120000 farms (Alam, 1997, p. 274). Applying a drop out rate of 20–25 per cent for dairy farms and 25–30 per cent for poultry farms, Alam (1997, p. 257) argues that 70 per cent of these farms were still operational two years later.

5.6 CONCLUDING COMMENTS

The non-crop sector in Bangladesh agriculture as a whole has remained neglected relative to the crop sector over the years. This notwithstanding, the value added of non-crop agriculture has grown at a faster rate than the crop sector over the 1972–97 period.

The livestock sector has undergone significant changes over the years. In recent years, the growth has been faster, due primarily to significant increases in the number of poultry and goats, while the rate of growth of the cattle population remains sluggish. Incentives for establishing livestock farms in the private sector and financial profitability have both contributed to this pattern of growth. Given the pivotal importance of cattle in the Bangladesh livestock sector, the slow growth in cattle population has arrested its overall growth rate.

Per capita supply of food products from the livestock sector has remained stagnant and is far short of requirements. Furthermore, Bangladesh suffers from an acute shortage of draught power, this shortage also having a regional dimension. This is because of slow cattle growth, caused by shortage of fodder, an inadequate artificial insemination programme and a poor disease control and vaccination programme. Natural disasters have also claimed a large number of livestock animals over the years, especially the devastating cyclones of 1970 and 1991, and the floods of 1974, 1988 and 1998.

The growth in the non-crop sector, especially livestock, has significant implications for improvement in dietary conditions and rural poverty alleviation. The Department of Livestock Services, in collaboration with three NGOs of Bangladesh introduced a Small Farmers Livestock Development Project in 1993. It has resulted in a significant and positive impact on the poultry population, adoption of HYVs, disease control and mortality, employment and income generation and poverty reduction in rural Bangladesh (Alam, 1997, p. 259). Given the limited employment potential of the crop sector (Alauddin and Tisdell, 1995), this achievement is significant.

In conclusion, the development strategy for the livestock sector must consider the following essential elements:

- adequate farmer training for management of livestock resources
- strengthening institutional capacity for extension services and research
- improved fodder supply
- improved breeds, feed concentrate, vaccine and medicine
- regulation of the illegal import of cattle across the Indian border
- strengthening and intensifying of the artificial insemination programmes
- improved marketing, especially adequate provision for processing and preservation of output
- livestock and poultry development at farmers' level on the basis of the principle of integration of the different components of the farming system and nutrient recycling, through optimum utilization of indigenous resources.

NOTES

1   Draws on Mosharaff Hossain (1991, pp. 61–5).
2   The cost–benefit ratio for vaccination is estimated to be about 1:90 and that for deworming is about 1:25 (Mosharaff Hossain, 1991, p. 66).

6. Ancillary Sectors within Agriculture: Fisheries

6.1 INTRODUCTION

Against the background of the analysis in Chapter 5, this chapter focuses on the fisheries sub-sector of the non-crop complex of Bangladesh agriculture. Development activities in fisheries have, over the years, focused on increased production to meet growing domestic needs, export and employment generation (see, for example, BPC, 1998, p. 20).

Fish is an essential item of food. It is an important source of protein and it constitutes nearly four-fifths of the animal protein in the average Bangladesh diet. The fisheries sub-sector is of critical importance to the economy of Bangladesh, accounting for 3 per cent of gross domestic product (GDP) and 10 per cent of export earnings. It employs 1.2 million people on a full-time basis, and employs another 11 million people on a part-time basis (Alam, 1997, p. 261; BPC, 1998, pp. 19–20). Given this scenario, the importance of the fisheries sub-sector extends far beyond its contribution to GDP.

Bangladesh possesses vast inland, coastal and marine waters with great potential for fisheries. Its inland water resources are in the form of rivers, canals, depressions (*haors* and *beels*), reservoirs, ox-bow lakes (*baors*), ponds, tanks and seasonally flooded areas. It is estimated (Mosharaff Hossain, 1991) that inland water areas comprise an aggregate of 1.45 million hectares. Moreover, there are about 2.83 million hectares of paddy fields that remain under water for some 3–6 months in the year. This provides feeding and breeding grounds for various species of fishes. Thus with a land area of 142780 km^2 and 4.28 million hectares of inland water, the water–land ratio of Bangladesh is one of the highest in the world. This means that Bangladesh is endowed with one of the world's richest fisheries resource systems with very favourable ecological conditions for aquaculture (M. Ahmed, 1988).

Bangladesh has a 480 km long coastal belt in the southern zone. It also has about 1 million hectares of territorial waters extending up to 19 km into the Bay of Bengal (Rahman, 1993). The continental shelf, commonly known as the land under the sea, is very extensive and supports a variety of important species of fish and other aquatic life.

This chapter proceeds with a brief review of the planned development of the fisheries sub-sector in terms of production targets and achievements and an analysis of the growth and change in the fisheries sector with an explanation of the patterns observed. After critically examining the process of coastal shrimp farming, this chapter discusses some implications of the overall analysis of the development of this sector.

6.2 A REVIEW OF PLANNED DEVELOPMENT

Since Bangladesh gained independence in the early 1970s, the government has sought to accelerate the development of fisheries through economic planning. Mosharaff Hossain (1991, pp. 73–5) provides an overview of the earlier efforts for planned development of the fisheries sub-sector.

Against the background of a decline in the per capita consumption of fish, the First Five Year Plan (1973–78) set forth an ambitious programme to increase the level of fish production by about 26 per cent by 1977–78. The plan document emphasized both inland and marine fishery resources (BPC, 1973). It envisaged augmenting fish output from 810 000 tonnes in 1969–70 to 1.02 million tonnes by 1977–78. However, fish production actually declined to about 640 000 tonnes.

The Two Year Plan (1978–80) (BPC, 1978) restated the importance of fisheries and proposed the intensification of fish culture in ponds and tanks. The plan envisaged a fish production target of 808 000 tonnes and sought to increase export of shrimp and fish to the extent of 10 000 tonnes during the plan period. However, actual production fell far short of expectations in that it showed very little or no improvement over the 1977–78 level of production.

The principal objective of the Second Five Year Plan (1980–85) (BPC, 1980) was to improve the supply of fish for the domestic market in order to raise the per capita consumption of fish and fish products. Other specific objectives of the plan were to expand employment opportunities and improve the socio-economic conditions of rural people in general and fishermen and fish farmers in particular, and also to increase export earnings from fishery products including shrimp and frogs' legs. The plan set the target of production at 1 million tonnes by 1984–85, the terminal year of the plan. Like all its predecessors, the second plan targets fell far short of expectations and an increasing supply of fish per capita remained an elusive goal. By 1984–85, overall fish production stood at 766 000 tonnes.

A combination of social, economic and institutional factors led to the under-fulfilment of the planned targets of fish production up to 1984–85. Reduced investment, overfishing, lack of infrastructural facilities for the culture of fish, organizational weaknesses and the environmental effects of irrigation and chemical use in crop production all contributed to the decline in fish production and continued to inhibit the sector.

It was only towards the end of the second plan period that fisheries came to be recognized as an integral part of water sector development projects. Not only did irrigation and water control structure impact on fisheries but also the use of chemicals in agriculture and industrial wastes adversely affected fish population. Lack of knowledge about the ecology and natural habitat of major fish species in the country accentuated the problem of ecological degradation. The Water Sector Master Plan known as MPO was commissioned to address the problem of a coordinated approach to water use.

The main thrust of the Third Five Year Plan (1985–90) (BPC, 1985) was to take advantage of the up-turn in the fish output of the second plan and consolidate its base for gathering momentum. The third plan envisaged a fish production target of 1 million tonnes by the end of 1989–90. This included 772 000 tonnes from inland water and 228 000 tonnes from the sea. By 1989–90, the overall fish production stood at 848 000 tonnes. The marine fish production marginally exceeded its target while inland fisheries fell short by 159 000 tonnes.

The development of the fisheries sub-sector Fourth Five Year Plan (1990–95) (BPC, 1991) embodied the principal objectives of:

• Increasing fish production for domestic consumption
• Improving the socio-economic conditions of the fishing community
• Enhancing the fisheries resource base
• Improving the management technology and
• Augmenting foreign exchange earnings through export of fish and fish products (BPC, 1998, p. 20).

Actual fish production during the fourth plan exceeded its target of 1.17 million tonnes and by 1994–95, actual production stood at approximately 1.2 million tonnes. The fisheries sub-sector continued to receive priority during both 1995–96 and 1996–97 with an emphasis on aquaculture because of the shortfall of inland fisheries during the fourth plan as well as its potential for development. This included fish culture in derelict tanks, paddy fields, open water areas and other bodies of water (BPC, 1998, p. 20). In 1996–97, the export of fisheries stood at 43 300 tonnes consisting of 28 000 tonnes of shrimp, 9800 tonnes of fish and fish products and 5500 tonnes of fish related products (BPC, 1998, p. 258).

The Fifth Five Year Plan (1997–2002) envisages a fish production target of 2.075 million tonnes (1.675 million tonnes inland, 0.40 million tonnes marine) by the 2001–02 financial year. The export target is set at 95 000 tonnes, comprising in the main 70 000 tonnes of shrimp and 20 000 tonnes of fish and fish products (BPC, 1998, p. 258).

6.3 GROWTH AND CHANGE IN THE FISHERIES SUB-SECTOR

6.3.1 Broad Patterns

Table 6.1 sets out information on the changing importance of the fisheries sub-sector relative to the broader context of national accounts, overall agricultural value added and the non-crop agricultural complex. The trend in the overall fisheries value added is also provided. Figure 6.1 graphically illustrates the process of these changes. The salient features can be summed up as follows:

- The relative share of fisheries value added in GDP declined to less than 3 per cent in the period of two decades to the early 1990s. In the last few years, this sector has regained some lost ground. This pattern permeated the other relevant indicators such as the share of fisheries in noncrop agriculture, in agricultural value added and the relative importance of the non-crop sector cluster in overall agriculture.
- The fisheries sub-sector value added remained stagnant until 1976–77, then consistently remained below the 1972–73 level until 1989–90. Since 1990–91, it has increased at a compound rate of more than 8 per cent per annum. The overall growth for the 1972–97 period using a semi-logarithmic trend is estimated to be 1.86 per cent (significant at 1 per cent level). This is below the overall growth rates of the overall agricultural value added and valued added in other components of the non-crop sector (see Chapter 5).

6.3.2 Fish Production: A Disaggregated View

Fisheries in Bangladesh are broadly classified as inland and marine fisheries. Table 6.2 portrays the changing pattern of the relative importance of the fisheries from two sources: inland and marine. Inland fisheries are predominant sources of domestic supply. For nearly a decade and a half to 1977–78, fish production remained stagnant or at best increased very slowly. This was due to very slow growth both in inland and marine fisheries even though the relative growth in the latter was marginally faster. For nearly a decade thereafter, fish production remained depressed. This was due primarily to a poor performance of inland fisheries compensated only partially by a relatively faster growth in marine fisheries. The combined effect was that fish production remained below the late 1960s level. During the late 1980s fish production increased very slowly. In the 1990s, however, fish production registered a much faster growth rate. It must be emphasized that it was not until 1992–93 that the output of inland fisheries exceeded the

Table 6.1   Trends in fishery value added, its relative shares in gross domestic product (GDP), non-crop value added, agricultural value added and the relative importance of non-crop in agricultural value added at constant 1984–85 market prices, Bangladesh 1972–97

Year	Relative share (%) of fishery in			Share of non-crop in agriculture	Index of fishery value added
	GDP	Non-crop agriculture	Agriculture		
1972	5.22	42.71	10.48	24.54	100.0
1973	4.77	43.58	9.88	22.67	100.3
1974	5.00	44.29	10.39	23.47	100.7
1975	4.72	43.30	9.42	21.76	98.9
1976	4.59	43.92	9.92	22.59	100.4
1977	4.34	41.44	9.32	22.49	101.7
1978	3.05	32.67	6.90	21.12	74.8
1979	3.07	33.05	6.99	21.14	75.9
1980	2.98	32.72	6.74	20.59	76.2
1981	3.11	33.03	7.11	21.52	80.5
1982	3.12	33.28	7.18	21.57	84.8
1983	3.01	34.13	7.06	20.67	86.3
1984	3.00	34.94	7.18	20.56	88.5
1985	2.92	34.51	7.07	20.48	89.9
1986	2.87	34.61	7.20	20.80	91.9
1987	2.82	33.94	7.33	21.60	92.9
1988	2.76	33.41	7.44	22.27	93.3
1989	2.64	33.23	6.90	20.76	95.2
1990	2.70	34.03	7.19	21.12	100.7
1991	2.76	34.77	7.49	21.53	107.2
1992	2.82	35.19	7.84	22.28	114.4
1993	2.94	35.67	8.49	23.80	124.2
1994	3.08	36.33	9.41	25.90	136.3
1995	3.10	36.23	9.61	26.53	144.3
1996	3.18	36.73	9.81	26.71	156.7
1997	3.27	37.56	10.49	27.93	172.8

Notes: 1997 means financial year beginning July. Figures for financial year 1997 are provisional.

Sources: Based on data from BBS (1993b, pp. 66–71; 1998b, pp. 489–91).

1977–78 level. Since 1992–93, inland fisheries have experienced a surge in growth of production.

The process of fish production for a period of 33 years up to 1996–97 is characterized by a slow growth in inland fisheries (50 per cent) and a consistently faster growth in marine fisheries (258 per cent), albeit from a very small base. But the combined effect is a manifestly slow growth in fish production. The composition has undergone a significant change. The relative importance of marine fish has increased from around 10 per cent up until 1977–78 to more than 20 per cent. One can notice some decline in the relative share of marine fish production since its peak of 28 per cent in 1988–89. Figure 6.2 illustrates these changes in sharp focus. Note that the left-hand scale on the vertical axis represents respective output trends while the right-hand scale measures the relative share of marine and inland fisheries.

There exist over 200 species of finned fish in inland waters. Among the principal commercial species of finned fishes are: several Indian carp species such as rohu (*Labeoruhita*), katla (*Catla catla*), mrigal (*Cirrhina mrigala*), shad (*Hilsailisha*), catfish such as magur (*Clarions Batrachus*), shingi (*Heteropnoustes fossils*), air (*Mystus acr*), rita (*Rita*), boal (*Wallago attu*), feather back or chital (*Notopterus chitola*), snake's heads such as shole and other allied fishes of the genus *ophicephalus*, punti (*Puntias Spp*); fresh water eels known as bain (*Nastacembalus spp*).

Reliable data on the abundance of various species of inland fisheries are not readily available. Table 6.3 sets out information on the distribution of inland fisheries by major species for two decades to 1991–92. A dearth of disaggregated data prevents any analysis for subsequent years. Note that:

- Hilsa is the single most important species of inland fish that accounts for more than 50 per cent of the total catch. Hilsa production fell significantly in the late 1970s. However, by 1991–92 it was close to the level in the earlier part of our time series.
- A similar pattern of output growth applies to the other major species in inland fisheries. Consequently, the relative importance of each of the major species in inland fisheries has remained virtually unchanged.

Inland fisheries have two broad components – capture and culture fisheries. Table 6.4 presents information on the growth of both forms of inland fisheries for fifteen years to 1994–95. Figure 6.3 graphically illustrates the information contained in Table 6.4. While both forms have experienced growth relative to the 1980–81 level, culture fisheries have grown at an appreciably higher rate than capture fisheries. The process of growth in inland fisheries has significantly changed the output mix from the two sources. As of 1994–95, nearly two fifths of inland fisheries originate from marine sources. This is a significant rise from its share of about a quarter in the early 1980s.

Table 6.2 Trends in production of inland and marine fisheries in Bangladesh, 1964–96

Year	Production (tons)			% share in total		Index of production (1964 = 100)		
	Inland	Marine	Total	Inland	Marine	Inland	Marine	Total
1964	718000	81000	799000	89.86	10.14	100.0	100.0	100.0
1965	720000	81000	801000	89.89	10.11	100.3	100.0	100.3
1966	721000	81000	802000	89.90	10.10	100.4	100.0	100.4
1967	723000	81000	804000	89.93	10.07	100.7	100.0	100.6
1968	726000	82000	808000	89.85	10.15	101.1	101.2	101.1
1969	727000	83000	810000	89.75	10.25	101.3	102.5	101.4
1970	729000	85000	814000	89.56	10.44	101.5	104.9	101.9
1971	729000	95000	824000	88.47	11.53	101.5	117.3	103.1
1972	731000	87000	818000	89.36	10.64	101.8	107.4	102.4
1973	733000	88000	821000	89.28	10.72	102.1	108.6	102.8
1974	735000	90000	825000	89.09	10.91	102.4	111.1	103.3
1975	733000	89000	822000	89.17	10.83	102.1	109.9	102.9
1976	733000	89000	822000	89.17	10.83	102.1	109.9	102.9
1977	739910	95000	834910	88.62	11.38	103.1	117.3	104.5
1978	520000	114173	634173	82.00	18.00	72.4	141.0	79.4
1979	524000	122000	646000	81.11	18.89	73.0	150.6	80.9
1980	525001	125000	650001	80.77	19.23	73.1	154.3	81.4
1981	556000	130000	686000	81.05	18.95	77.4	160.5	85.9
1982	583000	141000	724000	80.52	19.48	81.2	174.1	90.6
1983	568912	174000	742912	76.58	23.42	79.2	214.8	93.0
1984	585000	181000	766000	76.37	23.63	81.5	223.5	95.9

1985	586000	207000	793000	73.90	26.10	81.6	255.6	99.2
1986	597000	218000	815000	73.25	26.75	83.1	269.1	102.0
1987	599000	228000	827000	72.43	27.57	83.4	281.5	103.5
1988	599000	233000	832000	72.00	28.00	83.4	287.7	104.1
1989	613000	235000	848000	72.29	27.71	85.4	290.1	106.1
1990	654937	239000	893937	73.26	26.74	91.2	295.1	111.9
1991	701600	244500	946100	74.16	25.84	97.7	301.9	118.4
1992	776000	250491	1026491	75.60	24.40	108.1	309.2	128.5
1993	827000	253044	1080044	76.57	23.43	115.2	312.4	135.2
1994	922000	264650	1186650	77.70	22.30	128.4	326.7	148.5
1995	976398	280264	1256662	77.70	22.30	136.0	346.0	157.3
1996	1079000	290000	1369000	78.82	21.18	150.3	358.0	171.3

Note: 1964 indicates financial year beginning July 1964 etc.

Sources: Based on data from BBS (1979, p. 227; 1993b, p. 263); Shahabuddin and Rahman (1998, p. 34); GOB (1998, p. 39).

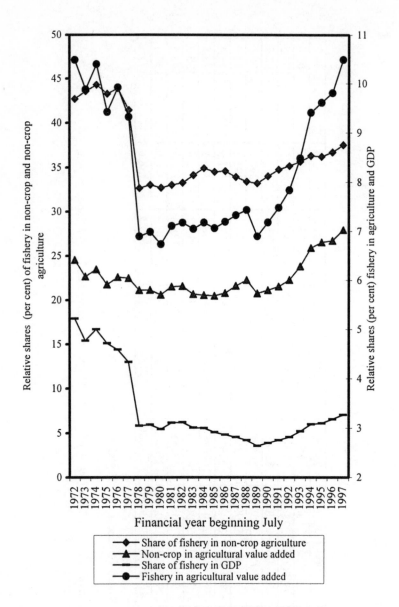

Figure 6.1 Trends in relative shares of fishery in gross domestic product, in agricultural value added and in non-crop agricultural value added in Bangladesh at constant 1984–85 market prices, 1972–97

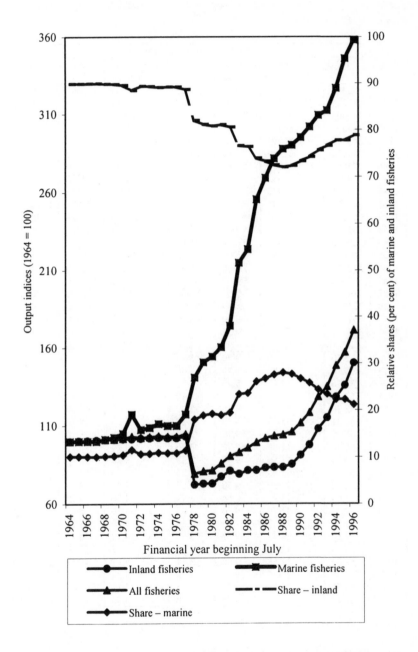

Figure 6.2 Trends in output indices of various types of fisheries in Bangladesh, 1964–96

Table 6.3   Distribution of inland fisheries production by species in Bangladesh, 1972–91

Year	Production by species (tons)						
	Hilsa	Rohu, Katla, Mrigal	Boal, Air Pangas	Chingri	Koi, Magur, Singhi etc.	Others	Total
1972	382313	86258	70907	24123	30702	136697	731000
1973	383359	86494	71101	24189	30786	137071	733000
1974	384405	86730	71295	24255	30870	137445	735000
1975	383359	86494	71101	24189	30786	137071	733000
1976	383359	86494	71101	24189	30786	137071	733000
1977	387020	87230	71780	24420	31080	138380	739910
1978	271960	61360	50440	17160	21840	97240	520000
1979	274052	61832	50828	17292	22008	97988	524000
1980	274576	61950	50925	17325	22050	98175	525001
1981	290788	65608	53932	18348	23352	103972	556000
1982	304909	68794	56551	19239	24486	109021	583000
1983	301771	68086	55969	11041	24234	107811	568912
1984	306000	69000	57000	19000	24000	110000	585000
1985	307000	69000	57000	19000	24000	110000	586000
1986	312000	70000	58000	20000	25000	112000	597000
1987	313000	71000	58000	20000	25000	112000	599000
1988	313000	71000	58000	20000	25000	112000	599000
1989	321000	72000	59000	20000	26000	115000	613000
1990	342937	77000	64000	22000	27000	122000	654937
1991	366937	82789	68055	23153	29467	131199	701600
Relative share of individual species in total inland fisheries (per cent)							
1972	52.30	11.80	9.70	3.30	4.20	18.70	100
1973	52.30	11.80	9.70	3.30	4.20	18.70	100
1974	52.30	11.80	9.70	3.30	4.20	18.70	100
1975	52.30	11.80	9.70	3.30	4.20	18.70	100
1976	52.30	11.80	9.70	3.30	4.20	18.70	100
1977	52.31	11.79	9.70	3.30	4.20	18.70	100
1978	52.30	11.80	9.70	3.30	4.20	18.70	100
1979	52.30	11.80	9.70	3.30	4.20	18.70	100
1980	52.30	11.80	9.70	3.30	4.20	18.70	100
1981	52.30	11.80	9.70	3.30	4.20	18.70	100
1982	52.30	11.80	9.70	3.30	4.20	18.70	100
1983	53.04	11.97	9.84	1.94	4.26	18.95	100
1984	52.31	11.79	9.74	3.25	4.10	18.80	100
1985	52.39	11.77	9.73	3.24	4.10	18.77	100
1986	52.26	11.73	9.72	3.35	4.19	18.76	100
1987	52.25	11.85	9.68	3.34	4.17	18.70	100
1988	52.25	11.85	9.68	3.34	4.17	18.70	100
1989	52.37	11.75	9.62	3.26	4.24	18.76	100
1990	52.36	11.76	9.77	3.36	4.12	18.63	100
1991	52.30	11.80	9.70	3.30	4.20	18.70	100

Note: 1972 indicates financial year beginning July 1972 etc.

Source: Based on data from BBS (1993b, p. 263)

Table 6.4 Production of inland fisheries in Bangladesh, 1980–94: capture and culture

Year	Production (000 tons)			Relative share (%)			Production Index (1980 = 100)		
	capture	culture	total	capture	culture	total	capture	culture	total
1980	388	137	525	73.9	26.1		100.0	100.0	100.0
1981	411	145	556	73.9	26.1		105.9	105.8	105.9
1982	431	152	583	73.9	26.1		111.1	110.9	111.0
1983	464	118	582	79.7	20.3		119.6	86.1	110.9
1984	463	124	587	78.9	21.1		119.3	90.5	111.8
1985	442	145	587	75.3	24.7		113.9	105.8	111.8
1986	431	166	597	72.2	27.8		111.1	121.2	113.7
1987	424	176	600	70.7	29.3		109.3	128.5	114.3
1988	424	184	608	69.7	30.3		109.3	134.3	115.8
1989	420	193	613	68.5	31.5		108.2	140.9	116.8
1990	443	211	654	67.7	32.3		114.2	154.0	124.6
1991	429	277	706	60.8	39.2		110.6	202.2	134.5
1992	533	243	776	68.7	31.3		137.4	177.4	147.8
1993	552	275	827	66.8	33.2		142.3	200.7	157.5
1994	576	346	922	62.5	37.5		148.5	252.6	175.6

Note: 1980 indicates financial year beginning July 1980 etc.

Source: Based on data from sources mentioned in Table 6.3.

Open water capture fishery and closed water culture fishery constitute two production systems of inland fisheries. Similarly, marine fisheries consist of two components, namely industrial (trawling) and artisanal.

Inland fishing activities are carried out in a variety of water bodies. The floodplains, rivers, lakes and reservoirs comprise the largest inland resources of Bangladesh. Let us briefly discuss the sources of the inland fisheries system.

Capture fishery

Riverine, estuarine and canal fisheries. Riverine fisheries in Bangladesh comprise three major systems, namely the Padma, the Brahmaputra–Jamuna and the Meghna. Rivers and canals cover roughly 5.8 per cent of the total area of Bangladesh. The river systems in Bangladesh with their tributaries constitute the main sources of capture fisheries for several species of fish such as carp, catfish, the feather backs and freshwater prawn. Fishing of principal fishes in the rivers and tributaries continues throughout the year and it is at its peak during the winter months when the water level of the rivers is low and the current comparatively slow. During the monsoon, however, the popular fish *hilsa* is available in large quantities. The area of water available for this source of fisheries is 1.032 million hectares (Alam, 1997, p. 280).

Haors and beel fishery. Haors and *beels* are areas of natural depression situated in the floodplain and provide a good habitat for fish. They are found mainly in the old Sylhet and Mymensingh Districts. *Beels* are also present in Faridpur, Comilla and Dhaka districts. A recent survey gives an estimate of 114 000 hectares (Alam, 1997, p. 280) of *beel* area. *Beels* and *haors* in Mymensingh and Sylhet districts are estimated to cover 62 000 hectares. Major carp, catfish and minor carp are the important fish in *beel* areas.

The floodplains. A vast area of 2.83 million hectares (Alam, 1997, p. 280) remains under water for 3–6 months annually, and serves as a feeding, growing and spawning ground for many fish and shellfish. This area is flooded every year contributing to subsistence fishery for the villagers.

Reservoir fishery: Kaptai Lake. Kaptai Lake with an area of about 69 000 hectares (Alam, 1997, p. 280) constitutes 1.5 per cent of the total inland water area. Bangladesh Fisheries Development Corporation (BFDC) manages the lake.

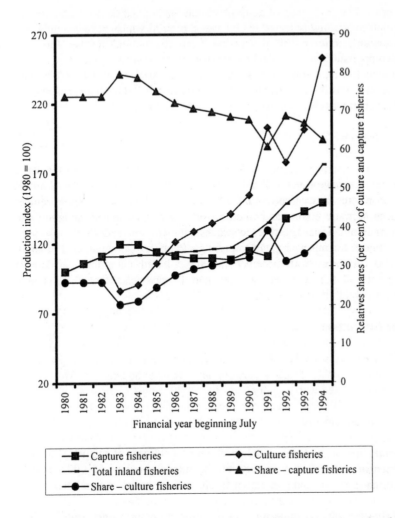

Figure 6.3 Trends in the growth of capture (left-hand cale) and culture fisheries and their relative shares (right-hand scale) in total inland fish production in Bangladesh, 1980–94

Culture fishery

Water resource development projects, particularly drainage and flood control schemes, have affected the aquatic environment of the floodplains to the detriment of the inland capture fisheries, which have traditionally yielded the bulk of the domestic fish supply. However, with increasing demand and relative scarcity of fish, and with a decrease in fishing areas due to irrigation and flood control activity, fisheries development should be based on culture fisheries. The principles of aquaculture can be applied to the production of fish in the various types of inland water bodies, which have potential for substantially raising fish production from the natural levels. The carp spawn/fry fishery plays a vital role in freshwater fish culture in Bangladesh. It is found in the Padma, the Brahmaputra, the Arial Khan, the Madhumati, the Kumar and the old Brahmaputra rivers. In the Halda River, spawns are collected and hatched out in earthen pits on riverbanks.

Pond fishery

There are innumerable ponds and tanks in the country and also a large number of irrigation tanks. Ponds thus constitute an important type of inland fishery resources which provide the bulk of the fish catch. However, returns from these water bodies depend on the fertility of the soil and the inputs and efficiency of the management techniques adopted. Small ponds are also used as nurseries for raising fry and fingerlings. Ponds constitute an area of about 147 000 hectares. Note, however, that the cultured, culturable and derelict constitute 52 per cent, 31 per cent and 17 per cent of total pond area respectively (BBS, 1997b, p. 250).

Baor fish culture

The *baor*s are suitable for aquaculture. There are about 84 *baor*s in the Jessore and Kushtia districts covering an area of 5488 hectares. Most of the *baor*s are stocked with carp fry.

Coastal aquaculture

Shrimp farming constitutes the most important form of culture fishery in Bangladesh. It caters primarily to the export market and is the most important foreign exchange earner in the primary sector. Section 6.5 briefly examines the process of shrimp aquaculture in Bangladesh.

Table 6.5 sets out relevant data on production from open water, closed water and marine sources for the 1983–95 period. Floodplains, together with riverine and estuarine fisheries are the two main components of open water fishery. Between them they account for nearly 90 per cent of the total open water fishery catch. *Beel* fishery has maintained an almost constant share of around 10 per cent of open water fishery production. The relative share of the riverine and estuarine component of open water fishery has been rapidly declining from around 40 per cent in 1983–84 to about 26 per cent in 1995–96. In absolute terms, the output has fallen from 216 000 tonnes in 1983–94 to 131 000 tonnes in 1991–92, but has recovered to over 150 000 tonnes more recently. Floodplain fishery has nearly doubled in 13 years, after initially declining in the late 1980s.

The total catch of the closed water fishery has more than trebled between 1983–84 and 1995–96. This is primarily due to a rapid increase in pond fishery and shrimp farming. Pond fishery accounted for about 80 per cent of culture fishery in 1995–96, while shrimp output accounted for the remainder of the total closed water catch.

The contribution of open water fish production has declined from more than 60 per cent in 1983–84 to less than 50 per cent in 1995–96. Artisanal fishery is the primary form of marine fishery accounting for more than three-quarters of the total marine catch. These changes are highlighted in Figure 6.4.

Table 6.6 sets out data on area, total catch and productivity of inland fishery open water capture and closed water culture components. Trends in productivity per hectare are illustrated in Figure 6.5. Yield per hectare of open water fishery is very low. Furthermore, it declined from 117 kg in 1983–84 to 105 kg in 1987–88. In the 1990s, it showed an upward trend, and as of 1995–96 it stood at 152 kg. The productivity of closed water culture fishery increased from 568 kg in 1983–84 to nearly 1400 kg in 1995–96. The growing divergence in productivity between the two forms of inland fishery is particularly noteworthy.

6.4 EXPLAINING THE OBSERVED PATTERN

In the not-too-distant past, supply and availability of different varieties of freshwater fish was relatively plentiful. This scenario has changed quite significantly in recent decades. In the light of the preceding discussion, some pertinent questions arise:

- What factors underlay the pattern of growth and change in the fisheries sub-sector over the last three decades?
- Why did fish production initially decline?
- What factors led to the subsequent recovery in fish production in the 1990s?

A combination of many factors, both man-made and natural, has reduced the total habitat of, or has degraded physio-chemical and biological environments for, aquatic organisms in inland water. The most important of these factors affecting open water capture fisheries as identified by Mosharaff Hossain (1991, p. 76) are:

- Large-scale siltation and shoaling in rivers resulting in loss of fish habitat
- Large-scale and systematic reclamation of land for agriculture resulting in continuous loss of fisheries

Table 6.5 Fish production from different types of water bodies in Bangladesh, 1983–94

Year	Open water (000 tons)					Closed water fisheries				Marine fisheries (000) tons		
	River	*Beel*	Kaptai Lake	Flood plain	Total	Pond	*Baor*	Shrimp	Total	Trawling	Artisanal	Total
1983	216.0	51.0	4.0	201.0	472.0	108.0	1.0	8.0	117.0	14.0	150.0	164.0
1984	220.0	46.0	3.0	194.0	463.0	112.0	1.0	11.0	124.0	12.0	175.0	187.0
1985	207.0	45.0	2.4	187.0	441.4	124.0	1.0	20.0	145.0	12.0	196.0	208.0
1986	201.0	42.0	3.9	184.0	430.9	143.0	1.1	22.0	166.1	12.0	205.0	217.0
1987	192.0	46.0	4.0	182.0	424.0	149.0	1.2	25.0	175.2	10.0	217.0	227.0
1988	188.0	47.0	3.4	186.0	424.4	155.0	1.3	27.0	183.3	10.0	223.0	233.0
1989	180.0	47.0	3.7	194.0	424.7	164.0	1.4	28.0	193.4	11.0	228.0	239.0
1990	142.0	48.0	4.4	249.0	443.4	181.0	1.5	28.0	210.5	9.0	233.0	242.0
1991	131.0	49.0	4.2	295.0	479.2	195.0	1.7	30.0	226.7	10.0	236.0	246.0
1992	146.0	53.0	4.1	330.0	533.1	202.0	1.8	34.0	237.8	12.0	238.0	250.0
1993	151.0	56.0	6.6	361.0	574.6	223.0	2.2	39.0	264.2	12.0	241.0	253.0
1994	159.0	58.0	5.6	368.0	590.6	267.0	2.5	47.0	316.5	12.0	253.0	265.0
1995	155.0	63.0	7.0	390.0	615.0	310.0	3.0	77.0	390.0	25.0	254.0	279.0

	Relative share (%)					Relative share (%)				Relative share (%)		
1983	45.8	10.8	0.8	42.6	100	92.3	0.9	6.8	100.0	8.5	91.5	100.0
1984	47.5	9.9	0.6	41.9	100	90.3	0.8	8.9	100.0	6.4	93.6	100.0
1985	46.9	10.2	0.5	42.4	100	85.5	0.7	13.8	100.0	5.8	94.2	100.0
1986	46.6	9.7	0.9	42.7	100	86.1	0.7	13.2	100.0	5.5	94.5	100.0
1987	45.3	10.8	0.9	42.9	100	85.0	0.7	14.3	100.0	4.4	95.6	100.0
1988	44.3	11.1	0.8	43.8	100	84.6	0.7	14.7	100.0	4.3	95.7	100.0
1989	42.4	11.1	0.9	45.7	100	84.8	0.7	14.5	100.0	4.6	95.4	100.0
1990	32.0	10.8	1.0	56.2	100	86.0	0.7	13.3	100.0	3.7	96.3	100.0
1991	27.3	10.2	0.9	61.6	100	86.0	0.7	13.2	100.0	4.1	95.9	100.0
1992	27.4	9.9	0.8	61.9	100	84.9	0.8	14.3	100.0	4.8	95.2	100.0
1993	26.3	9.7	1.1	62.8	100	84.4	0.8	14.8	100.0	4.7	95.3	100.0
1994	26.9	9.8	0.9	62.3	100	84.4	0.8	14.8	100.0	4.5	95.5	100.0
1995	25.2	10.2	1.1	63.4	100	79.5	0.8	19.7	100.0	9.0	91.0	100.0

Notes: *Beels* indicate depressed inland water bodies while *baors* refer to oxbow lakes. 1983 indicates financial year beginning July 1983 etc.

Sources: Based on data from Alam (1997, p. 280); BBS (1997b, p. 252; 1999a. p. 83).

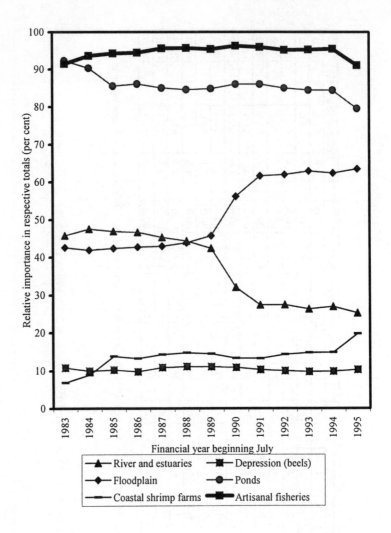

Figure 6.4   Relative importance of open water, closed water and marine fisheries in Bangladesh, 1983–95

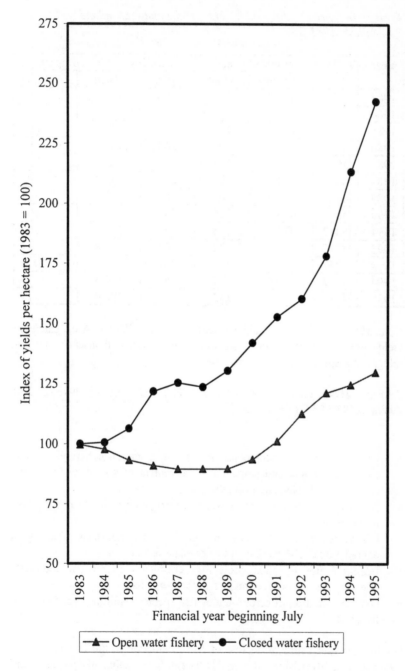

Figure 6.5 Trends in yields per hectare of open and closed water fisheries in Bangladesh, 1983–95

Table 6.6   Area, total catch and productivity of inland fisheries in Bangladesh, 1983–95

Year	Open water inland fishery			Closed water inland fishery		
	Area	Catch	Yield	Area	Catch	Yield
1983	4047	472.0	117	206	117.0	568
1984	4047	463.0	114	217	124.0	571
1985	4047	441.4	109	240	145.0	604
1986	4047	430.9	106	240	166.1	692
1987	4047	424.0	105	246	175.2	712
1988	4047	424.4	105	261	183.3	702
1989	4047	424.7	105	261	193.4	741
1990	4047	443.4	110	261	210.5	807
1991	4047	479.2	118	261	226.7	869
1992	4047	533.1	132	261	237.8	911
1993	4047	574.6	142	261	264.2	1012
1994	4047	590.6	146	261	316.5	1213
1995	4047	615.0	152	283	390.0	1378

Note: 1983 indicates financial year beginning July 1983 etc. Area, catch and yield are expressed in terms of thousand hectares, thousand tons and kilograms respectively.

Sources: Based on data from Alam (1997, p. 280); BBS (1997b, p. 252, 1999a. p. 83); BPC (1998, p. 260).

- Construction of embankments, dykes and irrigation structures causing change of habitat and stoppage of movement of migratory fishes and destruction of spawning grounds
- Excessive removal of surface water for irrigation resulting in shrinkage of fish habitat
- Discharge of untreated effluents in rivers by industries resulting in degradation of fish habitat and large-scale fish mortality
- Increased use of plant protection chemicals directly or indirectly affecting the fish production or fish food organism
- Over-exploitation of certain major fish species resulting in depletion of fisheries.

Thus the root cause of decline of fish production in the late 1970s and 1980s lies in 'overfishing through indiscriminate fishing of spawners and spawns, the destruction of breeding grounds by blocking the migration route through erection of dams, the reduction of water areas due to flood control and irrigation structures as well as the indiscriminate use of agro-chemicals and pesticides etc' (Alam, 1997, p. 262).

As indicated in section 6.2, policy makers in the mid-1980s recognized the need for arresting the decline in fish production, especially in open water capture fisheries. Some measures have been introduced since then. Following Shahabuddin and Rahman (1998, pp. 37–8) and Alam (1997, pp. 262–4), these can be summed up as follows:

- More recently, the government has launched a programme of artificial stocking of open waters such as rivers, floodlands, *beels, haors* and lakes with fish fingerlings. During the 1988–94 period, 378 million fingerlings were stocked. Furthermore, new water control structures, including redesigned sluice gates and submergible embankments, have been introduced to facilitate fish migration.

- Improved fish culture in closed water bodies has been introduced to augment fish production. For example, species of native carp (such as *rohu, katla* and *mrigal*), Chinese carp (such as silver carp, grass carp); European common carp and mirror carp are often cultured in different combinations in ponds and *baors*. In addition, Thai *sar puti* and *nilotica* have been cultured.

- In the mid-1990s, some measures in respect of property rights and fisheries management were introduced. These include (a) long-term leasing of *beels* and *baors*; and (b) transfer of management of 300 *jalmohals* (state managed water bodies, in place since 1986) from the Ministry of Lands to the Department of Fisheries. The policy embedded in (a) has been introduced with a view to encouraging conservation of fish and improved fish culture practices. On the other hand, the management policy under (b) was designed to replace *jalmohal* leasing by allowing only genuine fishermen to establish fishing rights under a system of licensing. The results under (a) are yet to be observed, while the results under (b) indicate only partial success. 'Only a part of the intended *jalmohals* have so far been released from their leases and transferred to licentiate fishermen. In practice many of the former leaseholders have retained control over the *jalmohals* by using licentiate fishermen as their frontmen' (Alam, 1997, p. 263).

- Bangladesh Krishi Bank (BKB) and some commercial banks have extended credit facilities to farmers with a view to encouraging improved fresh water aquaculture. Some non-governmental organizations (NGOs) such as the Bangladesh Rural Advancement Committee (BRAC), Proshika and Prism and other organizations such as the Grameen Bank and Bangladesh Rural Development Board (BRDB) have supplemented these efforts. The combined effect of these has been a significant improvement in closed water fish production and productivity per hectare. The fishponds, which have benefited from the funds made available to them by the above institutions have registered productivity more than twice as high as the national average (Alam, 1997, p. 263).

- Based on a sample survey, a study by Alam (1997, p. 297) shows that freshwater pond aquaculture is a highly profitable enterprise and on average the benefit–cost ratio is of the order of 1.65, even though there are regional variations.

On the whole, therefore, the turnaround in fisheries output in the 1990s has resulted from a combination of circumstances, the most prominent among them being the combined effect of policy, institutional arrangements and technology in improved fish production including higher prices of fish relative to other cereal and non-cereal commodities as discussed in Chapter 4. This is reminiscent of the process of the green revolution in crop production in which technology, price and policy all played their part (see for example, Dantwala, 1973).

6.5 COASTAL AQUACULTURE

6.5.1 The Process

The last two decades have witnessed a prolific growth in coastal aquaculture in many countries of the developing world (Goldburg, 1996; Lucien-Brun, 1997; ADB/NACA, 1996; FAO/NACA, 1995; FAO, 1994a; 1995). Bangladesh is no exception. Over a period of a decade to the mid-1990s, the area under shrimp farming in Bangladesh has more than doubled to over 130000 hectares (Alauddin and Hamid, 1996; BPC, 1998). This is against the background of a shrimp area of next to nothing until the mid-1970s. Bangladesh now produces around 30 000 tonnes of shrimp. Productivity per hectare of cultured shrimp in Bangladesh is one of the lowest in the world, together with that of Vietnam (Alauddin and Hamid, 1996; BPC, 1998). Bangladesh primarily depends on the extensive method of shrimp farming practices even though the semi-intensive method is gaining grounds in recent years (Alauddin and Tisdell, 1998).

Nearly 80 per cent of the area under shrimp farms is located in the south-western districts of Satkhira, Khulna and Bagerhat. The remainder of the shrimp farming area is located in the south-eastern district of Cox's Bazaar (Alauddin and Tisdell, 1998). In the south-eastern coastal areas of Bangladesh, shrimp production alternates with salt production (Alauddin and Hamid, 1996; Mazid, 1995). In some parts of the south-east tidal area, rice alternates with shrimp and fish production (ESCAP, 1988). In the south-west Khulna region, shrimp farming alternates with rice farming (Alauddin and Tisdell, 1998).

6.5.2 The Impact: The Positive Side

Shrimp represents a significant change in the structure of Bangladesh's export trade. Over a period of a decade to the mid-1980s, export earnings from shrimp and frozen fish overtook the once-dominant raw jute in the category of primary export goods. As of 1996–97, export earnings from items in the frozen foods category (85–90 per cent being shrimp) accounted for more than 7 per cent of Bangladesh's total export earnings. Over the last few years, frozen foods have been elevated to the second largest export earning group of commodities after ready-made garments (BFFEA, 1995; GOB, 1998; BPC, 1998). Shrimp also accounts for around 60 per cent of the export earnings from the primary goods category. Figure 6.6 illustrates the process of this phenomenal change.

Shrimp culture, through a network of backward and forward linkages, has created a substantial volume of employment. The backward linkage activities in the shrimp industry include, *inter alia,* shrimp hatcheries, shrimp fry collection, shrimp nurseries, shrimp feed mills and backyard shrimp feed manufacturers. The forward linkage activities surround those in shrimp depots, processing plants and cold storage, exporting and shipping agents and so on. Ancillary activities include, among other things, production and delivery of ice, supply of packaging materials, supply of raw materials for farm construction, supply of agri-business products such as shrimp feeds, shrimp fry and farm product trading, shrimp fry and harvested crop transportation, shrimp feed such as snail collection and supply of farm implements such as aerators.

The most important source of employment is shrimp fry collection followed by on-farm employment in shrimp farms as well as ancillary activities like trade/commerce, processing, marketing and exporting. It has been estimated that in 1983, 4.1 million person days of on-farm employment were created for 51 000 hectares of shrimp farms in the coastal areas of Bangladesh. Off-farm employment was 5.9 million person days (MPO, 1986). Based on the projected expansion of shrimp farming areas, MPO estimation for both on- and off-farm labour requirements for 1990 were 22.6 million person days. The corresponding figure for 2005 is expected to be 59.4 million person days (MPO, 1986), much of this employment effect being with the female work force (Hamid and Alauddin, 1998).

Bangladesh, with 4.2 per cent of the world production of farmed shrimp, is the world's seventh largest cultured shrimp producer. Bangladeshi farmed shrimp is well recognized for its flavour, taste and texture since it is grown primarily under natural environment (BFFEA, 1995). Cultured shrimp primarily caters for the international market. Open water shrimp catches that are not exclusively destined for overseas market cater for domestic demand. Shrimp is a popular food item all over the world because of its taste and boneless meat. Bangladesh exports frozen foods (shrimp constitutes 85–90 per cent of this category) to about 40 countries of the world with the USA, Japan and the European Union countries the major importers of Bangladesh shrimp (BFFEA, 1995). In recent years, the European Union has become the largest buyer of Bangladesh shrimp, accounting for nearly half the total export. The USA and Japan respectively account for 34 per cent and 11 per cent of the total export (BFFEA, 1995). Although Japan and the USA are two of the largest buyers of Bangladesh shrimp, Bangladesh accounts for less than 2 per cent of the combined Japan and US shrimp market (ASCC, 1995). As the single largest importer of Bangladesh shrimp, the US market has shown a downward trend in recent years while Japan's relative share has been on the increase (Alauddin and Hamid, 1999).

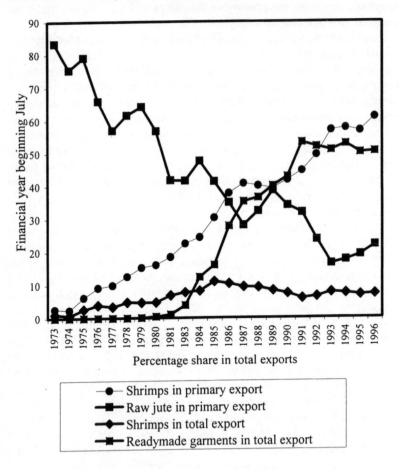

Figure 6.6 Shrimp in the export trade of Bangladesh, 1973–96

6.5.3 The Impact: The Negative Side

The positive impact of shrimp farming portrayed in the preceding section must be juxtaposed alongside its negative impact. The process has entailed high environmental costs. These include, among other things, destruction of mangrove forests, reduction in crop production (especially paddy), increased water pollution and destruction of green vegetation. Based on Alauddin and Tisdell (1998), Asaduzzaman and Toufique (1997) and Rahman *et al.* (1995) some of the negative impacts of shrimp farming can be summed up as follows:

- lower paddy production due to declining yield per hectare
- destruction of trees and vegetation due to salinity
- decline in household incomes from non-farm sources, especially those of ecological reserves
- decline in the production of poultry and livestock
- various forms of social conflict
- uneven gains between Bangladeshi (shrimp farm) owners and land owners especially the small land-owning households
- adverse environmental spillovers in the form of loss of green vegetation (for example, vegetables, coconut trees, bamboo plantation) and also of other crops, loss of genetic diversity (loss or extinction of indigenous species of fish), declining rice yields.

The process of shrimp cultivation, therefore, epitomizes conflicting resource use patterns. It has also set in motion socio-economic changes. All these may have serious implications for the sustainability of shrimp farming itself, of rural livelihoods and communities in the coastal belt of Bangladesh.

The evidence from Bangladesh is supported by evidence from elsewhere in South Asia as well as other shrimp producing countries (Alagarswami, 1995; Jayasinghe, 1995). According to Menasveta (1997, p. 41) over a period of 32 years to 1993 more than 54 per cent of Thailand's mangrove forests were destroyed to make way for shrimp farming. Hambrey (1999, p. 1), however, argues that 'shrimp farming is only one of the many pressures on mangroves and is rarely the most significant'.

In Bangladesh, mangrove has been reduced by, *inter alia,* expansion of shrimp farming in the coastal areas of Bangladesh (Mazid, 1995; Mahmood, 1986). While mangrove destruction has been a ubiquitous feature of shrimp farming in Bangladesh, it is particularly severe in its south-eastern region. As Mazid (1995, p. 77) reports 'Once the Chakaria Sundarban had a dense mangrove forest of 18 200 ha. With the expansion of shrimp farming since the 1970s, over 50 per cent of mangroves have been cleared for the establishment of shrimp farms and now only a small patch of forest remains in the interior. ... The conversion of mangrove forests would appear to be uneconomic if the potential yields are compared with the combined yields of the forests and traditional fisheries, which are now both lost'.

The environmental issues stemming from the process of shrimp culture have serious consequences for the shrimp industry. The livelihoods of many could be unsustainable if the environmental issues are not addressed and remedial measures not undertaken. These issues, however, stem from, *inter alia,* externalities engendered by the process of shrimp culture but are *internal* to the shrimp-farming country.

Overall, therefore as Lockwood (1997, p. 52) rightly argues:

> the conflict resulting from the remarkable expansion of shrimp farming has aquaculture poised at the threshold of a historic moment in which aquaculture, as one of the world's newest yet basic industries, must be transformed to a higher level of environmental and social sustainability. ... Aquaculture sustainability requires full accommodation of market economics, people struggling in subsistence economies, and the nature's economy – the environment.

6.6 SOME IMPLICATIONS AND CONCLUSIONS

The fisheries sub-sector is of critical importance to the Bangladesh economy in terms of its contribution to exports, employment, gross domestic product and above all, as a source of animal protein for human consumption. Yet, this sub-sector remains the most neglected facet of agricultural development in Bangladesh.

Significant changes have taken place in the fisheries sub-sector over the last few decades. Fish production initially declined and in the late 1970s, remained more or less stagnant until the mid-1980s. Since then, it gradually recovered to regain the early 1970s level by the end of the 1980s. In the 1990s, fish production increased quite significantly. This process of initial decline, subsequent recovery and acceleration is underpinned by a combination of both man-made and natural factors. These include among other things, the destruction of habitats, over-exploitation, favourable policy, changes in cultural practices, institutional arrangements and high profitability. Both governmental and non-governmental organizations have played an important role.

Open water capture fishery in respect of riverine and estuarine fishery has suffered significantly throughout the period under consideration. The increased catch of floodplain fisheries has compensated for this decline. The most remarkable feature of inland fishery is the prolific growth in pond culture and coastal aquaculture. The environmental impact of the former is benign (Smith, 1973) while that of the latter is adverse. As Alauddin and

Hamid (1999, p. 289) argue:

> Experiences in many countries suggest that coastal aquaculture exceeds the carrying capacity of the coastal waters resulting in lower production and often complete destruction of the yield. Thus the process of coastal aquaculture seems to have stressed the fragile environment to the limit and has resulted in significant changes in the overall socio-economic milieu.

Shrimp-producing countries of the developing world engage in shrimp farming primarily for export purposes. They export shrimp to the high-income countries of Western Europe, North America and Japan. Other emerging markets are Singapore, Hong Kong and Malaysia. The exporting countries have to adhere to the rules and regulations of the importing countries. These include, *inter alia,* various non-tariff barriers including health and environmental standards, labour laws and so on. The consumers, and hence importers, are highly sensitive to the quality of the products that they are importing. For example, 'green consumerism' in the western world is a potent force that can hardly be ignored. Similarly, customers or lobby groups in developed countries can wage campaigns to boycott products that use child labour. This could be a potential public relations setback to market access for the exporting country.

In conclusion, while there are encouraging signs of development in the fisheries sub-sector, there is very little room for complacency. The physical environment, which is already badly damaged, has been stressed to the limit, especially in the case of shrimp culture. A viable fisheries industry needs to be based on sound government policy embracing incentives, technology, marketing and value adding. Of paramount importance is the need to address environmental issues resulting from the process of growth of the fisheries sub-sector.

7. Ancillary Sectors within Agriculture: Forestry

7.1 INTRODUCTION

With increasing population and economic production throughout Asia, the utilization of natural resources has risen considerably. This is manifested in Asia by an increase in the area under crop production, a rise in land area under human settlement and a decline in area under forests and woodland. Forests all over the world, especially in Asia, are rapidly disappearing. Overall, the extent of deforestation in East Asia is greater than in South Asia even though deforestation in Bangladesh is proportionately very large (Tisdell and Alauddin, 1997, pp. 142–3; WRI, UNEP and UNDP, 1994). Given this scenario, the tropical forests of Southeast Asia will be largely diminished before long if immediate measures are not undertaken to ensure their sustainability along with a more rapid afforestation programme (Mosharaff Hossain, 1991, p. 87).

The forests are ecologically important and play an important role in the economy, those of the region being an important source of food, fodder, fuel, fibre and timber. The forest resources, apart from their economic benefit, are useful from the point of view of balanced agro-ecological development and natural growth. Forests maintain an ecological balance by their beneficial effects on water catchment areas, soil conservation, and control of siltation of dams and canals, and also of wildlife habitats. The effects of deforestation manifest themselves, *inter alia,* in (BBS, 1999a, p. 8):

- Losses of habitat, biodiversity and carbon sink
- Changes in local ecology and micro-climate
- Soil erosion and increased incidence of flooding
- Loss of water-retention capacity of soils.

The forestry resources of Bangladesh are under considerable environmental strain from the intensification and extension of agriculture as facilitated by the green revolution technologies (Alauddin and Tisdell, 1991,

1998; see also Alauddin *et al.*, 1995), deforestation and loss of natural vegetation cover. Population increase (combined with attempts at least to maintain the already low per capita income) is the main underlying cause of such pressure. Industry and urbanization put added environmental pressures on forestry resources.

This chapter proceeds with a brief overview of the Bangladesh forestry sub-sector in terms of its past performance and its present state. Homestead/household and social forestry issues are then discussed. This is followed by a discussion on policy issues relating to forestry development in Bangladesh.

7.2 THE BANGLADESH FORESTRY SUB-SECTOR: PERFORMANCE AND TRENDS

7.2.1 Broad Patterns

Table 7.1 sets out information on the changing and relative importance of the forestry sub-sector within the broader context of national accounts, overall agricultural value added and the non-crop agricultural complex. Trends in the overall forestry value added are also provided. Figure 7.1 graphically illustrates the process of these changes. A close inspection of the information contained in Table 7.1 and Figure 7.1 indicates the following salient features:

- The relative share of forestry value added in GDP declined to less than 2.5 per cent in the period of more than two and half decades to 1997–98. There does not seem to be an upward trend in recent years. After showing some increasing tendency to rise in the mid-1980s after initially falling in the 1970s, the relative share of forestry in GDP seemed to be on the decline in the 1990s. This pattern has permeated other relevant indicators such as the share of forestry in non-crop agriculture. Its share in agricultural value added has increased marginally. Its share in non-crop agricultural value added is just above 25 per cent which is slightly below the low 30 per cent mark it reached a few years ago.
- The forestry sub-sector value added has declined and remained significantly below the 1972–73 level until 1976–77. Since then it has registered consistent increases, albeit with occasional fluctuations. Since 1990–91, it has increased at a compound rate of nearly 4 per cent per annum. The overall growth for the 1972–97 period, using a semi-logarithmic trend, is estimated to be 3.27 per cent (significant at 1 per cent level). This growth rate compares favourably with those in the

overall agricultural value added and valued added in other components of the non-crop sector (see Table 5.2, Chapter 5).

Table 7.1 Trends in forestry value added, its relative shares in gross domestic product (GDP), non-crop value added, agricultural value added and the relative importance of non-crop in agricultural value added in Bangladesh at constant 1984–85 market prices, 1972–97

Year	Relative share (%) of forestry in			Relative share of non-crop in agriculture	Index of forestry value added
	GDP	Non-crop agriculture	Agriculture		
1972	3.18	26.07	6.40	24.54	100.0
1973	2.64	24.13	5.47	22.67	91.0
1974	2.54	22.51	5.28	23.47	83.9
1975	2.48	23.11	5.03	21.76	86.5
1976	2.29	21.94	4.96	22.59	82.2
1977	2.66	25.33	5.70	22.49	101.8
1978	2.88	30.90	6.53	21.12	115.9
1979	2.76	29.79	6.30	21.14	112.0
1980	2.71	29.79	6.13	20.59	113.6
1981	2.85	30.23	6.51	21.52	120.7
1982	2.88	30.70	6.62	21.57	128.1
1983	2.93	33.15	6.85	20.67	137.3
1984	2.69	31.33	6.44	20.56	130.0
1985	2.69	31.75	6.50	20.48	135.5
1986	2.52	30.47	6.34	20.80	132.6
1987	2.64	31.86	6.88	21.60	142.9
1988	2.64	31.95	7.11	22.27	146.1
1989	2.53	31.84	6.61	20.76	149.4
1990	2.50	31.45	6.64	21.12	152.5
1991	2.45	30.89	6.65	21.53	156.1
1992	2.42	30.19	6.73	22.28	160.7
1993	2.41	29.29	6.97	23.80	167.1
1994	2.41	28.43	7.36	25.90	174.7
1995	2.39	27.91	7.41	26.53	182.1
1996	2.35	27.14	7.25	26.71	189.7
1997	2.32	26.25	7.33	27.93	197.9

Notes: 1997 means financial year beginning July etc. 1997 figures are provisional.

Sources: Based on data from BBS (1993b, pp. 66–71; 1998b, pp. 489–91).

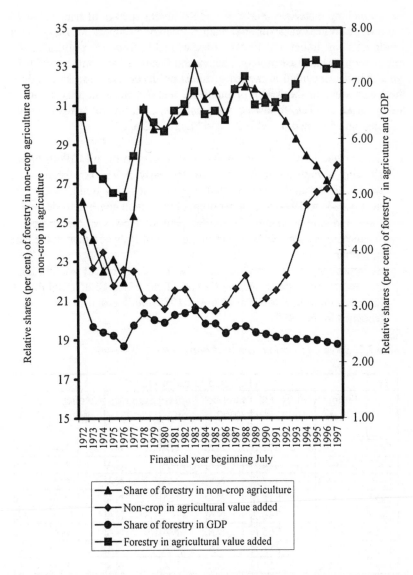

Figure 7.1 Trends in relative shares of forestry in gross domestic product, in agricultural value added and in non-crop agricultural value added in Bangladesh at constant 1984–85 market prices, 1972–97

7.2.2 Forest Products

The forestry sub-sector supplies a number of products such as timber, firewood, bamboo and raw materials for industries. It also supplies honey,

wax, thatching materials, wild fruits and different species of fish. Table 7.2
provides information about the major forestry products in Bangladesh.
While data on timber and firewood are available from 1948–49, available
information on sungrass, *golpata*, honey and fish date back only to 1970–71.
Note that fish included in the list of forest products refers to fish caught in
the water areas in the forests. Figures 7.2 and 7.3 illustrate time trends in
these variables. The following patterns emerge from an analysis of the
information contained in Table 7.2 and Figures 7.2 and 7.3:

- Timber output rose steadily to its highest level in the mid-1960s before
  showing a tendency to decline until the early 1970s. For more than a
  decade to the mid-1980s, it then registered a rising trend. Within the
  next decade to 1994–95, timber output has been in continuous decline.
- Firewood output exhibits a similar pattern. However, the degree of
  fluctuation is appreciably higher in the case of firewood than in the case
  of timber.
- Sungrass output, as measured along the left-hand vertical axis in Figure
  7.3, increased initially and with a considerable degree of instability. It
  has been on a decline for most of the 1980s but has shown some rising
  tendency in the 1990s.

Table 7.2 Selected forest products of Bangladesh, 1948–94

Year	Selected forest products						
	Timber (000 m³)	Firewood (000 m³)	Bamboo (000 canes)	*Golpata* (ton)	Sungrass (000 bundle)	Honey (ton)	Fish (ton)
1948	257.7	371.0	NA	NA	NA	NA	NA
1949	167.1	424.8	NA	NA	NA	NA	NA
1950	116.1	438.9	NA	NA	NA	NA	NA
1951	135.9	818.4	NA	NA	NA	NA	NA
1952	121.8	736.2	NA	NA	NA	NA	NA
1953	186.9	965.6	NA	NA	NA	NA	NA
1954	215.2	883.5	NA	NA	NA	NA	NA
1955	303.0	914.6	NA	NA	NA	NA	NA
1956	331.3	872.2	NA	NA	NA	NA	NA
1957	436.1	855.2	NA	NA	NA	NA	NA
1958	470.1	1087.4	NA	NA	NA	NA	NA
1959	430.4	954.3	NA	NA	NA	NA	NA
1960	481.4	866.5	NA	NA	NA	NA	NA
1961	540.9	1067.6	NA	NA	NA	NA	NA
1962	580.5	1027.9	NA	NA	NA	NA	NA
1963	637.1	957.1	NA	NA	NA	NA	NA

1964	696.6	996.8	NA	NA	NA	NA	NA
1965	713.6	767.4	NA	NA	NA	NA	NA
1966	699.4	781.5	NA	NA	NA	NA	NA
1967	557.8	880.7	NA	NA	NA	NA	NA
1968	589.0	911.8	NA	NA	NA	NA	NA
1969	563.5	659.8	NA	NA	NA	NA	NA
1970	474.5	514.1	52658	56	463	54	1861
1971	138.5	72.4	74328	42	3020	159	667
1972	198.8	240.6	103351	73	2109	235	2236
1973	335.8	473.7	74387	73	1438	117	1364
1974	214.0	310.0	67083	67	1574	203	1335
1975	234.5	309.5	48352	75	1327	156	1163
1976	289.8	381.3	62579	71	6831	240	6399
1977	343.8	630.6	73568	67	1784	228	7218
1978	436.7	552.8	60135	84	1534	176	10442
1979	388.6	647.9	78115	70	3795	213	9028
1980	433.4	679.8	74028	68	6706	311	8147
1981	490.9	744.2	77865	69	2432	225	9748
1982	437.6	862.2	92335	64	1390	233	9396
1983	554.1	903.4	92061	63	1279	260	9374
1984	493.4	888.2	76989	61	1295	256	8260
1985	560.6	989.7	75786	62	859	225	8146
1986	361.4	670.0	92616	71	1710	229	6856
1987	398.5	739.4	105050	80	1525	225	6332
1988	349.9	787.8	140636	68	1384	100	7788
1989	191.2	376.8	119131	67	1117	146	5074
1990	238.4	1082.9	84240	72	641	210	8472
1991	186.9	368.1	80000	72	458	159	4715
1992	230.0	188.7	119206	67	1016	182	5528
1993	191.6	268.5	90466	68	1092	107	5093
1994	171.7	161.9	73251	63	2146	90	5328

Note: 1948 refers to financial year beginning July 1948 etc. NA indicates not available.

Sources: Based on data from BBS (1975, p.50; 1981a, p.267; 1988a, p.217; 1993a, p.194; 1997b, p.222; 1998b, p.171).

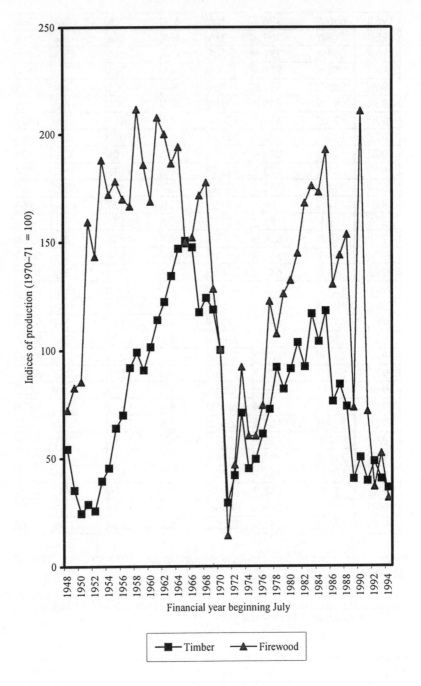

Figure 7.2 Trends in the production of timber and firewood in Bangladesh,
1948–94

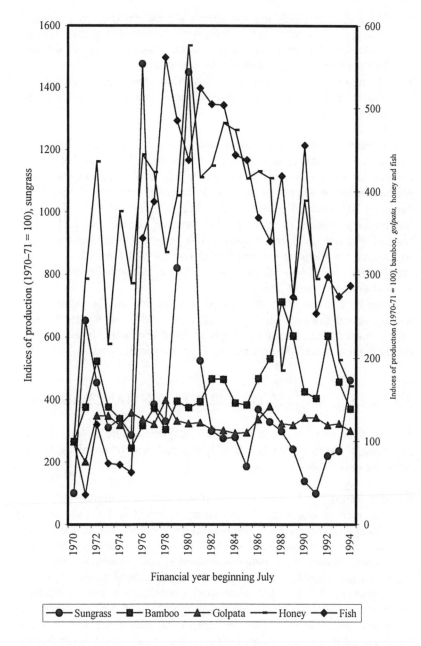

Figure 7.3 Trends in production of selected forest products in Bangladesh, 1970–94

- The output of honey has not shown a great tendency to increase in recent years. Its output in the 1990s is much lower than in the 1970s and 1980s. *Golpata* output has initially increased but subsequently declined. This declining tendency seems to be continuing.
- The fish catch from forest areas has overall been on the decline. The amount in the 1990s is significantly lower than the amount a decade before.

It is quite clear that the supply of forest products has been on the decline over time. Per capita production figures of timber, fuelwood and bamboo are set out in Table 7.3 and illustrated in Figure 7.4. Per capita timber production has registered the sharpest decline over the years. The supply of fuelwood has declined steadily. According to Alam (1997, p. 267), this 'forced the population to resort to other forms of biomass fuel such as crop residues (60 per cent) and cow-dung (20 per cent). Supplies from these sources are not adequate for the ongoing process of deforestation'. The per capita supply of bamboo has been on the decline, although the decline is not as rapid as in the case of timber.

In the light of the above, the gap between the demand for and supply of forest products has been on the increase (Roy, 1987). Several factors have been at work for the dwindling supply of forest products. The next section discusses these as well the present state of forestry in Bangladesh.

7.3 PRESENT STATE OF FORESTRY IN BANGLADESH

Table 7.4 presents the distribution of Bangladesh forests by type and geographical location. The forests of Bangladesh may be broadly classified into three main types:

- *Hill Forests:* This class consists of the tropical evergreen and semi-evergreen or deciduous types which are found in the hilly areas of Chittagong and Sylhet Divisions. The important species are *garjan, chapalish, civit, gamar, jarul, dhaki jam, champa, chundul, telsur* and *chetim*. Besides these indigenous species, teak, mahogany, nageswar, rosewood, sandalwood, rubber and pine are found to thrive well in plantations. Bamboo and other species are found in the undergrowth. The area under hill forests constitutes more than 56 per cent of the total forest area. Twenty seven per cent of the total forest area is under managed forest while 29 per cent is unclassed state forest (scrub forest).
- *Tidal Forests:* The tidal or mangrove forests occur in the south-western part of the country. They are tropical evergreen forests. The principal species in these mangrove forests are *sundari, gewa, amur, dhundal, pasur, baen, kankra, keora,* and *golpata*. Near the lower reaches of the

Matamuhuri and Naf rivers, small patches of poorly stocked mangroves
are also found.

- *Inland* Sal *Forests:* The uplifted old alluvium tracts of the Dhaka and
  Rajshahi Divisions are the locations of these forests. In addition to *Sal*
  trees, *ajuli, kaika, kimbhi, sidha* and *chaplash* are found. Many of these
  standards are in depleted condition. These are plain land (moist
  deciduous) forests. The total area of these forests constitutes about 5 per
  cent of the total forest area.

*Table 7.3   Trends in per capita production of some important forest
products in Bangladesh, 1972–94*

Year	Per capita production of		
	Timber (m^3)	Firewood (m^3)	Bamboo (number of canes)
1972	0.00268	0.00324	1.39
1973	0.00440	0.00620	0.97
1974	0.00274	0.00397	0.86
1975	0.00293	0.00387	0.61
1976	0.00354	0.00466	0.77
1977	0.00411	0.00753	0.88
1978	0.00510	0.00646	0.70
1979	0.00443	0.00739	0.89
1980	0.00482	0.00756	0.82
1981	0.00536	0.00812	0.85
1982	0.00468	0.00922	0.99
1983	0.00580	0.00946	0.96
1984	0.00506	0.00911	0.79
1985	0.00564	0.00996	0.76
1986	0.00356	0.00660	0.91
1987	0.00385	0.00715	1.02
1988	0.00332	0.00747	1.33
1989	0.00178	0.00351	1.11
1990	0.00218	0.00988	0.77
1991	0.00167	0.00330	0.72
1992	0.00202	0.00166	1.05
1993	0.00165	0.00231	0.78
1994	0.00145	0.00136	0.62

Sources: As in Table 7.2

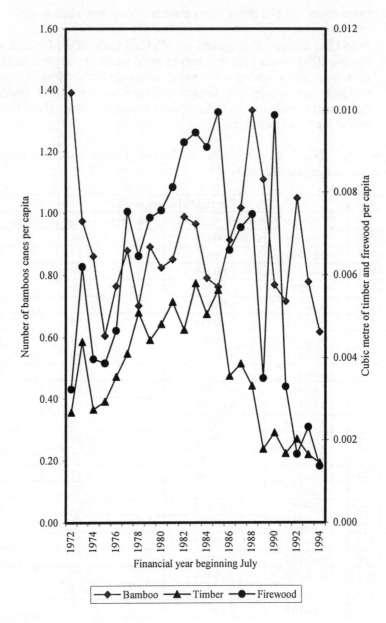

Figure 7.4 Per capita production of some important forest products in Bangladesh, 1972–94

Table 7.4 Distribution of Bangladesh forests by type and location

Forest type	Location	% of total forest area	Major forest products
Mangrove (tropical evergreen) Sundarban	South-west	22.98	Timber, poles, firewood, pulpwood, thatching materials
Coastal	Along the coast	4.84	Firewood, pulpwood
Hill forest (tropical evergreen) Managed	Eastern part	27.02	Large saw log, poles, firewood, bamboo, thatching materials
Unclassed state forests (scrub forest)	Hill tract districts	29.44	Bamboo, thatching materials and firewood
Plain land forest (tropical moist deciduous)	Central and north-western regions	4.84	Indigenous *Gazari* and plantation of short rotation exotics for poles and firewood
Village forests	Spread all over the country on homestead land	10.88	Timber, poles and firewood

Sources: Shahabuddin and Rahman (1998, p. 217); Alam (1997, p. 284).

Eighty-nine per cent of the total forest area is state owned while the remaining 11 per cent constitutes the village forest/private forest category. The distribution of forest resources in Bangladesh is highly uneven, as can be seen from Figure 7.5. More than 90 per cent of the state forest land is concentrated in 12 districts in the south and south-eastern region of Bangladesh. Twenty-eight of the total 64 districts have very little or no public forest cover at all. It can be clearly seen that the north-western and western regions have the least forest cover.

Table 7.5 presents information on forest area by management category for the 1960–94 period. The forest area as a percentage of total land area of Bangladesh is also presented. Reserve forests and unclassed state forests are the two major categories that constitute the bulk of the total forest area. One can notice a significant decline in the total forest area due primarily to a considerable decline in the area labelled unclassed state forests. The increase in the area under reserve forest has only partly compensated for the decrease in the area of unclassed state forest. Forest area as a percentage of land area has been on the decline over the years, although of late, it has shown some signs of increase. Figures 7.6 and 7.7 capture the representation of this changing phenomenon.

It is widely recognized that maintaining an ecological balance requires that forests constitute approximately 25–30 per cent of the total land area (Alam, 1997, p. 266). In that sense, at no stage during the last few decades has Bangladesh had the desirable ratio of forest to total land area. Bangladesh has, at best half that ratio, in that only about 17 per cent of the total land area is actually or potentially under forest. This area, as can be seen from Table 7.5, has come down to around 13 per cent in the 1990s.

Thus, over the years, the process of deforestation has been at work. The estimates of deforestation annually vary somewhat according to sources. Some of the estimates are as follows:

- Alam (1997, p. 267) estimates that 37 000 hectares of land are deforested annually and argues that currently only 61 per cent of the government forest is productive. Given that this area is over-exploited the present tree-covered area could be below 8 per cent of the total land area (BBS, 1996).
- BBS (1999a, p. 17) provides an equally if not more dismal picture of the extent of deforestation. It estimates that over a period of two decades to 1990, Bangladesh has lost at least 50 per cent of its natural forests. Only 6 per cent of the total land area (about 1 million hectares) is under natural forest cover consisting of deciduous forests, evergreen forests, mangrove forests and scattered patches of forests, as portrayed in Figure 7.5.
- WRI and CIDE (1990) estimate that per capita forestland declined from 0.035 hectares in 1969 to 0.020 hectares in 1990. WRI, UNEP, UNDP

and World Bank (1997, pp. 216–17) estimate that natural forests in Bangladesh are being depleted at an annual rate of 3.3 per cent.

The cutting down of trees for fuel, timber, shifting cultivation and other purposes is decimating the existing forest areas. The watershed areas of Chittagong Hill Tracts are facing population pressure and the Barind Tract is threatened by desertification. Even the central plain forest zone is ecologically degraded, which affects the socio-economic conditions of the populace. The forest resources in the private homestead areas are also being rapidly depleted.

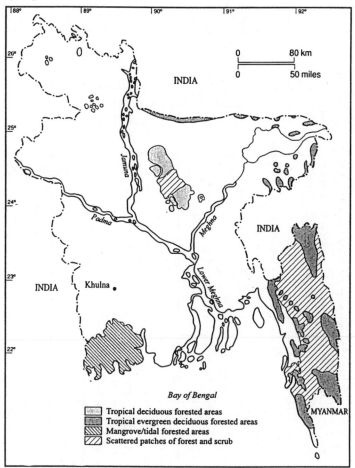

Source: BBS (1999a, p. 19)

Figure 7.5 Location of forested areas in Bangladesh

Table 7.5 Area under forest by type in Bangladesh, 1960–95

Year	Area under different types of forest (000 hectares)							Forest area as % of total land area
	Reserve forest	Acquired forest	Protected forest	Unclassed state forests	Vested forest	Others	All forests	
1960	1015	90	32	810	27	7	1980	13.95
1961	1015	90	46	810	27	6	1994	14.04
1962	1016	75	44	810	27	1	1973	13.89
1963	1032	75	46	810	29	1	1993	14.04
1964	1032	75	46	810	30	1	1994	14.04
1965	1032	76	46	804	30	6	1994	14.05
1966	1032	76	47	804	30	6	1995	14.05
1967	1032	76	47	804	30	6	1996	14.05
1968	1032	76	47	804	30	6	1996	14.05
1969	1032	79	50	804	29	5	1999	14.07
1970	1011	85	47	804	23	8	1978	13.93
1971	1011	85	45	804	23	10	1979	13.94
1972	1004	86	51	962	9	1	2114	14.89
1973	1006	86	51	962	9	2	2116	14.90
1974	1011	86	51	807	9	2	1967	13.85
1975	1020	84	51	806	9	11	1982	13.96
1976	1175	84	51	806	9	11	2137	15.05
1977	1175	85	51	809	9	11	2139	15.07
1978	1181	79	51	810	10	11	2141	15.08

1979	1250	80	51	811	10	11	2212	15.58
1980	1248	92	51	792	9	11	2204	15.52
1981	1248	91	51	805	10	11	2217	15.61
1982	1249	72	51	358	10	11	1750	12.32
1983	1127	70	51	332	9	181	1770	12.47
1984	1300	62	53	407	8	11	1841	12.96
1985	1317	60	48	562	8	13	2008	14.14
1986	1124	83	47	363	8	11	1637	11.53
1987	1174	103	47	364	8	13	1708	12.03
1988	1002	113	44	320	22	12	1653	11.64
1989	1166	36	33	302	20	92	1649	11.61
1990	1158	36	47	307	20	85	1653	11.64
1991	1172	114	45	330	12	12	1686	11.87
1992	1080	139	33	326	7	111	1696	11.95
1993	1176	119	44	316	7	35	1697	11.95
1994	1299	86	34	424	8	63	1948	13.72
1995	1299	86	34	424	8	63	1948	13.72

Note: 1960 refers to financial year beginning July 1960 etc. The category marked 'Others' includes WAPDA (Water and Power Development Authority) and *khas* (government) land, private forests, village forests etc. The Ministry of Land controls unclassed state forest. The Forest Directory under the Ministry of Forests and Environment controls all forestry areas except for private forests and unclassed state forests.

Sources: As in Table 7.2.

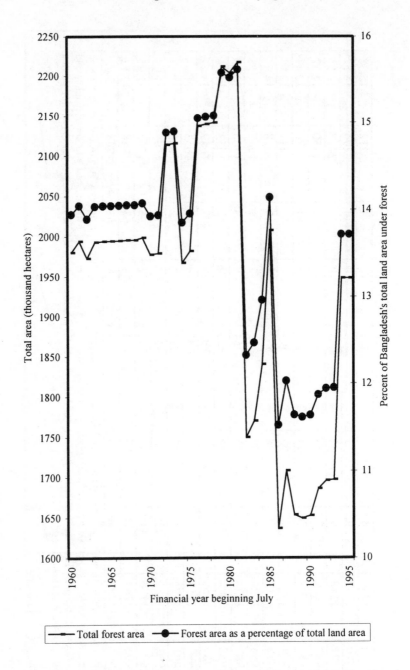

Figure 7.6   Trends in total forest area (thousand hectares) and its share (per cent) in Bangladesh's total land area, 1960–95

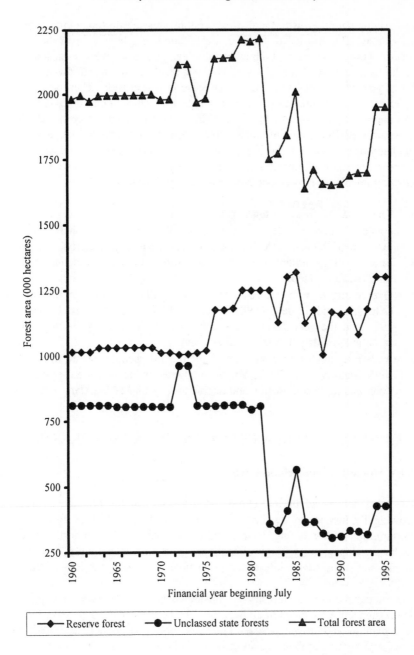

Figure 7.7 Trends in areas under major categories of forest in Bangladesh, 1960–95

Due to population growth, there is tremendous pressure on forest land in the hilly areas. This has led to the over-exploitation of a huge area of the hill forests. Timber extraction, both legal and illegal, has also greatly contributed to the decline in total forest cover. This has resulted not only in the loss of forest growth potential but also the increase in soil erosion. There are also other causes of deforestation, including industrialization, rapid urbanization and natural factors such as floods and droughts. The village forests, which have supplied 70 per cent of timber, 90 per cent of fuelwood and 90 per cent of bamboo consumed in Bangladesh, have also been subjected to deforestation as reafforestation initiatives are not sufficient to make up the growing imbalance between demand and supply. To sum up:

- The state of forest resources in Bangladesh is a matter of serious concern. There is intense pressure on land for crop production and extension of human settlement because of increasing population.
- There is illegal felling of trees in state forests and an encroachment on reserved forest lands
- Overcutting of village forests occurs especially for fuel in brick kilns (Alauddin and Tisdell, 1998). Hussain (1990) estimates that between 1981 and the year 2000, over-cutting will have reduced the growing stock in the village forests by 35 per cent.
- Access to unclassed state forests by the hill people has resulted in shifting cultivation. This is also accompanied by uncontrolled felling of trees leading to soil erosion and degradation (Gain, 1998; Alam, 1997).

7.4 HOUSEHOLD/HOMESTEAD AND SOCIAL FORESTRY

7.4.1 Homestead/household Forestry

The term homestead or household forestry refers to the practice of tree growing by homestead dwellers. Trees provide fuel, fodder or fruits for consumption and/or selling. Homestead forestry can play an important role in the developmental strategy of motivating the rural community to strive toward self-sufficiency while at the same time, combating the loss of trees and forest cover.

Although homestead forestry is considered a relatively new concept, it has existed since the dawn of civilization. The homestead dwellers have long been planting and growing trees not only for food, fuel, fodder and fibre but also for protection of their houses against wind, storms and soil erosion.

In Bangladesh, homestead forests play a vital role in providing fuelwood, fodder, fruits and timber. It is estimated that about 65 per cent to 70 per cent of saw logs and 90 per cent of fuelwood and bamboo come from homestead forests.

Bangladesh is a small, densely populated country. Because of the shortage of land, homestead forestry is one important option for bridging the gap between demand and supply of forest products. It is necessary to improve and develop homestead forestry in ways that could enhance the supply of forest resources in the rural areas. The promotion of homestead forestry could reduce fuelwood deficits as well as providing revenue to homesteaders. This would also benefit all of the rural community because trees offer other amenities such as shade, shelter and recreation and, very importantly, help sustain a balanced agro-ecological growth.

7.4.2 Social Forestry

In Bangladesh there is little scope to extend the forest area controlled by the government. The scarcity of forest cover, acute land shortage, and lack of access to public lands are the main constraints to traditional forestry development. These constraints have led to the concept of social forestry, a forestry approach that is dependent on the participation of local people. Social forestry in Bangladesh includes community forestry and farm forestry.

This approach involves the growing of trees for fuel, timber, fodder and other products by local people. Often this is done on available under-utilized lands such as on homesteads or in strip plantations along roadsides, railways, canals, embankments, or in public places like schools, mosques and office compounds.

There are approximately 5000 kilometres of highways, 3000 kilometres of railways, 4000 kilometres of coastal embankments and 6500 kilometres of local district council roads in Bangladesh. All these available spaces constitute an area equivalent to about 30 000 hectares. This large area holds great potential for putting into practice the new concept of social forestry.

Social forestry has transformed the traditional concept of forestry that dealt only with reserved forest areas. Presently, tree growing is practical on waste lands, fallow marginal lands, grazing areas or in association with agricultural crops. This is possible only with the cooperation and participation of the people involved. The success of social forestry would benefit not only the people directly concerned but would help restore an ecological balance between soil, water, flora and fauna.

For the successful implementation of any social forestry programme, the people concerned must be convinced of its usefulness and be guaranteed that they will reap the benefits. It requires a thorough investigation of the area in question and the people involved. This will identify their needs, their problems and possible solutions. This information would facilitate the ability of the government and the Forest Department to provide timely advice and input and thereby gain the confidence of the local people. This would in turn, develop responsibility and awareness among the community, a prerequisite for success.

7.5 FORESTRY DEVELOPMENT: POLICY ISSUES

7.5.1 A Review of Planned Development

Successive development plans in Bangladesh have recognised the importance of forestry sector development. Following Mosharaff Hossain (1991, pp. 98–99) and BPC (1985, pp. 200–201; 1998, pp. 18–19) public sector efforts to plan development of the forestry sub-sector can be summed up as follows:

- The First Five Year Plan (1973–78) (BPC, 1973) focused on resource development and the exploitation of natural forests. It envisaged maintaining the 1965–70 level of per capita production of timber and fuelwood. The plan emphasized intensive resource management practices in terms of extending the area under forestry, rather than planned and higher maintenance of existing forestland.
- The Two Year Plan (1978–80) (BPC, 1978) basically pursued the programme laid down in the objectives of the First Five Year Plan rather than any new programme. The priority areas, however, included: (1) extraction of wood and bamboo from the inaccessible area of the Chittagong Hill Tracts; (2) plantation of exploited hill forests; and (3) a coastal afforestation programme.
- The Second Five Year Plan (1980–85) (BPC, 1980) envisaged (1) maximizing output of forest products from existing stock; (2) development of the forest resources in government-owned forests; (3) assistance in developing the homestead woodlot, particularly through fast growing species and fruit trees and strip plantation of roads, highways, railways, canal and embankment sides; and (4) stabilization of the accretion of land in the coastal area through plantation.
- The Third Five Year Plan (1985–90) (BPC, 1985, p. 203) set the broad goals of (1) augmenting state and homestead forestry production of both timber and non-timber crops through afforestation, reafforestation and social forestry programmes; (2) accelerating the programme of short-cycle plants in order to protect more valuable fruit and timber crops in the rural areas; and (3) optimally exploiting the forest resources, without disturbing the ecological balance in order to meet the increasing demand for timber fuel, fodder, rubber and raw materials for industries.
- The Fourth Five Year Plan (1990–95) (BPC, 1991) discouraged extraction of forest resources for environmental conservation and accorded priority to afforestation of newly accreted land. The major

thrust of the fourth plan put the emphasis on a participatory approach and private sector investment in the management and development of forestry resources.

The development plans up to and including the fourth plan emphasized quantitative expansion of forestry in order to augment supplies of wood and wood products. However, qualitative expansion of natural forests through afforestation also formed an important element of this strategy.

Forestry sub-sector programmes emphasized (1) the expansion of forest resources, (2) making forests adequately productive and developing institutional capabilities including human resources; and (3) participatory approach to forestry with people-oriented programmes covering forestry on marginal lands and *charlands*, with roadsides being the central plank.

The Fifth Five Year Plan (BPC, 1998, pp. 263–7) emphasizes a more integrated approach to forestry development in terms of its focus, *inter alia,* on (1) multiple land use technology such as agro-forestry to support and supplement overall agricultural development; (2) conservation and development of forestry resources through participatory approach; and (3) expansion and rehabilitation of forest resources to increase productivity.

On the whole, the policy focus has belatedly but gradually recognized the importance of conservation, even though it is far from adequate. Let us now consider the trends in area afforested and its composition on an annual basis since the 1970s. This information is presented in Table 7.6 and illustrated in Figures 7.8 and 7.9. The following important points can be noted:

- Overall afforested area increased initially for a decade to the mid-1980s and continued to decline until 1990. In the last few years, it has begun to increase even though it is still below the mid-1980s level.
- Hill forests, coastal afforestation and unclassed state forest seem to be the major focus of the programme despite high year-to-year variations.
- Overall, the relative importance of hill forest and coastal forest is on the decline while that of unclassed state forest is on the rise. Of late, afforestation of *sal* forestry has gained considerable importance. However, Gain (1998, p. 6) argues that 'commercial plantation, mainly of exotic species with the Asian Development Bank soft loans has taken much of the traditional *sal* forests'.

7.5.2 Non-governmental Organizations and Forestry in Bangladesh

There are about 110 foreign and local non-governmental organizations (NGOs) working in Bangladesh. Most of them are localized and work in rural areas, but some have a broad geographic focus. The NGOs mainly concentrate on various income-generating activities for the rural community.

Some of the important NGOs taking part in this initiative are: Bangladesh Rural Advancement Committee (BRAC), Rangpur, Dinajpur Rehabilitation Service (RDRS), the Cooperative for American Relief Everywhere (CARE), Mennonite Central Committee (MCC), Kushtia Social Services Committee (KSSC), *Proshika*, Youth Project BARD, and CARITAS.

Table 7.6 Afforestation programme by type of forest in Bangladesh, 1974– 93

Year	Area by forest type (hectares)				
	Hill Forest	*Sal* forest	Coastal afforestation	Unclassed state forest	Total
1974	2643.5	80.9	1968.8	286.5	4979.8
1975	3092.3	522.1	4864.0	1214.1	9692.4
1976	3361.0	1140.0	6727.2	1780.7	13008.9
1977	4339.1	1022.7	4942.5	1651.2	11955.5
1978	4619.2	957.1	6606.6	1123.5	13306.4
1979	5986.2	809.4	6518.0	2225.4	15539.1
1980	7367.1	688.3	6242.0	1983.0	16280.3
1981	8207.2	1193.9	6322.5	6151.4	21875.0
1982	7222.6	1058.7	8093.9	3844.6	20219.8
1983	7437.1	1038.5	10117.4	3744.4	22337.3
1984	5232.7	615.1	9996.0	6960.7	22804.5
1985	4106.4	1052.2	8114.1	6253.3	19526.1
1986	3476.7	1028.3	8093.9	4643.5	17242.4
1987	3367.9	217.7	8195.1	4534.6	16315.3
1988	3698.5	590.9	3806.2	3669.4	11764.9
1989	5163.5	2562.5	4168.4	945.0	12839.3
1990	3781.9	3265.1	2865.2	94.7	10006.9
1991	3628.1	3323.4	3565.4	1347.6	11864.4
1992	4235.1	4550.0	4325.0	4134.0	17244.0
1993	4239.2	5423.7	4989.1	4134.0	18785.9
Percentage share of respective components in yearly total					
1974	53.08	1.63	39.54	5.75	100
1975	31.90	5.39	50.18	12.53	100
1976	25.84	8.76	51.71	13.69	100
1977	36.29	8.55	41.34	13.81	100
1978	34.71	7.19	49.65	8.44	100
1979	38.52	5.21	41.95	14.32	100
1980	45.25	4.23	38.34	12.18	100
1981	37.52	5.46	28.90	28.12	100
1982	35.72	5.24	40.03	19.01	100
1983	33.29	4.65	45.29	16.76	100
1984	22.95	2.70	43.83	30.52	100
1985	21.03	5.39	41.56	32.03	100

1986	20.16	5.96	46.94	26.93	100
1987	20.64	1.33	50.23	27.79	100
1988	31.44	5.02	32.35	31.19	100
1989	40.22	19.96	32.47	7.36	100
1990	37.79	32.63	28.63	0.95	100
1991	30.58	28.01	30.05	11.36	100
1992	24.56	26.39	25.08	23.97	100
1993	22.57	28.87	26.56	22.01	100

Note: 1974 indicates financial year beginning July 1974.

Source: Based on data from Alam (1997, pp. 285–6).

RDRS

The RDRS has worked in Bangladesh since 1972. They have been in touch with about 5100 farmers and have organized over 500 small-farmer groups. In the social forestry sector, they have worked under two components: private nursery development and roadside strip plantations. There are over 120 nurseries in business and about 430 farmers have received training. RDRS also took up the task of strip planting 35 miles of major district roads with the help of the rural poor women. Each of them was responsible for half a mile of the roadway and was paid a daily wage.

MCC

The Mennonite Central Committee has a small tree-planting programme, and about 40 000 seedlings have been planted on public and private areas. These were mostly timber species but some fruit trees were planted on private sites. The outcomes on the private sites were encouraging and MCC plans to emphasize private domestic planting. MCC also introduced fruit and spice trees into their horticultural programme for homesteads and has a training programme for the landless to manage nurseries.

KSSC

The Kushtia Social Services Committee of the Church of Bangladesh has a tree plantation programme. Mahogany and raintrees were planted along miles of roadside but these were damaged because of flooding and because of insufficient space for ox carts to pass between the rows of trees.

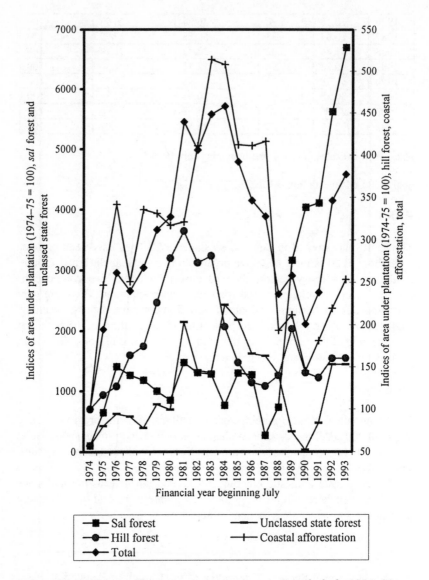

Figure 7.8 Trends in afforestation programmes in Bangladesh, 1974–93

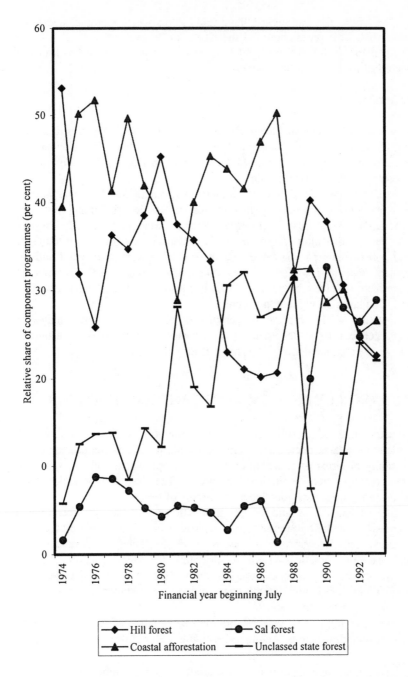

Figure 7.9 Changing composition of the Bangladesh afforestation programme, 1974–93

The KSSC also had eight village sale centres where seedlings and grafts were sold. This programme led the KSSC to believe that there is a strong demand for seedlings from local farmers who could not afford to transport seedlings from government nurseries.

Other NGOs

A number of NGOs including BRAC and CARITAS have subsidized the transportation cost of seedlings. They believe that there is a demand for good quality seedlings produced locally. Oxfam has a project for private coconut nurseries near Comilla.

Proshika has subsidized the training programme of 40 female nursery workers and is developing an agro-forestry project involving mulberry production. Bangladesh Rural Advancement Committee (BRAC) has also introduced horticultural activities in its women's activities programme. In addition to planting vegetables, some fruit trees were distributed and the present emphasis is on fast-growing trees for fuel wood. The Cooperative for American Relief Everywhere (CARE) has also introduced similar activities in 110 villages throughout the country.

On the whole, the non-governmental organizations have played a constructive role in development and conservation of forestry resources. They have complemented government efforts.

7.6 CONCLUDING COMMENTS AND IMPLICATIONS

Forestry. like other sub-sectors in the non-crop sector of Bangladesh agriculture is a neglected area. This is despite its crucial importance to the economy in terms of contribution to GDP, employment and, above all, to environmental and ecological resources. The last few decades have witnessed a progressive decline in the supply of forestry products.

Intense demand for land for crop production and human settlement due to increasing population pressure, together with lack of public policy focus on conservation of forestry resources, rapid deforestation, poor management and cultural practices have contributed to this situation. Several unprecedented floods and droughts during the last three decades, and frequent cyclones and natural hazards have exacerbated the process of destruction of forestry resources.

The alarming rate of deforestation and degradation of forestry resources have several dimensions. Among other things, deforestation entails:

- Declining supplies of main forest products such as timber, fuelwood and bamboo and subsidiary forest products such as fish, *golpata* and honey, which constitute a direct economic loss.

- Degradation of forestry resources that lead to loss of biodiversity and loss of ecological balance. Alauddin and Tisdell (1998) compute a biodiversity (conservation) index for Bangladesh to be 0.035, the lowest in a group of Asian countries which include: Thailand (0.63), Sri Lanka (0.595), Indonesia (0.51), Pakistan (0.23), India (0.20), China (0.16) and the Philippines (0.095)[1].

- Loss or depletion of livelihoods of the people who live in rural and hill areas (Alauddin *et al.*, 1995; Vyas, 1995; Gain, 1998). The crisis of fuelwood is indeed serious in Bangladesh as elsewhere in the developing world (Bowonder *et al.*, 1988).

- Decrease in water holding capacity and increased soil erosion which further lowers the capacity to sustain increased agricultural production.

The World Bank (1997) estimates that the adverse environmental impacts following or accompanying deforestation could be as high as a loss of 1 per cent of GDP in 1990 (quoted in BBS, 1999a, p. 17). Bangladesh, therefore, by all available accounts, seems to be in a state of environmental crisis (Ali, 1994; BBS, 1999a).

As indicated earlier in our discussion, a number of initiatives have been taken by the government and non-governmental organizations to create awareness and strengthen institutional capacity to handle multi-dimensional environmental problems. The problem is complex and one should not expect any simple or simplistic solutions. The concept of social/homestead forestry is very sound but faces some formidable constraints.

The major constraint on homestead forestry is the lack of available land. Small landowners are unable to expand because of the lack of homestead land. The very poor face insecurity of tenure, as at least 10 per cent of rural homesteaders do not own the land on which they live. Furthermore, the cost of transporting seedlings from central nurseries to homesteads is a burden to farmers, many of whom depend on natural regeneration as their source of seedling supply. There are influential local people who are destroying the forests for their own benefits. The settlement of migrants in forest areas has caused great harm as fallow periods are shortened due to land pressures. Uncontrolled grazing in both public and private forests hampers tree regeneration. There is also inadequate training and extension support services. Finally, the complete lack of awareness of ecological and environmental problems inhibits forestry development.

In social forestry, there is poor coordination between the local people and the Forest Department. The strip plantation programme implemented both by government and NGOs needed hired supervisors/guards for protecting the trees. This is because the local people use the strips for various other purposes. The cattle owners use the strips for grazing animals; in low-lying areas, the road embankments are used for shelter during flood periods and trees are often viewed as a hindrance. The farmers who worked the land adjacent to the strip often objected that trees would shade their crops and impede their access to the agricultural land near the strips.

Property rights have a significant bearing on resource use and environmental management. As Perrings (1995, p. 106) rightly argues, 'the less complete the property rights, the greater is the propensity for resources to be overutilized. The more environmental services/disservices associated with a given pattern of resource use are not the subject of well-defined rights, the greater is the risk of environmental damage'. Property rights are not well defined and management responsibilities often devolve on several departments, which frequently work in a piecemeal fashion rather than in any rationally coordinated way. As Alauddin and Tisdell (1998) put it:

> With too many ministries and departments running the environmental programmes the environmental administration in Bangladesh is not effective and resulted in expanding the bureaucratic machinery. The Department of Environment is supposed to coordinate all the activities relating to environmental management. But it does not have the authority over other ministries or departments dealing with environmental regulations and legislations. With different agencies and bodies having their respective chain of command, the coordination aspect of the Department of Environment or even the Ministry of Environment and Forestry becomes less effective. This state of play of environmental governance and management is reminiscent of the overall effectiveness and priorities of the Bangladesh agricultural research system (Alauddin and Tisdell, 1986).

The question of co-management involving government bodies and local communities needs serious consideration. It seems to have generated successful environmental management outcomes in India and other Asian countries (Alauddin and Tisdell, 1998, Chapter 6).

NOTES

1   Following Alauddin and Tisdell (1998, chapter 2), it is calculated as follows:

$V = \alpha HDI + (1 - \alpha) CI$, Where V refers to development valuation index; *HDI* refers to human development index; *CI* indicates conservation (or biodiversity) index. The value α reflects the relative weight placed on human development and the conservation of nature, using the protected areas variable as a proxy for the conservation of biodiversity (where $0<\alpha<1$). It is assumed that $\alpha = {}^2/_3$. This means that more weight is given to human welfare than to species conservation using this crude approach, but that the preservation of biodiversity is also ethically important. For further details and limitations of this approach see Alauddin and Tisdell (1998).

8. Agrarian Relations and Property Rights Issues[*]

8.1 INTRODUCTION

The ownership of land is of critical importance in rural Bangladesh. Agriculture still occupies a pivotal position in the structure of our economy even though its share in GDP has declined considerably during the last two decades. The economic and social life of people in rural Bangladesh revolves around agriculture. Land ownership and distribution is the singlemost important determinant of social, political and economic power in the rural society of Bangladesh.

The rural people of Bangladesh are becoming increasingly (functionally) landless and the pattern of land distribution is becoming increasingly skewed, due both to the high rate of population growth and the inability of the marginal peasants to earn enough for their survival (Banik, 1990; Hossain, 1986; Rahman, 1998). The pressure of population and the laws on inheritance lead inevitably to the disintegration of holdings (Cain, 1983). Since there is very little scope for an extension of the total area of net cultivable land, and in fact, more than 95 per cent of the total of about 9 million hectares of net cultivable land is now under the plough, the pressure of an ever-increasing demand for lands, can only result in an appreciation in the value of land assets. Only those people with surplus can hold on to their lands or buy more land. Even though the poor farmers are losing their lands, the reason that they are not forced out of agriculture is simply because there is little else for them to do.

Against this background, this chapter examines agrarian relations and property rights issues. It proceeds first of all with an analysis of these in a historical context. Land distribution patterns are analysed employing various agricultural census and survey data. Some implications of the above are also discussed.

8.2 AGRARIAN RELATIONS AND PROPERTY RIGHTS ISSUES IN A HISTORICAL CONTEXT

Historically speaking agrarian relations in present-day Bangladesh have gone through three distinct phases: (1) agrarian relations before 1950 (primarily the British period); (2) the Pakistan period (1950–71); and (3) the Bangladesh period (post-1972). We shall discuss each of these in turn.

8.2.1 Agrarian Relations before 1950: The British Period

In 1793, the British rulers introduced a new system of land revenue collection in the region that includes present-day Bangladesh. This was known as Permanent Settlement. Under this system, the landlords (known as *zaminders*) and rent collectors had the right to collect revenue on behalf of the government. These rights were permanent and the amounts to be paid to the government by the *zaminders* were also fixed in perpetuity.

The rights to collect revenue were hereditable and alienable. This meant that the *zaminders* could lease out these rights to subordinate interests who could do the same with the rights thus obtained. In this way, a chain of intermediaries grew up between the government and the cultivators who were bearing the full burden of rent and all the risks associated with agricultural production and other extractions.[1] Deprived of nearly every bit of surplus from land, a cultivator was destined to live in perpetual poverty, which more often than not forced him into bondage of indebtedness. A rapacious money-lending class alongside, or sometimes identical with, some of the landed interests emerged. A poor cultivator could hardly manage to escape the claws of either. The distrainment of his assets, including the landholding, was a logical as well as a real threat. Many a cultivator ended up joining the ranks of the landless and/or agricultural labourers during the period of British rule in India.

Losing the rights on their landholdings the cultivators were still committed to agriculture. Many of them moved to an inferior status to become sharecroppers and/or agricultural labourers. They were actually placed at the bottom or near-bottom of the hierarchy in agriculture. The sharecroppers (known as *bargadars*) lease land on an informal contractual basis from some landholders. A more common practice is to fix a *bargadar's* share at 50 per cent of the produce but it is not a general rule. In some cases, it is even much less, depending upon the custom and tradition of the locals and also upon the relative demand by the landless.

Even though the peasant farming system dominated cultivation in this region towards the end of the British rule, the area under sharecropping and the number of agricultural labourers grew to a considerable proportion. On the basis of the Floud Commission Report (GB, 1940) it is estimated that in 1938–40, about 19 per cent of the total area was cultivated by sharecroppers, and another 7 per cent by hired agricultural labourers. An estimated 12 per cent of the cultivating families lived mainly or entirely as sharecroppers while another 18.6 per cent were mainly or entirely agricultural labourers. Taken together, they constituted more than 30 per cent of the peasant population, cultivating about 26 per cent of the aggregate land. Ishaque's sample survey (Ishaque, 1946) also shows that approximately 30 per cent of the peasant population were absolutely landless or owned just homestead land. The size becomes much bigger if one includes households owning less than 0.40 hectare of land. Peasant households were fast becoming marginalized, but they continued to live on.

It appears that peasant households were becoming quite differentiated from each other from the point of view of the size of landholdings. The Floud Commission Report (GB, 1940) also shows that an overwhelmingly large number of the rural people, 45.8 per cent of the landowners, had less than 0.81 hectares per household, while 11 per cent had between 0.81 and 1.21 hectares, 16.8 per cent had between 1.21 and 2 hectares, 16.1 per cent between 2 and 4 hectares and the remaining 7.7 per cent had above 4 hectare holdings. The average size of holding per household thus came to 1.63 hectares. The marginal farming households were fast becoming unviable. The extraction of surplus by the superior classes of landowners and moneylenders hastened the process of the pauperization and proletarianization of these farming households.

Agrarian relations that evolved under the permanent settlement were not only unjust but also grotesquely inefficient. The long chain of intermediaries appropriated the surplus from land, but few of them accumulated enough to plough back the surplus into the system for socio-economic transformation. The different layers of middlemen mostly consumed rent. Those with very big estates indulged in luxury and ostentatious consumption. The usurious money-lending carried less risk and was more rewarding than investment in any productive activity. Consequently, production suffered, agriculture remained backward and the demand for industrial goods from the agricultural sector remained low and stagnant. There was very little diversification in the economy.[2]

8.2.2 Land Reforms since 1950: The Pakistan Era

The Floud Commission had recommended the abolition of the *zamindary* system along with the tenurial rights of other intermediaries. They also prescribed its replacement by direct settlement between the state and the cultivators. The recommendations could not, however, be immediately implemented because of the continuation of the Second World War and the political turmoil preceding the partition of India into two separate sovereign states, namely India and Pakistan. Bengal was also partitioned in the process and East Bengal became a part of Pakistan.

The mighty *zamindars* of the past had, in the meantime, lost all their power and glory. The permanent settlement was quite rightly thought to be the principal obstacle to agrarian change. A series of peasant movements, the last being the *Tebhaga* movement, continued raging through Bengal even after partition had shaken the base of the prevailing tenurial arrangements.

It is, therefore, no surprise that within less than three years after partition, the East Bengal Legislative Assembly passed the East Bengal Estate Acquisition and the Tenancy Act in February 1950. The Act contained the following salient features:

- The Act abolished the *zamindary* system with the government acquiring the rent-receiving interests in all lands. This marked the end of the numerous intermediaries created under the Permanent Settlement.
- The peasants became direct tenants under the government and got the proprietary rights on their lands, which were made permanent, hereditable and transferable.
- The ceiling to land holding was fixed at 100 standard *bighas* (about 13.35 hectares) of cultivable land per family or 10 standard *bighas* (1.34 hectares) per member of the family, whichever was the larger, in addition to homestead land up to 10 standard *bighas* (1.34 hectares) per family.
- The ceiling was able to be relaxed for plantation activities in tea, coffee, sugarcane and rubber, for cassia leaf gardens, orchards and large scale mechanized farming.
- The excess land, acquired by the state in the process was to be settled with bona fide marginal farmers holding not more than 1.21 hectares of land.
- A cultivator was allowed to buy or otherwise acquire additional cultivable land only if his holding did not exceed 13.35 hectares for himself and his family. The Act provided for suitable compensation for those whose excess lands were to be acquired.

The provisions of this Act underwent some significant amendments over time. The most important among them was a revision of the ceiling to landholding from 100 to 375 standard *bighas* (50 hectares) per family by an Ordinance in 1961. Accordingly, some of the acquired lands had to be given back to the previous owners after 1964. This modification was extended to cooperative societies, provided the individual members transferred unconditionally their ownership rights to the society.

For the redistribution of excess land acquired by the state, the Revenue Department, in 1957, laid down an order of priority that included even non-cultivators like ex-military men with long and meritorious service, refugees and ex-rent receivers with no land for consideration. The 1.21 hectare limit was not relaxed. It is to be noted that these lands were not freely redistributed. An applicant would get his share of land on payment of a sum of money, called *salami*, to the government, and provided his application for land was granted. In August 1957, the *salami* was set at 5–10 times the amount of annual rent. In

August 1958, it was made equivalent to 50 per cent of the current market price for land. In 1962, it was further enhanced to the full market value of the land.

It appears, therefore, that the great expectations of distributive justice and productive efficiency aroused by the Act of 1950 suffered considerable erosion in subsequent years. Given the socio-economic realities, the Act itself did not have much to offer in the way of change. It had actually given legal endorsement to the pattern of agrarian relations that had already been taking place. It did not do much in the matter of initiating fundamental changes of far-reaching consequences in land relations. There were emerging, in the meantime, some powerful interest groups whose self-seeking manoeuvres were leaving the Act emaciated and out of tune with the realities of the situation. In the absence of democracy, the army-bureaucracy power clique, like any other colonial and authoritarian rule, was looking for a support base of choice in the rural areas. The new landowning ruling elite from among the *jotdars* (rural landed gentry) became its chosen target for this purpose. The strategy was to win them over to its fold so that they could control the rural areas on their behalf. The raising of the land ceiling to 50 hectares per family was a deliberate act to that end. The large landholders were given the opportunity to expand their resource base and assume positions of influence. Since their newly-found powers and privileges were the creation of the authoritarian rule, it was quite likely that they would be relied on to act as trusted agents of the rulers for the distribution of patronage among the loyal few and the suppression of discontent among the rural masses. Ayub Khan, who seized power in a bloodless coup in October 1958, tried to institutionalize their position through the introduction of the system of 'Basic Democracy', wherein they were provided with political authority to exercise their socio-economic power.[3]

There was very little to be achieved in the matter of redistribution of acquired land. The popular belief that *zamindars* were, by and large, big estate holders and the acquisition of their land would release quite big areas of the aggregate cultivable area for redistribution, was not substantiated by any evidence of facts on the ground. Several factors were at work:

- Firstly, a small number of *zaminders*, barely 2 per cent, were big landlords.
- Second, lands settled with estate under any form of tenure holding could not be taken over for redistribution.
- Third, much of the excess land, if any existed, could be conveniently kept within the family members by way of land distribution among family members. This could be achieved through deeds showing each member as a separate household or even by way of fictitious transactions
- Fourth, the bigger landowners had the choice to keep the preferred plots to themselves and leave the inferior ones for government acquisition.

Consequently, much of the acquired land was uncultivated or uncultivable.

- Finally, the enhancement of the land ceiling to 50 hectares per family, by a 1961 Ordinance, eliminated even the residual possibility of land acquisition to a substantial level for redistribution among the poorer farmers. The *jotdars* acquired a pivotal position for land management and rural development.

It is known from the available statistics that the total area acquired under the Act of 1950 came to about 66 300 hectares (Abdullah, 1976, p. 85). It is also on the public record that total land acquired (through the Act of 1950 and other government measures) by 1959 was about 95 000 hectares, of which 68 per cent was wasteland. Assuming that roughly 60 per cent of the land acquired under the Act of 1950 was wasteland, Abdullah (1976, p. 85) estimates that the total arable land that the government could take over under the Act was no more than 26 500 hectares. Given that the net farm area of Bangladesh is 9 million hectares, this means that the Act could contribute to the acquisition of barely 0.3 per cent of the total cropped area in Bangladesh. Given also the number of landless and marginal farmers who constituted an overwhelming majority of rural households, the redistributive effect of the Act – if any real and honest attempt at redistribution was made – could not be other than negligible.

The partition of Bengal that accompanied the partition of India in 1947 led to a kind of redistribution. In its immediate aftermath, large-scale migration took place to and from this territory, resulting in substantial changes in entitlements to landholdings. This might have been a major factor contributing to the decline in landlessness or near landlessness. According to the 1951 Census (GOP, 1951) 17 per cent of agricultural households were found to be landless, while this category of peasant households constituted more than 30 per cent of the total in the Floud Commission Report for 1938–40 (GB, 1940). Once emigration slowed down, the forces determining the pattern of landholding changed. Landlessness, as a consequence, again showed an upward trend. By 1961, government policies began to be directed toward the interests of the farmers who owned in excess of the ceiling. Inequality was on the rise and there was very little gain in productive efficiency. The marginal farmers were losing out to bigger ones; and the affluent farmers, fed liberally on government subsidies and bounties, did not make much investment by themselves. Semi-feudal practices like usurious money-lending, land buying, hoarding, business in forward and backward purchases, and sales of agricultural commodities provided surer returns which were considered preferable to risky investments in agriculture.

8.2.3 Changes since 1972: The Bangladesh Period

Immediately after independence it fell to the new government to look into the problems of agrarian relations and to initiate measures for correction. Accordingly, in 1972, the government announced a programme whereby the ceiling to landholding was again brought down to 13.4 hectares per family. This was able to be relaxed in cases of cooperative farming and organized plantation. The *khas* (government) land was to be distributed among landless peasants and marginal farmers having not more than 0.61 hectare of land. The landless were to be especially encouraged to form cooperatives for settlement on large blocks of *khas* land. It was also decided that the recovered and accreted *charlands* by the rivers would not go back to original claimants, if there were any; rather, they would be vested with the government, who would be required to settle them among poor landless peasants. The government, in addition, declared exemption from payment of the land revenue for agricultural households owning less than 3.3 hectares of land.

It cannot be said that all these measures were fully and effectively implemented. Very little could be acquired through the reduction of land ceilings. The landowners with excess land were very few in number and could find enough loopholes in the land laws to help them hold on to their lands. There were no concerted efforts to distribute the government land among the landless and the marginal farmers. With more than 5 million households in the category of landless and marginal peasants, and the government having only about 182 000 hectares in aggregate for distribution, it could not have created much impact, even had it been a success.

The inefficiency of the measures of 1972 made the government realize that they would have to initiate changes of a more fundamental nature in agrarian relations, in order for there to be real, tangible improvements in agriculture. This was attempted in 1975 when the government declared a series of drastic measures for revitalizing the rural economy. The land ceiling was to be further reduced to 9.3 hectares per family. But measures of more far-reaching consequences were proposed in relation to the organization of production. The whole of agriculture was to be brought under a system of compulsory cooperatives. The total output would have to be distributed according to the ratio of one-third for land, one-third for labour and another one-third for the use of capital that included plough, bullock, seeds, fertilizer, irrigation and so on. In the management of cooperatives there would have to be proportional representation of land, labour and capital. The capital formation in agriculture would be used by the cooperatives for improvements in productive efficiency and also for diversion into rural industries, which would similarly be run under the overall management of the cooperatives. Landless labourers would thus be absorbed in a gainful process of production in rural activities. However, this policy could not be implemented owing to a change in government in 1975.

The deepening crisis in the economy and the sharpening of contradictions in the production relations, however, combined to exert pressure on the government to initiate land reform measures. Consequently, a Land Reform Committee was formed in 1982. On the basis of its recommendations, the government promulgated a new Land Reforms Ordinance in 1984, the main features of which are described below. The ceiling to ownership of agricultural land was reduced further to 8 hectares for a family. Excess land would be acquired by the state on the payment of compensation to the owners who would have the freedom to keep their preferred plots up to 8 hectares per family. A *bargadar* would be entitled to cultivate up to 2 hectares of land, his contract for cultivation on the *barga* land would remain valid initially for 5 years and would be renewed if he satisfied the terms and conditions of cultivation. The owner and the *bargadar* would each get one-third of the produce of the land. The remaining third was to be received by the owner or the *bargadar* or by both in proportion to the other costs of cultivation borne by them. In addition to reducing the ceiling of land holdings, the latest reforms, it appears, have shown greater interest in safeguarding the rights of the sharecroppers.

In spite of its promulgation in 1984, the provisions of the law are yet to be implemented fully. But the problem in Bangladesh today is so deep and complex that even if the law is fully implemented, it will touch only the fringes of the issue. A look into the cropping pattern of land distribution in rural Bangladesh will clarify this further.

8.3 THE PATTERN OF LAND DISTRIBUTION, 1960–84

8.3.1 The Aggregate Picture

It has already been noted that the concentration of landless or near landless peasants which stood at nearly 17 per cent in 1951 has since shown a continuous upward trend. According to the Census of Agriculture and Livestock (BBS, 1986b), the incidence of landlessness rose to 56.5 per cent of the rural households in 1983–84. Of those, 8.7 per cent claimed ownership of no land whatsoever, 19.6 per cent had claims only on homestead land, and another 28.2 per cent had at most 0.2 hectare of land, in addition to homestead land. Land reforms emphasizing only the tenurial arrangements can hardly be expected to solve the problem of access to land of these groups of people. The tenurial arrangements are showing some interesting shifts:

- Among the land holding population in 1951, about 41 per cent were estimated to be owner-cultivators, another 47 per cent owner-cum-tenants, and the remaining 12 per cent or so, were pure sharecroppers (GOP, 1951).

- The Land Occupancy Survey of 1978 shows the corresponding figure as 64.53 per cent, 28.06 per cent and 7.41 per cent respectively (BBS, 1981a; 1981b; see also Table 8.1). The 1983–84 Agricultural Census (BBS, 1986b) also shows similar trends. Compared to the number of owner-cultivators, it appears that the relative number of tenant farmers is also on the decline. About 19.1 per cent of cultivated land was still under sharecropping in 1978, but only 7.41 per cent of farmers holding only 3.7 per cent of cultivated land were pure sharecroppers. These figures seem to indicate two important trends: first most of the landowners prefer to keep all their land to themselves for cultivation (Bardhan, 1984, p. 189; Quasem, 1986, p. 18). Second, landlessness is gradually reducing the marginal peasants to agricultural labourers. Since sharecropping is being replaced by self-cultivation in the case of most farmers, and farming is being done mostly under the management of the landowners themselves, landless labourers are earning their living more and more as day labourers undertaking any work they can find.

Table 8.1   Number and area of rural households by type of tenancies in Bangladesh, 1960 and 1977

Year	Owner		Owner-cum-tenant		Tenant	
	House-hold (000)	Area (000 ha)	House-hold (000)	Area (000 ha)	House-hold (000)	Area (000 ha)
1960	3731	4716	2308	3978	100	97.94
1977	3646	4972	2575	3879	35	36.02
	Percentage of total					
1960	60.80	53.64	37.60	45.25	1.63	1.11
1977	58.30	55.95	21.20	43.66	0.55	0.41

Note: Total rented land areas in 1960 and 1977 were respectively 1.597 million hectares (18.16 per cent) and 1.490 million (16.76 per cent).

Sources: Based on data from BBS (1981b, pp. 41, 291).

The pattern of the distribution of size of holding, as it changes over time, is also indicative of an increasing rate of pauperization of peasant families in Bangladesh. We have already seen that the average size of a holding around 1938–40 was estimated at 1.63 hectares, which declined to 1.34 hectares in 1960 (ACO, 1962) and was further reduced to 0.93 hectare in 1983–84 (BBS, 1986b). Over the period of 45 years between 1938–40 and 1983–84, the average size of land held by a peasant family has been almost halved. The average size today has itself become a marginal size.

A farm household, as defined in the Agricultural Census is one, which has at least 0.02 hectare of land. Farm households are distributed into three categories: small (0.02 to 1.00 hectare), medium (1.00 to 3.00 hectares) and large (above 3.00 hectares).

Table 8.2 presents a comparative picture of farm size distribution in Bangladesh on the basis of statement of farm size distribution of the findings in Agricultural Census 1960 (ACO, 1962), Master Survey of Agriculture 1968 (BBS, 1972), Agricultural Census 1977 (BBS, 1981b) and Agricultural Census 1983–84 (BBS, 1986b).

In 1983–84, small farms accounted for more than 70 per cent of the total number of farm households. In 1960 they represented about 52 per cent of the total number of farms. Medium and large farms respectively constituted 37.7 per cent and 10.7 per cent in 1960, while the corresponding figures for 1983–84 are 24.7 and 4.9 per cent respectively (Figure 8.1) The shares of farm areas under different categories have also shown concomitant changes. The area under small farms has gone up from 16.25 per cent in 1960 to nearly 29 per cent in 1983–84,while that under large farms has decreased from about 38 per cent in 1960 to about 26 per cent in 1983–84 (Fgure 8.2).

The share of medium farms in terms of area has changed very little. Medium farms accounted for just over 45 per cent of the total cultivated area in 1983–84 compared to 45.69 per cent in 1960. More importantly, the average size of farms in each of the three categories has declined. For large and medium farms the shift is negligible, but for small farms the marginal worth of the change should be quite substantial: from about 0.45 in 1960 to 0.38 hectare in 1983–84, a decline of 16 per cent. This can be clearly seen from Table 8.3 and Figure 8.3.

A more detailed breakdown of farm distribution over the years is set out in the lower panel of Table 8.2. It shows the crisis that has been deepening in land–peasant relationships in Bangladesh agriculture. The majority of small farms are practically unviable. About a quarter of farms are below 0.20 hectare, and another 16 per cent lie between 0.20 and 0.40 hectare. Farms below 0.60 hectare constitute nearly 54 per cent of the aggregate number of farms. But together they account for only 14.78 per cent of the total farm area. Disparity in the most acute form is, of course, observable in the lowest category of farms below 0.60 hectare in size. Nearly 25 per cent of farms operate only 2.74 per cent of the cultivated area while at the other extreme, 0.17 per cent of farms covering about 2.70 per cent of farm area are in the size category of 10 hectares and above (Mosharaff Hossain, 1991, p. 135). Another 0.69 per cent in the 6–10 hectare group operate only 5.47 per cent of the area under cultivation. Inequalities are obviously very distinct and are becoming even more so. But the point to note is that even the bigger farms are not very big by standards of neighbouring countries. A farm of 3 hectares in size is now defined as large.

Table 8.2 Size distribution of farm households in Bangladesh, 1960, 1968, 1977 and 1983–84

Farm size	Total number of farms (000)				Total farm area (000 hectares)			
	1960	1968	1977	1983–84	1960	1968	1977	1983–84
Small 1	803	842	342	2417	83.0	101.2	44.1	251.7
Small 2	690	873	648	1644	201.9	268.7	191.0	466.2
Small 3	1677	2175	2121	3005	1143.7	1490.5	1431.0	1942.1
All Small	**3170**	**3890**	**3111**	**7066**	**1428.6**	**1860.4**	**1666.1**	**2660.1**
Medium	2314	2439	2556	2483	4017.8	4165.5	4345.6	4138.4
Large	656	539	590	496	3346.4	2700.1	2875.4	2379.2
All farms	**6140**	**6868**	**6257**	**10045**	**8792.8**	**8726.0**	**8887.1**	**9177.7**
Farm size	Percentage of farms				Percentage of farm area			
Small 1	13.08	12.26	5.47	24.06	0.94	1.16	0.50	2.74
Small 2	11.24	12.71	10.36	16.37	2.30	3.08	2.15	5.08
Small 3	27.31	31.67	33.90	29.92	13.01	17.08	16.10	21.16
Small	51.63	56.64	49.72	70.34	16.25	21.32	18.75	28.98
Medium	37.69	35.51	40.85	24.72	45.69	47.74	48.90	45.09
Large	10.68	7.85	9.43	4.94	38.06	30.94	32.35	25.92
All farms	**100.00**	**100.00**	**100.00**	**100.00**	**100.00**	**100.00**	**100.00**	**100.00**

Notes: Small 1, Small 2 and Small 3 respectively refer to size classes of farms under 0.20 hectare, between 0.20 and 0.40 hectare and between 0.40 and 1 hectare. Medium refers to farm size ranging between 1 and 3 hectares while Large refers to farms above 3 hectares. The figures in bold refer to totals of relevant categories.

Sources: Based on data from ACO (1962, p. 32); BBS (1972, table 1(a); 1981b, pp. 41, 291; 1986b, p. 32).

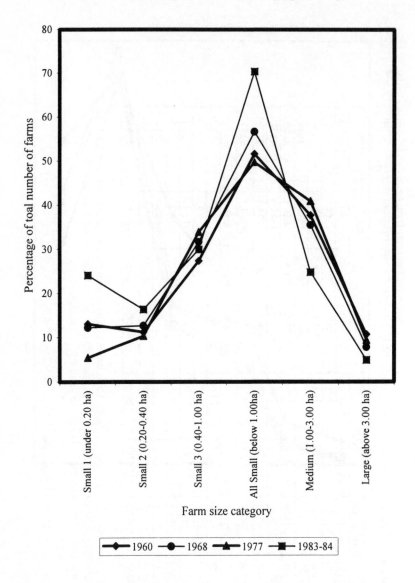

Figure 8.1 Size distribution of total number of farms in Bangladesh, 1960, 1968, 1977 and 1983–84

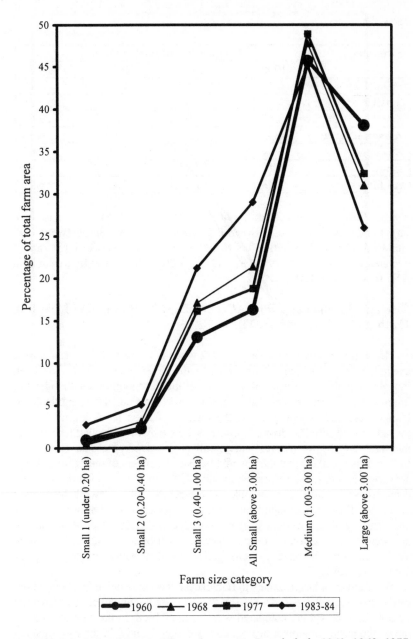

Figure 8.2 Size distribution of farms by area in Bangladesh, 1960, 1968, 1977 and 1983–84

Table 8.3 Trends in average farm size in Bangladesh, 1960, 1968, 1977 and 1983–84

Size category	Average size of farms (hectare)			
	1960	1968	1977	1983–84
Small 1	0.10	0.12	0.13	0.10
Small 2	0.29	0.31	0.29	0.28
Small 3	0.68	0.69	0.67	0.65
All small farms	**0.45**	**0.48**	**0.54**	**0.38**
Medium	1.74	1.71	1.70	1.67
Large	5.10	5.01	4.87	4.80
All farms	**1.43**	**1.27**	**1.42**	**0.91**

Notes: Small 1, Small 2 and Small 3 respectively refer to size classes of farms under 0.20 hectare, between 0.20 and 0.40 hectare and between 0.40 and 1.00 hectare. Medium refers to farm size ranging between 1.00 and 3 hectares while Large refers to farms above 3.00 hectares. The figures in bold refer to totals of relevant categories.

Sources: Based on data from ACO (1962, p.32); BBS (1972, Table 1(a); 1981b, pp. 41, 291; 1986c, p. 32).

This was probably not the case in 1972 when farms up to 3.34 hectares were exempted from payment of any rent to the government. They were then thought to be just self-sufficient. It is not that their economic strength today has improved. But in an overall situation of losses in land entitlements, landlessness and general poverty, the owners of these farms are now being treated as well-off. The distribution also shows why the so-called land reform measures are, by themselves and for all practical purposes, an exercise in futility. It is not likely that there would be even 1 per cent of the cultivated area acquirable as per Land Reform Ordinance, 1984. In reality, much of that 1 per cent also will remain unacquirable, as the process of its lawful distribution continues. There is not much land above the 8 hectare ceiling of farm holdings as fixed by the government that may become acquirable after making allowance for prospective or retrospective distributions within the family. Table 8.2 shows the pattern of changes in size distribution of holdings since 1960 more clearly.

The number of large farmers in Bangladesh has come down by about 24 per cent between 1960 and 1983–84. But the decrease is only 8 per cent when the figures for 1983–84 are compared with those of 1968. In the case of medium farms, the absolute number has not changed significantly. In the case of small farms, there has been an 81 per cent increase in the number of farms if we compare the 1983–84 data with that of 1968 and 123 per cent if the 1960 data were taken into account. Not only has the number of farms increased but the area under small farms has also risen sharply. The area under the medium and the large farms, however, has changed very little. Table 8.4 shows clearly that the peasants of Bangladesh hold on to their tiny plots of land even when the farm size becomes unviable. It is also evident from this table that with more than 95 per cent of the farming households owning less than 3 hectares, which also accounts for nearly 75 per cent of the total cultivated areas, government policies and programmes in agriculture must be designed primarily to help the small and medium farms increase their productivity.

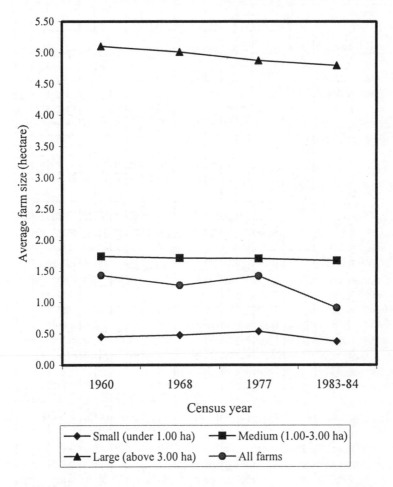

Figure 8.3 Trends in average farm size in Bangladesh, 1960, 1968, 1977 and 1983–84

Table 8.4 Land distribution by farm households, area and relative concentration ratios for different farm size categories for Bangladesh and its districts, 1983–84

Geographical entity	Percentage of number of farms			Percentage of farm area			Relative concentration ratio in farm category		
	Small (2)	Medium (3)	Large (4)	Small (5)	Medium (6)	Large (7)	Small (8)	Medium (9)	Large (10)
Bangladesh	70.34	24.72	4.94	28.99	45.09	25.92	0.41	1.82	5.25
Bandarban	38.46	50.00	11.54	12.50	57.69	29.81	0.33	1.15	2.58
Chittagong	79.77	18.14	2.09	43.53	42.15	14.33	0.55	2.32	6.86
Chittagong Hill Tracts	45.65	46.74	7.61	14.63	57.62	27.74	0.32	1.23	3.65
Comilla	84.40	14.49	1.11	53.17	38.31	8.51	0.63	2.64	7.67
Noakhali	83.43	14.23	2.34	44.11	36.09	19.80	0.53	2.54	8.46
Sylhet	67.11	25.34	7.14	23.60	41.75	34.65	0.35	1.65	4.85
Dhaka	78.89	18.79	2.32	41.21	43.38	15.41	0.52	2.31	6.64
Faridpur	70.49	25.04	4.17	29.66	47.01	23.32	0.42	1.88	5.59
Jamalpur	69.67	26.00	4.33	29.31	47.43	23.46	0.42	1.82	5.41
Mymensingh	69.83	25.36	4.86	29.58	45.19	25.24	0.42	1.78	5.19
Tangail	72.31	24.42	3.26	33.91	47.72	18.37	0.47	1.95	5.63
Barisal	75.61	20.79	3.60	33.19	44.43	22.39	0.44	2.14	6.22
Jessore	59.14	33.61	4.23	20.84	50.22	28.94	0.35	1.49	6.84

Khulna	66.17	26.43	7.40	22.27	43.30	34.43	0.34	1.64	4.65
Kushtia	62.30	29.92	7.79	20.41	46.26	33.33	0.33	1.55	4.28
Patualkhali	66.67	26.07	7.26	20.89	42.93	36.18	0.31	1.65	4.98
Bogra	71.15	24.73	4.12	32.26	45.41	22.33	0.45	1.84	5.42
Dinajpur	51.46	38.83	9.71	17.13	49.13	33.75	0.33	1.27	3.48
Pabna	64.83	28.49	6.69	24.23	45.35	30.42	0.37	1.59	4.55
Rajshahi	60.26	31.27	8.47	20.66	45.53	33.83	0.34	1.46	3.99
Rangpur	67.21	27.66	5.13	27.96	47.53	25.50	0.42	1.72	4.97

Note: Relative concentration ratio = Percentage of farm area/Percentage of number of farms i.e.
Column 8 = Column 5/Column 2.

Sources: Based on data from BBS (1986b); Mosharaff Hossain (1991, pp. 139–41).

If land reform is to make any sense, the land ceiling will have to be reduced to something between 2.7 to 4 hectares per family. This means that there would be no large farms as the term is understood today. From the point of view just of economic efficiency it makes sense, as the smaller farms in Bangladesh are found to be more intensely and efficiently cultivated. Landholdings will continue to break up into pieces in natural course of subdivision among the inheritors. As a consequence, perhaps many of the large farms will disappear from the scene. But simultaneously, almost all farms will end up being too small to be of proper economic use. As there should be a limit to the large size of farms, there has to be also a limit to the small size if efficiency considerations are to be satisfied. More than 53 per cent of farm households, that is, those below 0.40 hectare in size, are already threatened with disintegration. If this process is to continue, more than 90 per cent of the farm households may face the same fate in the next two decades.

8.3.2 A Brief Analysis of District-level Data, 1983–84

The pattern of distribution of farm households is not uniform throughout Bangladesh. It is true that an overwhelming majority of farm households is small in almost every region, yet they cover quite a wide range of sizes. The relevant information is set out in Table 8.4.

Comilla has the highest percentage of small farms – 84.40 per cent of the total number of farm households, followed closely by Noakhali with 83.43 per cent of total farms in the small farm category. In six of the 19 old districts, the percentage varies from 70 to 80 per cent. In descending order they are Chittatgong (79.77 per cent), Dhaka (78.9 per cent), Barisal (75.61 per cent) Tangail (72.31 per cent), Bogra (71.15 per cent) and Faridpur (70.89 per cent). In nine other old districts, namely Mymensingh, Jamalpur, Rangpur, Sylhet, Patuakhali, Khulna, Pabna, Kushtia and Rajshahi, the small farm concentration ranges between 60 to 70 per cent. Jessore (59.14 per cent) and Dinajpur (51.46 per cent) are the two districts with the small farm concentration ranging between 50 and 60 per cent. In only two of the old districts, namely Chittagong Hill Tracts (45.65 per cent) and Bandarban (38.46 per cent) is the percentage of small farms less than 50 per cent. The topography of these areas is, of course, atypical since in the hilly region all the lands are not sufficiently suitable for cultivation.

The distribution of the number of large farms is likewise uneven. Apart from Bandarban, nowhere is it higher than 10 per cent. Yet it ranges between 1.11 per cent in Comilla to 9.71 per cent in Dinajpur. For six other older districts, namely Rajshahi, Chittagong Hill Tract, Kushtia, Khulna, Patuakhali and Sylhet, this ratio is above 7 per cent. The distribution of the number of medium size farms also shows a similar diversity, ranging from just over 14 per cent in both Comilla and Noakhali, to nearly 47 per cent in Chittagong Hill Tracts and 50 per cent in Bandarban. In the other old districts of Dinajpur,

Jessore and Rajshahi, the ratio of concentration of medium farm households ranges between 30 and 40 per cent.

It appears that from the point of view of viability of size of landholdings, the distribution problem is slightly more favourable in Dinajpur and Rajshahi. The problem is quite acute in the districts of Comilla, Noakhali, Chittagong and Dhaka (Table 8.4).

It is already noted that the share of the total area under small farms in Bangladesh has been on the rise over time, while that under large farms is on the decline. Yet the distribution under different categories of farms is not uniform and varies widely across Bangladesh. Predictably, the aggregate area under small farms is higher in the districts which have a higher percentage of small farms. Comilla tops the list with over 53 per cent. Other regions with significantly large areas under small farms are Noakhali (44.11 per cent), Chittagong (43.53 per cent) and Dhaka (42.21 per cent). Small farms cover only 12.5 per cent of the area in Bandarban and 14.6 per cent in Chittagong Hill Tracts. In the northern district of Dinajpur, the corresponding figure is just over 17 per cent. In four other older districts, namely Rajshahi, Kushtia, Jessore and Patuakhali, it is around 20 per cent. Large farms covering above 30 per cent of the aggregate area, are in Patuakhali, Sylhet, Khulna, Rajshahi, Kushtia and Pabna. Patuakhlai with large farms covering over 36 per cent of the land tops the list, while Comilla with a corresponding figure of 8.51 per cent comes last.

If we define the relative concentration ratios of landholding distribution as ratios of the percentage area held relative to the percentage of small, medium and large farms in the regions, another perspective emerges. For Bangladesh as a whole, the relative concentration ratios are 0.41, 1.82 and 5.25 for small, medium and large farms respectively. This means that 1 per cent of small farms have command over only 0.41 per cent of the cultivable land, while the corresponding figure for medium and large farms are respectively 1.82 and 5.25. The weakness of the small farm households in Bangladesh is manifestly reflected in their low relative concentration ratio. It is even lower, ranging between 0.30 and 0.40 in ten older districts, namely, Bandarban, Chittagong Hill Tracts, Sylhet, Jessore, Khulna, Kushtia, Patuakhali, Dinajpur, Pabna and Rajshahi. For Comilla, Noakhali, Dhaka and Chittagong, the corresponding ratios are relatively higher, but still below 1.0 (the highest being 0.63 for Comilla). These are also the districts where large farm households have higher concentration ratios, the highest being 8.61 in Noakhali, followed by Comilla (7.74), Chittagong (6.65) and Dhaka (6.69). All these figures seem to indicate the degrees of inequality and relative strengths of different categories of farm households in Bangladesh. These aspects come into sharper focus when illustrated in Figure 8.4.

8.4 CONCLUDING COMMENTS AND IMPLICATIONS

Land is of central importance to the social, political and economic life in rural Bangladesh. The preceding discussion has demonstrated a process of growing landlessness and near-landlessness. This process has not only marginalized the rural peasantry but also made the poor increasingly dependent on wage employment for their subsistence. While landlessness per se may not necessarily be a major problem if adequate income-generating opportunities for the landless are provided, the crux of the problem is that economic growth in Bangladesh, especially in the agricultural sector, has not been high enough to gainfully absorb the bulk of the landless population (H.Z. Rahman, 1998, p. 69).

Previous land reform policies have failed or have been only partially successful, because they have only taken a view of the land policy debate where it has primarily emphasized the redistributive aspects. On the whole, the East Bengal Estate Acquisition and Tenancy Act 1950 provided the basis for better defined property rights and better security of land ownership. However, what it failed to achieve was an equitable land ownership and distribution system, and it also failed to stem the growing tide of landlessness. Subsequent land reform measures have not fared any better. The real issue is that very little surplus land can be acquired.

Previous land reform measures have paid little or no attention to the myriad of problems including, *inter alia,* major flaws in land record keeping, registration procedures, court processes and land administration. These provide a recipe for violence and social instability in rural Bangladesh. Furthermore, despite the close linkage between property rights and environmental management, this aspect has remained neglected in previous land policy agenda although of late there is a growing recognition of such neglect. As Rahman (1998, pp. 67–8; cf. Abdullah, 1978) rightly argues, an effective national land policy for Bangladesh must embrace the following four aspects:

- *Productivity aspect*: Given that land is a fundamental factor of production, its optimal use must constitute a critical policy priority.
- *Equity aspect:* Given that land is a critical element in social and economic empowerment, its equitable access to the rural poor needs to be ensured.
- *Land administration*: The issue of good land administration and governance is vitally important to ensure social stability in rural areas and reduce land-related legal disputes.

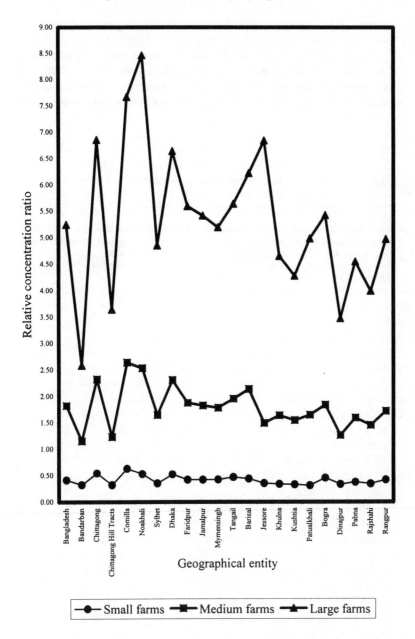

Figure 8.4 Land ownership concentration in Bangladesh and its districts, 1983–84

- *Environmental and ecological aspect*: This is an extremely important issue as sound environmental management results from well-defined property rights. These can prevent environmental degradation by reducing (1) the extent of deforestation, and (2) wasteful and unsustainable land and water resource use practices. On the whole these will have an ameliorating effect both on the rural environment and on rural poverty.

NOTES

*   A significantly modified version of chapter 7 from Mosharaff Hossain (1991).
1   For an excellent analysis of the process whereby this long chain of intermediaries was created and survived for more than 150 years, see Abdullah (1976). See also Abdullah *et al.* (1976).
2   For a detailed analysis of the process of agricultural stagnation and technological backwardness in Bengal, which during the British period comprised the Indian State of West Bengal and present-day Bangladesh, see Boyce (1987) and Islam (1978).
3   For an excellent analysis of the process of rural development under Basic Democracy, see Sobhan (1968).

9. Agrarian Change, Sustainable Resource Use and the Rural Environment in Bangladesh

9.1 INTRODUCTION

There is a growing body of evidence that agricultural and environmental problems are taking a turn for the worse in the face of the rapid pace of industrialisation and growth in GNP (Tisdell and Dragun, 1999, p. 1).[1] For instance, the World Bank (1996, p. 4) notes with concern that 'many environmental problems continue to intensify and in many countries there are few grounds for optimism'. In expressing its concern on global problems in agriculture and environment especially in developing countries, the World Bank (1996, p. 5) further notes that 'the costs of inappropriate economic policies on the environment are very high'. Recent evidence (see, for example, WRI *et al.*, 1997) suggests that adverse agricultural impacts on the environment manifest themselves, amongst other things, in the form of damage to ecological infrastructure, including extinction of species, loss of top soil, lowering of groundwater table, deforestation, disturbed and degraded ecosystems for fisheries.

As discussed in the preceding chapters, human activity critically impacts on the physical environment. Bangladesh faces a wide range of environmental problems that include both the urban and the rural environments. Figure 9.1 illustrates the interlinkages involving human activity and the manifestation of environmental impacts.

This chapter proposes to explore the linkages between agricultural growth and environmental changes. In the first place it provides an overview of the current state and trends in Bangladesh's rural environment. This is followed by an analysis of resource use with special emphasis on land and water, two fundamental resources used in agriculture. Both of these resources are under considerable strain due to various factors including, *inter alia*, intensive agricultural practices, widespread deforestation in upstream areas, soil erosion, siltation, inadequate recharge of aquifers, dumping of effluents in the river system, loss of tree cover and inappropriate government policies. These factors have affected both the quantity and quality of water. Trends in the use of

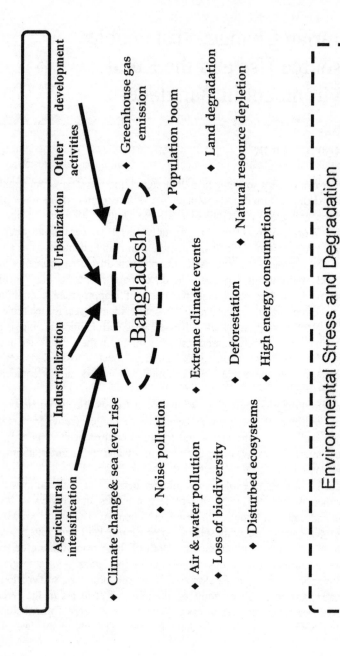

Figure 9.1 Environmental consequences of human activities in Bangladesh: a conceptual framework

ground and surface water are analysed. This is followed by an analysis of environmental implications of agricultural resource use.

9.2 STATE OF THE RURAL ENVIRONMENT IN BANGLADESH

Recent studies (Alauddin et al., 1995, pp. 222–24; Alauddin and Tisdell, 1998, pp. 80–96) have discussed the state of the environment in rural Bangladesh in greater detail. Their arguments are not repeated here.

Bangladesh's struggle for rapid development has exposed the fragility of the physical environment. The country is beset with a number of environmental problems, natural or man-made. These include, among others, 'frequent natural disasters, industrial pollution, poor health and sanitation, deforestation, desertification, changes in climatic conditions, salinity, deteriorating habitat of flora and fauna' (BPC, 1998, p. 181).

'To a considerable extent economic growth has magnified the effect of such natural disasters and has exacerbated environmental problems in rural Bangladesh' (Alauddin and Tisdell, 1998, p. 81). While this may be so, Bangladesh's environmental problems are also attributable in part to externalities or spillovers from economic developments and changes in neighbouring countries such as India and Nepal. Furthermore, some of the environmental problems in Bangladesh are transboundary. These include problems such as water pollution in the Indian part of the upstream Ganges and the presence of arsenic in the groundwater in the adjoining Indian State of West Bengal (Chakraborty, 1995; JU, 1994).

As discussed in earlier chapters the process of agricultural development in Bangladesh has emphasized grain production while other crops and, more importantly, the non-crop sector have remained virtually neglected. This is despite some changes in policy directions in recent years. There is little doubt that the ruthless pursuit of this policy has been economically detrimental to Bangladesh for it has failed to take adequate account of the importance of managing the two vital resources, land and water. The intensive use of land and water in agricultural production has entailed adverse environmental effects. Thus, on the whole, 'the environmental problems have originated mainly from population pressure, extreme poverty, natural disasters, depletion of forest resources, energy crisis, unplanned urbanization and industrialization, water pollution, air pollution in major cities, soil degradation etc.' (BPC, 1998, p. 268).

Based on Alauddin and Tisdell (1998, pp. 80–82) the following broad picture of Bangladesh's overall rural environment emerges:

- Bangladesh experiences an increased uncertainty in flows of rivers and streams, resulting both in greater severity of flooding and reduced availability of water during the dry season. These have adverse implications for navigation, aquatic life support systems especially fish stocks, siltation, water quality and so on.

- Bangladesh faces reduced availability of water and deteriorating water quality, such as salinization due to reduced inflows of freshwater into rivers and streams. This is also partly due to the leaching of nitrates into groundwater from chemical fertilizer-use in crop production.

- The increased intensity of cropping (greater incidence of multiple cropping) has led to declining soil fertility. Soils in many areas of Bangladesh suffer from declining micronutrients (see Section 9.3 for further details).

- Increased deforestation due to logging, extension of agriculture in some areas and intensification of slash-and-burn agriculture has reduced the length of the rotation cycle in *jhum* cultivation. Deforestation has a number of serious environmental consequences such as greater fluctuations in river flows, more rapid soil erosion and loss of wildlife with implications for reduced genetic diversity. Substantial reductions in stock of inland fish as a result of environmental changes such as reduced water availability and quality in streams and rivers, draining and filling of water bodies, and to some extent as a result of greater chemical use in agriculture associated with the adoption of green revolution technologies.

- Indigenous wildlife continues to disappear mainly as a result of over-harvesting and habitat alteration. Habitat alteration is brought about by expansion and intensification of economic activity and by rising levels of human population in Bangladesh. Out of a total number of 847 fauna, 17 are extinct while 136 are threatened (Task Force Report, 1991). More recent evidence points to a deteriorating situation (NFB, 1999). These include mammals, birds, reptiles and amphibians.

- As discussed in Chapter 6, the fisheries resource system has suffered a considerable degradation over the last three decades.[2] Asaduzzaman and Toufique (1997, p. 464) argue that the environmental degradation of the fisheries resource system has both qualitative and quantitative dimensions. Qualitative environmental degradation refers to a reduction in the area of fish habitat while qualitative environmental degradation of the fisheries resource system indicates deterioration in the quality of the fish habitat (for example, river pollution).

9.3 LAND AND WATER RESOURCE USE IN BANGLADESH

It is clear from the preceding discussion that the environmental problems in rural Bangladesh have manifested themselves in the form of degradation in the land and water resource systems. This section intends to provide an in-depth analysis of the land and water resource use patterns and the extent and gravity of the deterioration of the critically important resources for sustaining agricultural production.

Table 9.1 sets out relevant information that provides broad indicators of land and water resource use patterns in Bangladesh over a period of three decades since the late 1960s. The net cropped area (the area actually cultivated) has declined over the years while the effective (gross cropped) area has increased significantly during the period under consideration. This has been due to increased frequency of cropping during one calendar year. Land that once remained fallow during a significant part of the year is cropped primarily as a result of expansion of the irrigation during the *Rabi* (dry) season as a result of the advent of the green revolution technology. The increased intensification of agriculture via increased intensity of cropping comes into sharper focus when illustrated in Figure 9.2.

Table 9.1 also provides information on agricultural water use in Bangladesh over the same period. The introduction of the new agricultural technology has led to considerable increase in water use for production of agricultural crops. Even though Bangladesh adopted the strategy of expanding irrigation coverage in the early 1960s, it was not until the later part of the 1960s when the new high-yielding varieties (HYVs) of rice and wheat were introduced, that the use of irrigation assumed any real significance.

Total area irrigated has increased from around 1.1 million hectares in the late-1960s to nearly around 3.5 million hectares in the late 1990s signifying more than a three-fold increase. The phenomenal increase in land area irrigated has been due primarily to increases in the use of both surface water and groundwater. The use of surface water for irrigation has increased only slowly over the years (albeit with fluctuations) from just over 1 million hectares in the late 1960s to around 1.2 million hectares in the late 1990s and of late shows a declining tendency. On the other hand, the area under groundwater irrigation has registered a spectacular 76-fold increase from 32600 hectares in 1969–70 to about 2.5 million hectares in 1996–97. The ratio of groundwater to surface water use increased dramatically from only 3 per cent in 1969–70 to more than 200 per cent in 1996–97. Figure 9.3 highlights the changing relative importance of sources of irrigation water in terms of surface and groundwater sources.

Closely related to the increased pattern of ground–surface water use in Bangladesh is the phenomenal increase in the area irrigated by modern methods (shallow and deep tube wells, low-lift pumps and large-scale canal irrigation), that grew from 366 000 hectares in 1969-70 to 3.3 million hectares in 1996–97. On the other hand, the area irrigated using traditional methods has steadily declined from nearly 700 000 hectares in 1969–70 to 363 000 hectares in 1996–97. As a consequence, the ratio of the area irrigated by modern methods to the area irrigated by traditional methods has shown a spectacular increase from about 53 per cent in 1969–70 to more than 900 per cent in 1996–97.   Figure 9.4 illustrates the changing relative importance of the irrigation methods – modern vs. traditional.

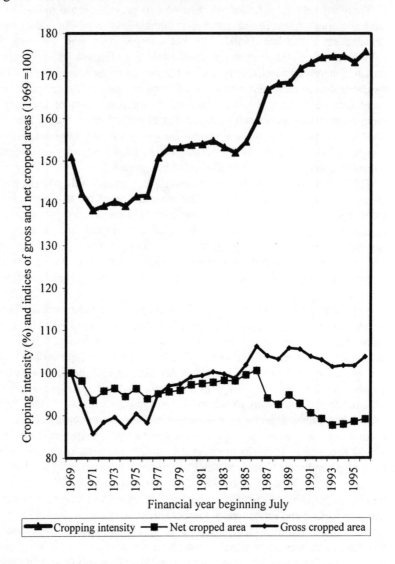

Figure 9.2 Trends in cropping intensity, net and gross cropped area under cultivation in Bangladesh, 1969–96

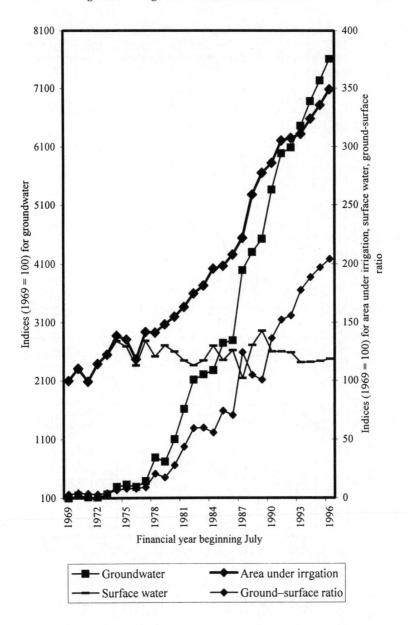

Figure 9.3 Trends in total area under irrigation, area under ground and surface water irrigation and ratio of ground to surface water irrigation in Bangladesh, 1969–96

Table 9.1 Land and water use in Bangladesh agriculture, 1969–96

Year	Cropped area (000 hectares)		Cropping intensity (per cent)	Area under irrigation (000 hectares)					Modern–traditional ratio	Ground–surface ratio
	Net	Gross		Total	Ground	Surface	Modern	Traditional		
1969	8807	13290	150.9	1057.9	32.6	1025.3	366.3	691.6	52.96	3.18
1970	8644	12292	142.2	1169.1	48.1	1121.1	569.4	599.7	94.94	4.29
1971	8244	11400	138.3	1050.9	38.0	1012.9	461.3	589.6	78.23	3.75
1972	8434	11752	139.3	1211.0	37.5	1173.5	604.5	606.4	99.69	3.19
1973	8489	11907	140.3	1295.9	53.1	1242.8	741.8	554.1	133.86	4.27
1974	8320	11589	139.3	1467.3	94.6	1372.7	814.6	652.7	124.80	6.89
1975	8485	12013	141.6	1432.4	106.8	1325.6	784.1	648.3	120.95	8.06
1976	8274	11727	141.7	1252.3	94.6	1157.7	737.6	514.7	143.31	8.17
1977	8374	12623	150.7	1501.0	127.1	1373.9	850.1	650.9	130.60	9.25
1978	8418	12888	153.1	1494.8	257.3	1237.5	937.5	557.3	168.22	20.79
1979	8447	12940	153.2	1569.1	235.6	1333.5	979.2	589.9	165.99	17.67
1980	8562	13160	153.7	1639.0	358.7	1280.3	1174.8	464.2	253.08	28.02
1981	8584	13208	153.9	1725.7	525.5	1200.2	1392.9	332.8	418.54	43.78
1982	8610	13316	154.7	1848.0	688.8	1159.2	1595.6	252.4	632.17	59.42
1983	8651	13250	153.2	1920.0	718.9	1201.1	1519.6	400.4	379.52	59.85
1984	8641	13126	151.9	2072.6	741.6	1331.0	1569.5	503.1	311.97	55.72
1985	8766	13541	154.5	2097.6	893.0	1204.6	1664.7	432.9	384.55	74.13
1986	8854	14117	159.4	2199.0	908.7	1290.3	1723.8	475.2	362.75	70.43
1987	8287	13820	166.8	2347.3	1300.8	1046.5	1943.1	404.2	480.73	124.30
1988	8154	13714	168.2	2737.4	1401.0	1336.4	2228.4	509.0	437.80	104.83
1989	8350	14063	168.4	2936.1	1473.2	1462.9	2306.8	629.3	366.57	100.70
1990	8174	14035	171.7	3026.8	1746.5	1280.3	2594.1	432.7	599.51	136.41

1991	7979	13809	173.1	3228.8	1949.4	1279.4	2804.7	424.1	661.33	152.37
1992	7858	13701	174.4	3252.2	1981.4	1270.8	2826.4	425.8	663.79	155.92
1993	7726	13482	174.5	3288.5	2104.0	1184.5	2927.2	361.4	809.97	177.62
1994	7743	13522	174.6	3428.6	2240.8	1187.8	3056.7	371.9	821.87	188.65
1995	7803	13513	173.2	3552.4	2356.5	1195.9	3187.0	365.4	872.09	197.06
1996	7851	13796	175.7	3692.4	2478.3	1214.1	3329.4	363.0	917.17	204.13

Notes: Modern irrigation refers to irrigation by shallow and deep tube-wells, low-lift pumps and large-scale canal irrigation.

Intensity of cropping indicates gross cropped area expressed as a percentage of net cropped area.

Sources: Based on data from BBS (1998b, pp. 120–28; 1999b, pp. 52–3); Alauddin and Tisdell (1998, table 3.1).

9.4 AGRICULTURAL RESOURCE USE: ENVIRONMENTAL IMPLICATIONS

This section concerns itself with some implications of resource-use in Bangladesh agriculture. As a prelude, let us present some information on the soil salinity and susceptibility of land to soil erosion.

Table 9.2 presents and Figures 9.5 and 9.6 illustrate the distribution of saline soils in the coastal and offshore areas of Bangladesh. More than 800000 hectares of land in Bangladesh are subject to various degrees of salinity. The most serious types of salinity occur in 14 per cent of the total salinity-prone area and are located in the greater Khulna region comprising districts of Khulna, Satkhira and Bagerhat. Table 9.3 sets out and Figures 9.7 and 9.8 illustrate the regional distribution of land susceptible to soil erosion in Bangladesh. Nearly 17 000 km^2 (more than 11 per cent of Bangladesh's total land area) is subject to various degrees of soil erosion. More than 72 per cent of this area is subject to very high risk of soil erosion. The highly erosion-prone areas are located in Chittagong Hill Tracts, Sylhet and the greater Chittagong region.

It is now widely recognized (see for example Ahmad and Hasanuzzaman, 1998, pp. 95–6) that agricultural intensification featuring increasing and indiscriminate use of agro-chemicals combined with poor irrigation management and waterlogging have resulted in a significant decline in organic matter. This process has led to a significant decline in soil quality. While all essential elements seemed to register a negative balance, the cases of nitrogen and potassium oxide were, as of 1988–89, particularly serious.

Table 9.4 provides a broad overview of the nutritient status of agro-ecological zones (AEZs) of Bangladesh. More than 50 per cent of Bangladesh's AEZs have a nutrient status ranging from poor to very poor. Young Brahmaputra and Jamuna Floodplain is the only AEZ whose nutrient status is classified as being good while that of the remaining AEZs is considered fair.

Table 9.5 sets out information on changes in the intensity of land use and some indicators of physio-chemical properties and organic matter in soils in various AEZs of Bangladesh over a period of two decades to 1989. Note that this period encompasses the period of the green revolution. These changes are also illustrated in Figure 9.9. The period has witnessed significant increases in cropping intensity across all AEZs except the Barind Tract. The period is also characterized by a significant decline in organic matter across all AEZs. The worst affected AEZs are those located in the highlands of the northern and eastern hills and the Old Meghna Estuarine Floodplain. A similar picture emerges in case of CEC (cation exchange capacity) content of soils.

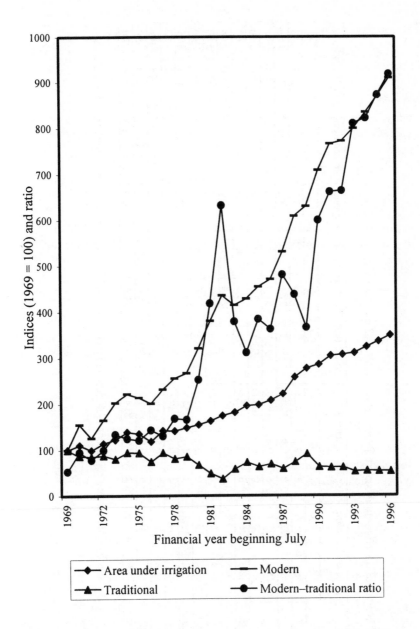

Figure 9.4　Trends in total area under irrigation, area irrigated by modern and traditional methods, and ratio of area under modern to traditional methods in Bangladesh, 1969–96

Table 9.2 Regional distribution of saline soils in the coastal and offshore areas of Bangladesh

District	Area under saline soils (000 hectares)					Percentage distribution across regions				Percentage distribution within a region			
	S_1	S_2	S_3	S_4	Total	S_1	S_2	S_3	S_4	S_1	S_2	S_3	S_4
Satkhira	16.5	85.6	33.4	10.9	146.4	11.3	58.5	22.8	7.5	6.0	20.4	42.7	27.3
Khulna	3.9	92.5	13.8	9.8	120.0	3.3	77.1	11.5	8.2	1.4	22.1	17.7	24.6
Bagerhat	28.3	77.1	2.6	0.0	108.0	26.2	71.4	2.4	0.0	10.2	18.4	3.3	0.00
Barguna	96.4	7.2	0.0	0.0	103.6	93.1	7.0	0.0	0.0	34.9	1.7	0.0	0.00
Patuakhali	68.5	46.6	0.0	0.0	115.1	59.5	40.5	0.0	0.0	24.8	11.1	0.0	0.00
Bhola	9.5	30.8	0.0	0.0	40.3	23.6	76.4	0.0	0.0	3.4	7.3	0.0	0.00
Perojpur	18.4	1.9	0.0	0.0	20.3	90.6	9.4	0.0	0.0	6.7	0.5	0.0	0.00
Chittagong	18.4	15.1	7.0	5.2	45.7	40.3	33.0	15.3	11.4	6.7	3.6	9.0	13.0
Cox's Bazar	7.2	16.2	17.3	14.0	54.7	13.2	29.6	31.6	25.6	2.6	3.9	22.1	35.1
Noakhali	6.3	39.9	3.4	0.0	49.6	12.7	80.4	6.9	0.0	2.3	9.5	4.4	0.0
Feni	1.6	6.7	0.7	0.0	9.0	17.8	74.4	7.8	0.0	0.6	1.6	0.9	0.0
Chandpur	1.5	0.0	0.0	0.0	1.5	100.0	0.0	0.0	0.0	0.5	0.0	0.0	0.0
Bangladesh	276.5	419.6	78.2	39.9	814.2	34.0	51.5	9.6	4.9	100	100	100	100

Notes: S_1, S_2, S_3, and S_4 respectively represent 2–4 ds/m (low)4–8 ds/m (moderate), 8–16 ds/m (high) and above 16 ds/m (very high).

Source: Based on data from BBS (1999a, p. 81)

Table 9.3 *Regional distribution of land susceptible to different degrees of soil erosion in the hill areas of Bangladesh*

Hill region	Area according to degree of risk of soil erosion (km^2)				Inter-regional distribution (%)			Intra-regional distribution (%)		
	M	H	VH	Total	M	H	VH	M	H	VH
Chittagong Hill Tracts	350	1814	10765	12929	2.7	14.1	83.3	37.8	48.4	87.6
Chittagong and Cox's Bazar	414	949	964	2327	17.8	40.8	41.4	44.8	25.3	7.8
Greater Sylhet	161	954	462	1577	10.2	60.5	29.3	17.4	25.4	3.8
Other areas	0	35	102	137	0.0	25.6	74.5	0.0	0.9	0.8
Bangladesh	**925**	**3752**	**12293**	**16970**	**5.5**	**22.1**	**72.4**	**100**	**100**	**100**

Notes: M, H and VH respectively indicate moderate, high and very high degrees of susceptibility to soil erosion. Other areas include, *inter alia*, Comilla, Brahmanbaria, Netrokona and Jamalpur.

Source: Based on data from BBS (1999a, p.81).

Table 9.4 Nutrient status of agro-ecological zones of Bangladesh

Nutrient status	Agro-ecological zones
Very poor	Active Teesta floodplain (2), Karatoya Bangali floodplain (4), Middle Meghna river floodplain (16), High Barind Tract (26).
Poor	Lower Atrai basin (5), Lower Purnabhaba floodplain (6), Active Brahmaputra-Jamuna floodplain (7), Ganges tidal floodplain (13), Gopalganj-Khulna Bil (14), Arial Bil (15), Lower Meghna floodplain (17), Young Meghna estuarine floodplain (18), Sylhet Basin (21), North and eastern piedmont plains (22) Chittagong coastal plain (23), St Martin's coral island (24), North and eastern hills (29).
Fair	Old Himalayan piedmont plains (1), Teesta meander floodplains, Old Brahmaputra floodplain (9), Active Ganges floodplain (10), High Ganges floodplain (11) Ganges tidal floodplain (13), Old Meghna estuarine floodplain (19), Eastern-Surma-Kushiyara floodplain (20), Level Barind Tract (25), North-eastern Barind Tract (27), Madhupur Tract (28).
Very good	Young Brahmaputra and Jamuna floodplain (8).

Note: Figures in parenthesis represent agro-ecological zone numbers.

Source: Adapted from Ahmad and Hasanuzzaman (1998, p. 97).

Table 9.5 Changes in land use intensity, physio-chemical properties and organic matter in agro-ecological zones of Bangladesh

Agro–ecologicalzZone	Average cropping intensity (%)			Organic matter (%)			CEC (me/100 gm soil)		
	1969	1989	Relativity (1969 = 100)	1969	1989	Relativity (1969 = 100)	1969	1989	Relativity (1969 = 100)
Madhupur Tract (28), HL	175	225	128.57	1.78	1.20	67.42	10.90	9.35	85.78
Barind Tract (25, 26), HL, MHL	150	150	100.00	1.45	1.15	79.31	9.50	8.25	86.84
Old Himalayan piedmont plain (1), HL	150	250	166.67	1.32	1.20	90.91	9.97	8.00	80.24
Tista Meander floodplain (3), HL, MHL	175	250	142.86	1.55	1.23	79.35	9.90	8.63	87.17
Northern and eastern hills (29), HL	150	200	133.33	2.04	1.32	64.71	12.53	9.00	71.83
Old Meghna estuarine floodplain (19), MHL	200	250	125.00	2.16	1.17	54.17	13.67	11.33	82.88
High Ganges river floodplain (11), HL	175	250	142.86	1.21	0.98	80.99	16.60	15.00	90.36
Old Brahmaputra floodplain (9), MHL	200	250	125.00	1.56	1.23	78.85	12.68	11.95	94.24

Note: Figures in parenthesis represent agro-ecological zone numbers. HL and MHL refer to highland and medium highland respectively. 1969 refers to financial year beginning July 1969 etc.

Source: Adapted from BBS (1999a, p.166).

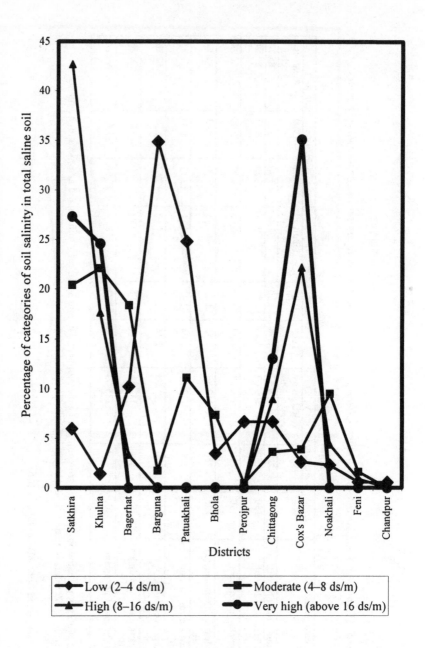

Figure 9.5 Regional distribution of different degrees of soil salinity in coastal and offshore areas of Bangladesh

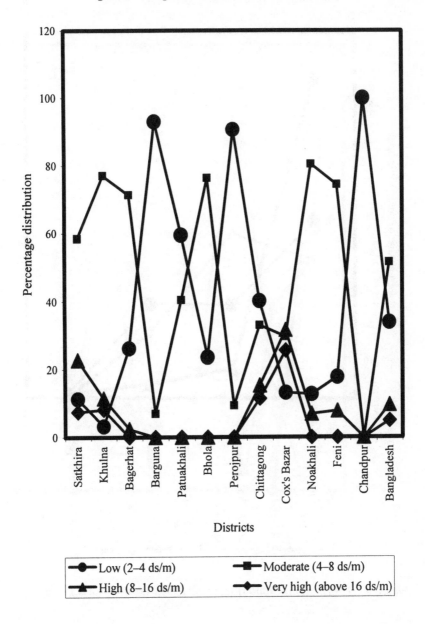

Figure 9.6 Distribution of saline soils within each region on the basis of degree of salinity

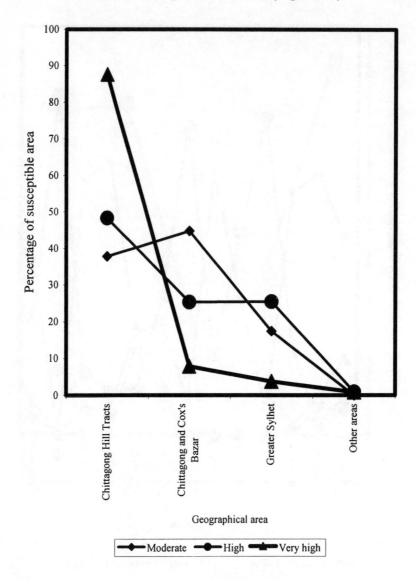

Figure 9.7 Distribution of land susceptible to soil erosion in Bangladesh

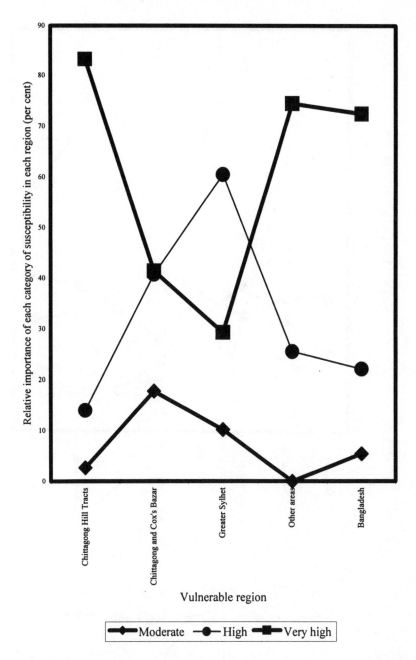

Figure 9.8 Distribution of land susceptible to soil erosion in total vulnerable areas

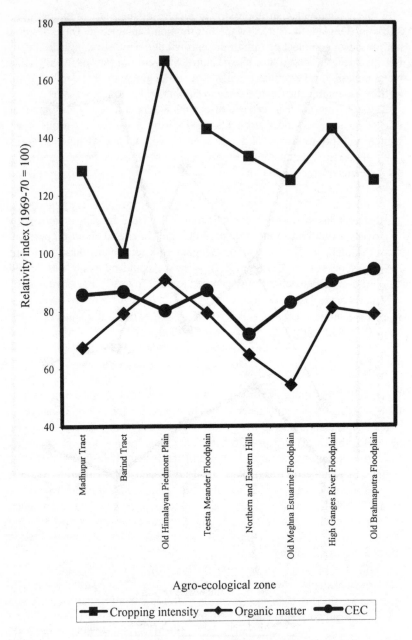

Figure 9.9   Status of selected physio-chemical properties and organic matter in different agro-ecological zones of Bangladesh, 1989–90 relative to 1969–70

Table 9.6 provides an approximate picture of the nutrient status of the AEZs in Bangladesh. Note that the information contained in Table 9.6 does not provide a complete picture of the nutrient deficiency in Bangladesh soils. For instance, the boron and magnesium levels are not known for all AEZs. Nevertheless, it reveals that problems of soil degradation and decline in soil fertility especially due to deficiency in sulphur and zinc seem severe.

Table 9.7 considers a scenario of changing temperature regimes and their effects on an area under droughts of differing severity in seasons – dry winter and pre-monsoon and monsoon. Two climatic change scenarios (CCS–1: a rise in temperature by 2°C and CCS–2: a rise in temperature by 4°C) are considered. Note that:

- Under CCS–1, the area under very severe to severe categories of drought taken together could increase from the existing level of just over 12 000 km^2 to more than 19 000 km^2 (a rise of about 60 per cent, equivalent to 13 per cent of Bangladesh's total area) during the pre-monsoon season. Under CSS–2, this area could be as high as 27 000 km^2 (an increase of 125 per cent, equivalent to nearly 19 per cent of the total area of Bangladesh).
- In the monsoon season, under CCS–1, the existing drought-prone area of 23 000 km^2 could increase to 29 000 km^2 (a rise of about 26 per cent). Under CSS–2, this area could increase to 33 000 km^2 (an increase of 43 per cent, nearly a quarter of Bangladesh's total area).

Table 9.8 sets out information on the incidence of drought-prone areas in Bangladesh. Taking the severe and the very severe drought categories together it is clear that well over 2 million hectares (nearly 30 per cent of the net cultivable area) are drought affected. The drought-affected areas are located primarily in the northern region (of Rajshahi Division) and western region (of Khulna division). Parts of Tangail and Dhaka districts are also susceptible to drought of severe intensity. About 0.58 million hectares of land in Rajshahi and Chapai Nawabganj districts that constitutes more than a quarter of the net cultivated area in these two districts are drought affected. No other areas of Bangladesh are exposed to the risk of intensity and extent of droughts as are these two districts.

Table 9.9 provides information on the effect of drought on yields of modern transplanted *Aman* rice (rainfed) in different geographical locations in Bangladesh. It is clear that stress due to droughts affects all stages of the production process. Its impact is particularly severe during the 'milk-to-maturity' stage. There are significant regional variations in respect of the impact of drought. Given the higher incidence of droughts in the northern districts of Bogra and Rajshahi and western districts of Jessore, these are more adversely affected than the central district of Dhaka and the eastern districts of Comilla and Sylhet. Note also that the duration of droughts is much longer in the northern and western parts of Bangladesh than in other parts.

This is due to several factors, including very low precipitation, high demand on underground water, and low flow of the Ganges water due to the Farakka barrage upstream.[3] As already mentioned, increased use of groundwater is causing serious environmental problems in Bangladesh. Water-tables have dropped in a number of areas in Bangladesh adversely affecting trees in the dry season and making access to water more difficult.

Not all underground aquifers are being fully recharged even during the wet season. Furthermore, several flood-mitigation works in Bangladesh may impede the recharging of groundwater. For example, flood control levy banks, by preventing the spread of floods, may reduce the supply of water to underground water bodies. The lowered level of streams in the dry season also reduces inflows of water to underground water bodies. Compared to the 1960s and 1970s the groundwater-table has become lower in many areas of Bangladesh especially the northern districts. Figure 9.10 provides information on the portion of useable recharge in different parts of Bangladesh. The problem in northern and western districts in Bangladesh seems particularly serious.

Environmental changes occur when freshwater diversion reaches 25–30 per cent of historic seasonal low flows. According to Feld (1995) these levels have been reached in many of Bangladesh's rivers. The three rivers worst affected by industrial pollution are Buriganga near Dhaka, Sitalakhya near Narayanganj and Karnafuli near Chittagong. As Jahan (1998, p. 212–13) argues:

> Sources of water pollution have multiplied with the country's recent drive for industrialisation. The main rivers inundate an extensive agricultural area and the industrial wastes that they carry are readily absorbed into ground water. Concentration of chromium originating from tanneries waste water, found in ground water at *Hazaribag* is 0.04 mg/L in early 1992, levels of mercury in the *Buriganga* river water were found at 0.01 mg/L i.e. ten times the limit proposed for Bangladesh (Feld, 1995). Mercury poisoning affects neurological functions and could be extremely serious.

Over 20 per cent of the net cultivable area of Bangladesh is in the coastal belt. At present most of the area is found under slightly saline conditions.

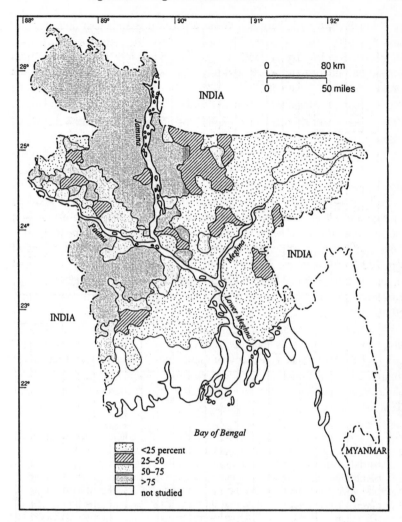

Source: MPO (1986)

Figure 9.10 Portion of usable recharge in different parts of Bangladesh

Table 9.6 Nutrient status of soils in different agro-ecological zones of Bangladesh

Agro-ecological zone	Nutrients							
	N	P	K	S	Zn	B	Mg	Ph
Old Himalayan piedmont plain (1)	L	M	M	L	H	H	L	4.6-5.4
Active Tista floodplain (2)	L	M	L	L	L	-	-	-
Tista meander floodplain (3)	L	H	H	L	L	H	M	4.5-5.5
Karotoya Bengali floodplain (4)	L	M	L	L	L	-	-	4.8-6.6
Lower Atrai Basin (5)	M	M	M	L	L	-	-	4.6-5.9
Lower Purnabhaba floodplain (6)	M	M	H	L	M	-	-	5.5-7.0
Active Brahmaputra floodplain (7)	L	L	M	M	M	-	-	-
Young Brahmaputra and Jamuna floodplain (8)	L	H	H	H	H	H	H	4.8
Old Brahmaputra floodplain (9)	L	M	M	L	M	H	H	5.0-5.6
Active Ganges floodplain (10)	L	L	H					
High Ganges river floodplain (11)	L	L	H	L	L	H	H	-
Low Ganges river floodplain (12)	L	L	H	L	L	H	H	6.1-8.0
Ganges tidal floodplain (13)	L	L	H	H	M	H	H	6.0
Gopalganj-Khulna Bils (14)	M	L	M	-	-	-	-	5.5-6.6
Arial Bil (15)	L	M	L	L	M	-	-	4.5-6.5
Middle Meghna river floodplain (16)	L	L	L	L	L	-	-	4.1-5.1
Lower Meghna river floodplain (17)	L	M	M	L	L	-	-	5.0-8.3
Young Meghna river floodplain (18)	L	L	M	L	L	M	H	6.5-8.0
Old Meghna river floodplain (19)	L	H	M	L	M	H	H	5.0-5.5
Eastern Surma-Kusiyara floodplain (20)	L	L	M	M	H	H	H	4.5-5.1
Sylhet Basin (21)	M	L	L	L	H	-	-	4.9-6.0

Northern and eastern piedmont plains (22)	L	L	M	L	L	H	L	4.5 -5.3
Chittagong coastal plains (23)	L	M	L	-	M	-	-	4.5-5.7
St. Martin's coral island (24)	L	L	H	L	L	-	-	6.5-8.0
Level-Barind Tract (25)	L	M	M	L	M	H	M	4.7-6.2
High Barind Tract (26)	L	L	L	L	M	-	-	4.8-5.8
North Eastern Barind Tract (27)	L	H	L	H	H	H	L	4.8-5.6
Madhupur Tract (28)	L	M	H	L	M	H	M	4.5-5.2
Northern and eastern hills (29)	L	L	L	L	M	-	-	4.7-5.2

Note: Figures in parenthesis represent agro-ecological zone numbers. L, M, H and – respectively refer to low, medium, high and no information. N = Nitrogen, P = Phosphate, K = Potassium, S = Sulphur, Zn = Zinc, B = Boron, Mg = Magnesium, Ph = Phosphate. For nutrient classification of soils see Appendix Table A9.1 at end of chapter.

Sources: Adapted from Ahmad and Hasanuzzaman (1998, pp.97-8); Bramer (1997, p.7).

Table 9.7 Change in area under different drought classes due to climate change scenario in dry winter and pre-monsoon and monsoon seasons (area in km²)

Drought type	Climatic change scenario (CCS): Dry winter and pre-monsoon					Climatic change scenario (CCS): Monsoon				
	Existing	CCS-1	% change	CCS-2	% change	Existing	CCS-1	% change	CCS-2	% change
Very severe	3639	8636	137.3	12220	235.8	5736	12066	110.4	22664	295.2
Severe	8581	10873	26.7	15303	78.3	17476	16898	-3.3	10540	-39.7
Moderate	32847	30380	-7.5	25465	-22.5	21783	16865	-22.6	13373	-38.6
Less moderate	14571	9747	-33.1	19814	36.0	-	-	-	-	-
Slight	43524	43524	0.0	30360	-30.2	25984	25120	-3.2	24271	-6.1

Notes: CCS-1 indicates rise in temperature by 2°C while CCS-2 indicates rise in temperature by 4°C.

Source: Adapted from Karim and Iqbal (1997, p.76).

Lowering of the water-table causes salt water intrusion and decreases dry season river flow, which adversely affects the productivity of aquatic resources and crops. The incidence and degree of salinity in groundwater-tables in the coastal belt of Bangladesh is depicted in Figure 9.11.

Table 9.8 Incidence of drought severity by location

Degree of severity	Affected area and location
Very severe	About 0.58 hectares in Rajshahi and Chapai Nawabganj districts
Severe	At least 1.7 million hectares in Dinajpur, Bogra, Kushtia, Jessore, Tangail and Dhaka districts
Moderate	About 2.18 million hectares in Dinajpur, Rangpur, Bogra, Kushtia, Jessore and Barisal districts

Source: BBS (1999a, p. 69).

Bangladesh faces an uphill battle in coping with the menacing problem of arsenic poisoning. The problem of arsenic at toxic levels has been detected since the mid-1990s (JU, 1994; Chakraborty, 1995). In India, as it is in Bangladesh, the problem of arsenicosis is widespread in several states especially in Bangladesh's neighbouring state of West Bengal. Even though the exact extent of the problem is not known with certainty, at least 20 million people are believed to be under serious threat while many more might be vulnerable. The arsenic affected areas are illustrated in Figure 9.12. The magnitude of the problem is clearly evident from the Figure. A vast area of Bangladesh is exposed to arsenic with a toxicity level higher than 0.05 ppm. Prolonged exposure to arsenic at toxic levels leads to diseases of a serious nature. Based on Jahan (1998, p. 213) one could identify some of the diseases at various stages (see Table 9.10).

Arsenic mitigation efforts to date have, primarily if not exclusively, concentrated on information related to toxicity at the scientific level. Much effort has gone into identifying tube wells whose water is more toxic than the acceptable level, labelling them to warn people of the dangers of arsenicosis and purification techniques. However, socio-economic implications have attracted very little attention.

Table 9.9 Effect of drought on yield of modern transplanted aman rice in different locations in Bangladesh

Location	PI to heading			Heading to milk			Milk to maturity			Drought stress yield	Drought yield–no stress yield ratio
	SD	SDI	SI	SD	SDI	SI	SD	SDI	SI		
Comilla	0	0.00	0.00	0	0.00	0.00	8	0.40	0.18	3.9	81
Bogra	4	0.13	0.06	2	0.20	0.12	12	0.60	0.26	2.9	57
Jessore	6	1.20	0.10	3	0.30	0.18	13	0.65	0.29	2.2	43
Dhaka	0	0.00	0.00	1	0.10	0.06	10	0.50	0.22	3.4	72
Sylhet	0	0.00	0.00	0	0.00	0.00	4	0.20	0.09	4.5	90
Rajshahi	8	0.27	0.13	3	0.30	0.18	13	0.55	0.29	2.0	38

Notes: PI = Pincale initiation, SD = Stress days, SDI = Stress day index, SI = Stress index

Source: Adapted from Karim and Iqbal (1997, p.75).

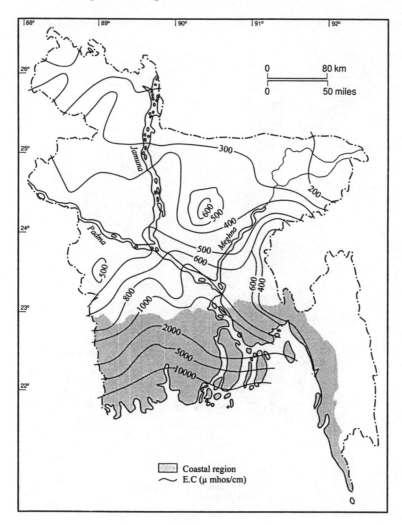

Source: BBS (1999a, p. 63)

Figure 9.11 Salinity in groundwater - table in Bangladesh

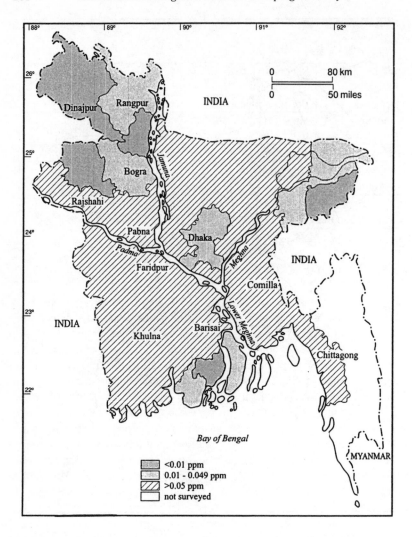

Source: BBS (1999a, p. 75)

Figure 9.12 Traces of arsenic in groundwater table of Bangladesh

Table 9.10 Diseases associated with prolonged exposure to arsenic at toxic levels

Primary stage	Secondary stage	Final stage
Dermatitis	Peripheral neuropathy	Gangrene of the limbs
Keratosis	Hepatopathy	Malignant dermatitis (cancer)
Brobchitis	Melanonis	
Conjunctivitis	Depigmentation	
Gastroenteritis	Hyperkeratosis	

Source: Jahan (1998, p. 213).

9.5 CONCLUDING OBSERVATIONS

The environmental resources of Bangladesh, more specifically land and water, are under considerable strain from intensification and extension of agriculture facilitated by the green revolution technologies, deforestation and loss of natural vegetation cover. Population increase (combined with attempts to at least maintain already low per capita income) is the main underlying cause of such pressure. A guiding principle of Bangladesh in pursuing economic development has been to attain self-sufficiency in grain supplies. But the 'one-eyed' pursuit of this policy has been economically detrimental to Bangladesh because adequate account had not been taken of spillovers or opportunity costs of increasing grain production.

Consequences of resource depletion and environmental pollution have not been given enough attention in many developing countries including Bangladesh. Unsustainable extraction of groundwater, indiscriminate use of pesticides and unbalanced use of chemical fertilizers led to degradation of the environment and the ecosystem. There has been a significant decline in soil quality across all agro-ecological zones.

Given that Bangladesh has very little or no scope for expanding agricultural production through extensive cultivation, agricultural intensification must take into account the adverse environmental effects. Pollution and resource degradation will affect the survival of subsequent generations. Alternatives should be developed to stop the indiscriminate use of agro-chemicals. Issues of environmental management warrant serious consideration, as the physical environment could become a limiting factor in sustaining future agricultural production. The signs are already evident (see for example, Pagiola, 1995; Asaduzzaman and Toufique, 1997).

NOTES

1   For an excellent review of the differing views on this, see Tisdell and Dragun (1999).
2   Ostrum (1990, p. 30) distinguishes between resource systems and resource units. 'Resource units are stock variables capable of producing a maximum quantity ... of a flow variable without harming the stock or the resource system itself.... Resource units are what individuals appropriate or use from a resource system' (Asaduzzaman and Toufique, 1997, p. 464). Examples of resource systems are fishing grounds, groundwater basins, grazing areas and so on, while those of resource units are fish catches from a fishing ground or the volume of water withdrawn from a groundwater basin and so on.
3   The treaty between India and Bangladesh entered into in December 1996 represents significant progress in sharing a transboundary natural resource (Alauddin, 1999b, p. 321). Note that in the absence of any agreement Bangladesh received a much smaller volume of the Ganges water. For instance in March 1993 flow in the Ganges at Hardinge Bridge was as low as 9761 cusecs (Crow *et al.*, 1995, p. 219). This notwithstanding, Bangladesh's share critically depends on augmented water supply much further upstream at the Farakka barrage (Ray, 1998).

Table A9.1 Nutrient classification of soils

Nutrient	Low	Medium	High
Nitrogen micro gm/ml soil	Up to 75	76-150	151-300
Phosphorous micro gm/ml soil	Up to 12	13-25	26-75
Sulphur micro gm/ml soil	Up to 12	13.25	26-75
Boron micro gm/ml soil	Up to 0.2	0.21-0.50	0.51-4.0
Copper micro gm/ml soil	Up to 1.0	1.1-3.0	3.1-10.0
Iron micro gm/ml soil	Up to 2.0	21-40	40-200
Manganese micro gm/ml soil	Up to 5.0	5.1-10.0	10.1-50.0
Zinc micro gm/ml soil	Up to 2.0	2.1-4.0	4.1-18.0
Calcium micro gm/ml soil	Up to 2.0	2.1-4.0	4.1-18.0
Magnesium micro gm/ml soil	Up to 0.8	0.81-2.0	2.1-19.0
Potassium micro gm/ml soil	Up to 0.2	0.21-0.40	0.41-1.5

Source: BBS (1999a, p. 166).

10. Agricultural Research and Extension[*]

10.1 INTRODUCTION

Technological innovations consistent with factor endowments and adaptable to ecological conditions are a critical factor determining sustained agricultural growth. Indigenous research and development efforts complemented by efficient extension services play a critical role in the generation and diffusion of technological innovations.

This chapter examines the role of research and extension in Bangladesh's agricultural development. It proceeds first of all with a brief history of agricultural research and extension in Bangladesh including an appraisal of the current state of play. The role of international organizations is also analysed with an emphasis on the complementarity between indigenous and international research organizations.

10.2 THE BANGLADESH AGRICULTURAL RESEARCH SYSTEM

10.2.1 Agricultural Research in a Historical Context

Agricultural research in Bangladesh commenced during British rule in 1880 when the Department of Agriculture was established. However, systematic agricultural research in Bangladesh began in the early twentieth century with the establishment of the Agricultural Research Institute (currently known as the Bangladesh Agricultural Research Institute, BARI) in 1909. The Livestock Research Directorate and the Jute Research Institute (BJRI) were established in 1932 and 1950 respectively.

However, it was not until the 1960s that agricultural research in Bangladesh assumed any real significance. The Bangladesh Agricultural University at Mymensingh was established in the early 1960s. The Bangladesh Rice Research Institute (BRRI), Bangladesh Sugarcane Research Institute (BSRI) and some other agricultural research institutes were also created in the late 1960s and early 1970s. By the early 1980s, a range of agricultural research organizations existed in Bangladesh. These are detailed elsewhere (Alauddin, 1981; Alauddin and Tisdell, 1986) and we do not wish to repeat them here. In addition to various agricultural research organizations, some agricultural research is also carried out in the Bangladesh Atomic Energy Commission and the Bangladesh Institute of Nuclear Agriculture (BINA). Furthermore, in recent years, some established universities have opened agricultural faculties which conduct research in agricultural and biological sciences. In addition, a new agricultural university (Haji Danesh Agricultural University) has been established in the northern district of Dinajpur. Postgraduate studies in agriculture are conducted at the Bangabondhu Agricultural University in Gazipur near Dhaka (formerly known as the Institute of Postgraduate Studies in Agriculture, IPSA). Research on non-crop agricultural sectors, that is, livestock, fisheries and forestry, is primarily conducted, respectively, by the Bangladesh Livestock Research Institute at Savar, Bangladesh Fisheries Research Institute at Mymensingh and Bangladesh Forestry Research Institute at Chittagong. Khulna University, established a decade ago, has a strong emphasis on forestry and coastal environment. Overall therefore, Bangladesh now has a network of agricultural research institutes.

10.2.2 Relative Roles of Indigenous and International Agricultural Research

Gains in agricultural productivity growth result from technological progress, which critically depends on research. CGIAR (1981) identifies four components of research:

- *Basic research*: Designed to generate new understanding (for example, influence on plant height on positioning of assimilates)
- *Strategic research:* Designed to solve specific research problems (for example, a technique for detecting dwarfing genes in rice seedlings)
- *Applied research:* Designed for the creation of new technology (for example, breeding new dwarf rice varieties highly responsive to fertilizer applications)
- *Adaptive research:* Designed to adjust technology to a specific set of ecological and environmental conditions (for example, adapting HYVs of rice to rain-fed areas).

It is broadly agreed that international agricultural research centres originally sought to concentrate on applied research requiring the national research centres to develop capabilities for adaptive research. While this division of relative research priorities of the two types of organizations was logical and rational in conception, reality seemed to differ from expectations. CGIAR (1981) subsequently found that the original plan regarding the relative research priorities of domestic and international research organizations research did not work in practice (see Alauddin and Tisdell, 1986, p. 12). This is because:

- National agricultural research systems were not able to carry out adaptive research adequately because they lacked the sophisticated science required, human resources and funding; and
- An inadequate supply of relevant research outcomes from strategic and basic research constrained the applied research of international organizations. Therefore they themselves had to enter these research areas.

Given Bangladesh's limited research capability in terms of research resources (Gill, 1981), the national research system is likely to be more effective when linked to the international system. As discussed in Chapter 3, the biological component of the green revolution technologies resulted from a close cooperation between the Bangladesh agricultural research system on the one hand and international agricultural research organizations on the other. The process of agricultural technology transfer to Bangladesh involved material, design and capacity transfers. Since the late 1960s, various international agricultural research organizations such as the International Rice Research Institute (IRRI) and the International Centre for Improvement of Maize and Wheat (CIMMYT) have played a critical role in strengthening the Bangladesh agricultural research system. Both IRRI and CIMMYT assisted the Bangladesh agricultural research system through:

- Human resource development by providing training to manpower engaged in agricultural research;
- Provision of scientific knowledge to expatriate scientists in various research organizations; and
- Supply of genetic resources.

Bangladesh agricultural research scientists are also involved in exchange with other international research institutes for research on non-cereal crops. The international organizations include, *inter alia*, International Potato Centre (CIP) in Peru, International Crops Research for the Semi-Arid Tropics (ICRISAT) in India, International Centre for Agricultural Research in Dry Areas (ICARDA) in Lebanon and International Institute of Tropical Agriculture (IITA) in Nigeria. Non-crop agricultural research in Bangladesh is also linked to relevant international bodies.

These linkages have enabled national research institutes access to genetic resource bases of the international research centres. This has further enabled national breeders to accelerate and intensify breeding programmes. This has resulted in the evolution of a good number of promising high-yielding varieties of rice, pulses, wheat, oilseeds, potato and so on. The central research stations have been supported by a number of recently strengthened regional stations and substations, all of which are meant to carry out adaptive trials with newly evolved technologies in the experimental stations.

10.2.3 The Bangladesh Agricultural Research System: Its Contribution and a Critical Appraisal

Agricultural research in Bangladesh received a new fillip after the establishment of the Bangladesh Agricultural Research Council (BARC), the Bangladesh Rice Research Institute (BRRI) and the Bangladesh Agricultural Research Institute (BARI) at Joydevpur in the early 1970s. Autonomous research institutes such as BRRI, BARI, BINA and BSRI were established with specific mandates for research on crop agriculture with a view to making agricultural research more dynamic and service-oriented (BPC, 1998, p. 243). The Bangladesh Agricultural Research Council is an apex organization which functions as a coordinating body for the agricultural research system comprising all agricultural research related institutions.

According to FAO (1978), three basic elements constitute the building blocks of an effective national agricultural research system:

- Policy, planning and coordination;
- Carrying out of research; and
- Training of research scientists.

'The problem with the Bangladesh agricultural research system is not their absence but their meaningful presence' (Alauddin and Tisdell, 1986, p. 14). The main deficiencies that epitomize the Bangladesh agricultural research system are:

- Organizational difficulties
- Lack of physical facilities and inadequate funds
- Low level of skill and ineffective training
- Inadequate linkages between agricultural education, extension and research; and
- Insufficient linkages involving research extension and farmers.

Agricultural research has for a long time been concentrated on a commodity-oriented basis and, in the case of many crops, has worked in a fragmentary manner, neglecting research on the cropping system as a whole and ignoring resource bases of different categories of farmers. Different technologies evolved through research were not tested in different agro-ecological conditions, which resulted in non-acceptance of high-cost technologies by small and marginal farmers, and technologies in many cases did not perform equally well in all agro-ecological zones.

There had also been unbalanced deployment of scientists in different disciplines and stations and also a dearth of trained and competent scientists in many priority areas. The Fifth Five Year Plan (BPC, 1998, pp. 243–4) recognizes that the Bangladesh agricultural research system needs to 'reexamine its focus and re-order its priorities, avoid fragmenting and duplicating its efforts, orient its approach from commodity-based to farming system and strengthening its planning, programme, monitoring and coordination'. More specifically, BPC (1998, pp. 244–5) identifies, *inter alia,* the following priorities for agricultural research:

- Improvement of food-grain quality with more digestible protein
- Increased efficiency in water use in grain production
- Technologies for maximum use of commodities and their byproducts for value addition
- Technology generation for rainfed crops
- Post-harvest technology
- Development of varieties tolerant to stresses
- Development of hybrid technology for vegetables, maize and sunflowers
- Conservation of soil, plant and genetic resources
- Management of agriculture in different agro-ecological zones, for example, hill areas in the eastern and south-eastern parts of Bangladesh and Barind tract in the north-western region
- Environmental issues and integrated pest management.

Investment in research and quality and quantity of manpower engaged in agricultural research are the two critical determinants of the level of scientific output, which ultimately manifests in productivity growth. On both counts, Bangladesh performs poorly. A newspaper report on a recent research (Reaz Ahmed, 2000) suggests that public investment in agricultural research in Bangladesh amounts to approximately US$20 million, which is only 0.25 per cent of its agricultural value added. This is far less than for the countries of South and Southeast Asia. India and Pakistan invest 0.50 per cent and 0.58 per cent of the respective agricultural components of their GDPs, while Malaysia, Taiwan and Thailand spend more than 1 per cent of their agricultural value added.

One adverse aspect of the Bangladesh agricultural research system is the lack of close cooperation among those involved in education, extension and research. Agricultural institutions are primarily training and teaching institutions where research is not a major activity. The highly trained manpower of the Bangladesh Agricultural University has not been properly harnessed by the agricultural research system (Mosemann *et al.,* 1980). A major problem facing the Bangladesh agricultural research system is the emigration of a large number of highly skilled agricultural scientists to Australia, Canada and New Zealand (Alauddin, 2000).

A good number of studies have estimated returns to agricultural research in Bangladesh (see, for example, Gill, 1983; Alauddin, 1982).[1] All of these studies demonstrate high returns to investment on agricultural research. Gill (1983) uses two sets of figures based on optimistic and pessimistic assumptions. Optimistic assumptions take into calculation the costs of only the period from the beginning of a particular experiment to the results in agricultural productivity. Optimistic assumptions also cover any projected future estimates accruing from agricultural research. By pessimistic assumptions Gill (1983) means calculations which take into account the cost of an experiment from the beginning of the research institute where the research is being conducted. Using Gill's (1983) system of estimates, the returns from agricultural research during the 1970s under most pessimistic assumptions are twice as much as the costs. Using optimistic assumptions, the returns are shown to be 20 times more than the costs. More recent studies (Pray and Ahmed, 1991; Dey and Evenson, 1991) confirm this. Jahan (1998, p. 85) examined the factors underlying total factor productivity growth in the Bangladesh crop sector. Expenditure on research and extension featured prominently as a significant explanatory variable (see also Jahan and Alauddin, 1996b).

10.3 AGRICULTURAL EXTENSION SERVICES

Agricultural extension, which aims at the transfer of more productive and useful technologies to the farmers, is essential for the growth and development of the agricultural sector. An efficient extension service can play (Siddiqui, 1998, p. 255) an important role through:

- Education to improve farming methods and techniques in order to increase production efficiency. It attempts to improve research information available to farming families and provides training and guidance to farmers to make meaningful use of this information.
- Enabling farmers to identify and resolve local agricultural problems. Problems that cannot be resolved locally by farmers and extension agents are brought to the attention of the research stations.

10.3.1 Agricultural Extension in a Historical Context

The origin of governmental extension services[2] can be traced back to 1870 when the Department of Agriculture was created as a part of the Department of Revenue to help rehabilitate farmers after the devastating effects of natural disasters. The Department of Agriculture became independent in 1906. It assumed an education role to broaden its scope of work and employed field agricultural personnel on demonstration farms at district headquarters in 1914.

In 1939, the Jute Regulation Department (JRD) was created to regulate jute growing and stabilize jute prices at the union level. In 1951, JRD was amalgamated with the Directorate of Agriculture and the regulators of jute cultivation became educators as extension workers but without required training. Their input-supply and credit functions became more prominent than their educational responsibilities. Though a programme of in-service training was introduced, it took a long time to re-orient the large number of field extension workers. The government, with the aid of the experts of USAID, tried to emphasize the educational role of the field extension service, but the system remained resistant to change.

In 1953 USAID, through its aid programme, established a new extension organization called Village Agricultural and Industrial Development (V-AID) parallel to agricultural extension. It was meant to be an integrated farm, home and youth development programme, but partly because of administrative problems, absence of an adequate system of input distribution, supplies, services and credit institutions, and partly because of socio-political reasons, this organization was abolished in 1961 and merged with agricultural extension organizations.

In 1961, the National Food and Agriculture Commission recommended the separation of agricultural extension services from input distribution and credit administration functions. As a result, the Bangladesh Agricultural Development Corporation (BADC) and the Bangladesh Krishi Bank (BKB) were established to handle input and credit functions respectively. On relinquishing input and credit functions, the Directorate of Agriculture should have initiated an effective extension programme for the farming community. However, an integrated extension programme was not developed and, as a result, the established services, commercial organizations engaged in livestock, forestry and fisheries cooperatives began to organize extension programmes in their respective fields. With few exceptions, most of them provided some material assistance and advice to the clients in specialized fields. Education remained neglected. The lack of integration of these independent extension services caused severe problems of coordination and control.

To overcome these problems, the Integrated Rural Development Programme (IRDP) emerged. The programme eventually became an independent organization providing inputs, credit and rural cooperative network. Its educational role, however, remained highly inadequate, as its educational programme consisted of one day's training in a fortnight for one model farmer in each cooperative society. The assumption was that the model farmer would educate other members of the cooperative society.

After the independence of Bangladesh, a good number of new organizations were established. Separate schemes for boosting intensive production and integrating extension, inputs, credit and training facilities were created for jute, sugarcane, tobacco, cotton, horticulture, tea, seed production, forestry, fisheries, agriculture and so on. These subsequently developed into independent organizations. At the same time, many external voluntary agencies like RDRS, CORR, CARITAS and others, which had originally come to help the rehabilitation and reconstruction work of the war-damaged country, expanded their activities to rural development programmes integrating production and supply of inputs, credit and training functions. Some local voluntary organizations financed by international agencies at project level also emerged. The government programmes were working through selective client approach, which resulted in orientation toward the privileged sector of the society. The non-governmental organizations (NGOs) were trying to reach less privileged people, giving priority to income-generating activities. These organizations can be considered as partners in a national agricultural extension system.

10.3.2 Bangladesh Agricultural Extension System: An Appraisal and its Contribution

A critical examination of the extension organization shows that extension work in Bangladesh has often been the victim of trial and error. Alternative concepts and methods of extension work and programme management were introduced at different times without proper examination of their validity. From the exposition of the historical perspective and review of some of the critical events, we may draw the following lessons, which may be useful for designing and operating the future extension systems.

- There was a lack of public demand and support for agricultural extension services. As a result, many initiatives grew and died down without establishing deep roots in the society.
- In the absence of a logically derived conceptual framework of an out-of-school educational system, different elements of an extension system were introduced in isolation and eventually dispersed to different organizations or ministries.
- Different approaches and models were introduced in different organizations at different points of time without giving a fair trial to any of the approaches.
- Instead of increasing the efficiency of existing systems by removing their weaknesses, parallel systems were created without setting aside or abolishing their predecessors. As a result, mutually competitive organizations became gradually weak through conflict and contradictions.
- The organizations eventually stretched up to village level without creating provisions for trained manpower, educational aids and working capital.
- Organizational structure was very frequently changed with the introduction of conflicting management practices.
- The educational role of the extension services could never be understood, resulting in frequent changes or in assigning of multiple or contradictory roles to the extension workers at the personal discretion of the administrators.

- Instead of employing professionally qualified field staff, amateurs were appointed as extension agents who could not be adequately trained through short in-service training programmes.

Currently, agricultural extension work is facing a number of serious problems arising both from outside and within the organizations. The problems are interlinked.

Exogenous problems

Exogenous problems are problems emerging from outside the extension systems over which the extension organizations have little control. These problems concern the prevailing economic and social situations and government policies regarding agricultural development.

Some of the socio-economic problems of agricultural extension are:

- Subsistence farming and the marginal resource base;
- Tenurial arrangements;
- Absentee landlordism;
- Multiple ownership;
- Credit inadequacy and complexity; and
- The poor law and order situation in the countryside.

Over-population in agriculture has not only led to rural underemployment and unemployment, but also to marginal farming in which farmers lack a sufficient resource base to profit from technological advances and prefer subsistence crops whose productivity is generally low. The benefits of technology diffusion are always disproportionately high to the richer farmers because they have more adequate resource bases.

Extension work can be greatly helped or hindered by government policies regarding agriculture. The policies of agricultural development programmes appropriate to agro-economic conditions, the concurrent operation of competitive development programmes in the same area, the level and balance of prices of inputs and outputs, subsidies or price supports and so on affect the efficiency of extension work.

Endogenous problems

Endogenous problems relate to the approaches, strategies, structures and managerial practices of the extension organizations. These problems could be overcome by improving the management system of extension work.

Disintegration and dispersion of programmes have resulted in isolation, ignorance about each other, conflict, and overlapping, thin distribution of scarce resources, absence of resource sharing and underuse of resources. They have also created problems of coordination and unity of direction toward the common goal of increasing productivity, income and level of living. Often they are counter-productive in effect. It is frequently observed that costly audio-visual aids are unused and highly trained specialized manpower is poorly utilized.

There is, however, no dearth of effort for increasing effectiveness of extension work. The government is seeking as well as receiving technical and financial assistance from international aid or credit-giving agencies from advanced countries through multilateral or bilateral agreements. Technical cooperation or assistance is being channelled through knowledge and translated into work programmes.

Organizations like the Department of Agricultural Extension (DAE) have been made functionally exclusive, but their contacts with farmers as well as technological bases were reduced by a few years when the Training and Visit (T & V) system was introduced. While more qualified personnel were employed at grassroots with increased resources, decision making became more centralized and operational units were at the same time reduced. The principle of client participation in decision making is accepted and pursued, but clients are rarely allowed to have representatives on technical and managerial committees or councils. Often their decisions or opinions are ignored. These contradictions and opposite forces make the extension system less effective.

Despite the above limitations, the Bangladesh agricultural extension system has contributed significantly to agricultural development. It has been a critical factor in the adoption and diffusion of HYV technologies. However, as seen in the preceding chapters, the singular emphasis on cereal production has had a negative impact on the non-cereal crops, non-crop agricultural sectors – livestock, forestry and fishery – and the physical environment.

In the light of the preceding discussion, it is clear that both research and extension face two broad categories of problems – under-investment and lack of coordination, management and appropriate focus. The issues that confront Bangladesh agriculture include, *inter alia*:

- Sustaining crop yields and crop diversification
- Environmental degradation following agricultural intensification
- Gender issues in rural development
- Irrigation and water development issues
- Appropriate technology for broad AEZs, especially hilly areas and coastal zones
- Poverty alleviation, especially through uplift of small and marginal farmers
- Environmental conservation.

In all of the above, agricultural research and extension can play an important role. The current and desired states of determinants of agricultural research and extension priorities in Bangladesh are set out in Figure 10.1. Note the discrepancy between the existing and desired situations.

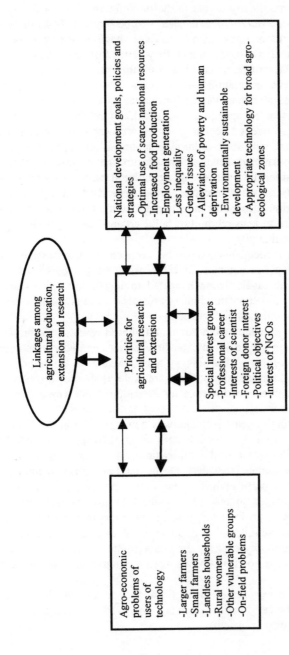

Notes: The thinner arrows portray the current situation (lower priorities) while the thicker arrows portray the desired priorities except for the special interest groups. For the special interest groups the thicker arrow represents the current situation (less desirable) while the thinner arrow represents the preferred priority.

Figure 10.1 Determinants of agricultural research and extension priorities in Bangladesh: current and desired states

10.4 CONCLUDING COMMENTS AND IMPLICATIONS

The foregoing analysis clearly points to the need for two vital and highly interrelated inputs – research and extension – to be reoriented. While both the research system and extension services have made significant contributions to agricultural development, they suffer from vital weaknesses that emanate from lack of resources, lack of coordination and, above all, appropriate focus. These manifest themselves in duplication and the fragmented nature of research and extension service.

Increased investment on spending on agricultural research is critically important. Bangladesh needs to enhance its research capability to generate technologies consistent with socio-cultural endowments and agro-ecological conditions. The government needs to weigh up the relative merits of subsidies involved in fertilizer marketing, agricultural output marketing and agricultural research spending. Despite being dependent on agriculture, Bangladesh suffers from a low human resource base in agricultural research and must invest more in research and to build up an expertise base (Reaz Ahmed 2000; Alauddin 2000).

Due to poor and inadequate linkages between research, extension and education, Bangladesh has not been able to derive the full benefits from strong international linkages. These have led to inefficiency in research resource allocation and transmission of research results both within Bangladesh and from international sources.

Bangladesh needs to switch from commodity-based research to farming systems-based research. Agricultural extension services and education need to be revamped accordingly. Farming systems research is an important factor in a country like Bangladesh. There are wide variations in physical, social and economic factors responsible for determining the way a farm is run.

Research on farming systems is a relatively new approach in the field of agriculture and the group that will benefit from this approach will be limited-resource family farms. In the family farms, the household and farm business is well coordinated because of the use of family labour for agricultural production, part of which is consumed and the rest sold. There is another group involved in the farm business known as agri-business farms. They form a more professional group, hiring more than 50 per cent of their labour force and selling off over 50 per cent of total production. A single member of the family controls the management of the agri-business farm and as such there is no close link between the household and the farm business.

Family farms possess some distinguishing features which are of considerable importance to the planners involved in research and development of the farming systems.

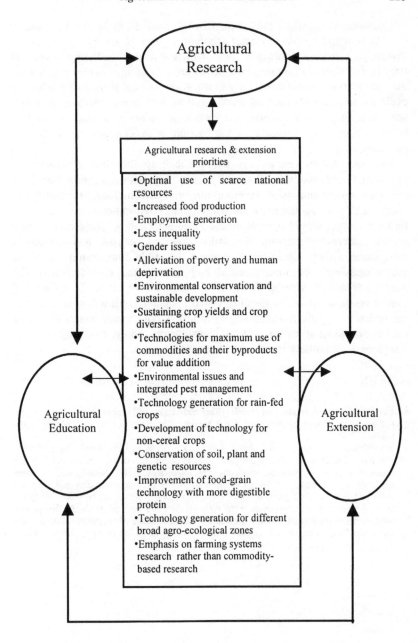

Figure 10.2 A conceptual model of agricultural research and extension in Bangladesh

Constrained by small land area, families have to make the best use of their land, avoiding risks by inter-cropping instead of using a monocrop, or diversifying crops according to local market demands. In family farms, not only is the whole family involved in the process of agricultural production, but they also involve other family farms at the critical phases of production cycle for joint efforts such as labour sharing and plough sharing. It is also seen that they often discuss and exchange opinions among themselves before taking any decision in connection with changes in production practices.

Farming system research is an approach to the new generation of agricultural technology for the family farms with resource limits. For this a thorough understanding of the environment, which includes the biological, social, cultural, economic and institutional environments in which the farming system would operate, needs to be established. There should be a smooth interaction among the crop produced, animal and household subsystems. Then again there should be right interaction of those subsystems with economic, social and institutional environments. The proper interactions among all the subsystems will result in the increase of overall productivity of the farming system, which in turn would take care of the welfare of individual farming families. A conceptual model involving linkages between agricultural research, extension and the emerging issues in Bangladesh agriculture is set out in Figure 10.2.

NOTES

* Partly draws on Alauddin and Tisdell (1986) and Mosharaff Hossain (1991).
1   For evidence of high returns to research for other countries see Arndt, Dalrymple and Ruttan (1977).
2   Agricultural extension services can be said to have begun in Bengal with the East India Company. The Company introduced crop varieties of commercial importance and provided financial support to increase production of exportable crops. Simultaneously, some landlords, as a hobby, had been collecting the seeds of new vegetables and fruit and cultivated those in their gardens. From there, some plants slowly found their way to the farmers. Rev. William Cary, through the Agro-Horticultural Society, made the first private institutional effort in agricultural extension in 1820. The scope of operations of the Society was limited and selective and, as such, it had little impact on the farming community as a whole (Mosharaff Hossain 1991).

11. Agricultural Growth and Rural Poverty

11.1 INTRODUCTION

This chapter examines the relationship between agricultural growth and rural poverty in Bangladesh. The present study argues that 'conventional indicators of poverty and its trends over time present the poor as a uniform mass – statistical entity. Such indicators obscure the varying identities of the poor and the different reasons they are poor' (Bernstein, 1992, p. 26). It takes a broader view of poverty and examines the economic and social relations that lead to and perpetuate poverty. Particular emphasis is placed on gender dimensions of rural poverty. The poverty–environment nexus is also examined.

11.2 IDENTIFYING THE POOR

According to the *World Development Report 1990* (World Bank, 1990, p. 26) poverty is the 'inability to attain minimal standard of living'. This is measured in terms of basic consumption needs or income required to satisfy them. The expenditure necessary to buy a minimum standard of nutrition and other necessities is the basis of the poverty line. The above definition of poverty lines, based on consumption, is concerned primarily with physical measures of relative well-being. Poverty, or more specifically absolute poverty or deprivation refers to the inability to attain minimal standards of consumption to satisfy the basic physiological criteria (Bernstein, 1992, p. 16).

World Bank (1990, p. 27) regards the consumption-based poverty line to consist of two elements:

- The expenditure to buy a minimum standard of nutrition and other basic necessities; and
- A further amount that varies from country to country reflecting the cost of participating in the everyday life of society.

Implicit in the World Bank (1990) discussion of poverty is the acknowledgement of the notion of relative poverty or deprivation. This is reminiscent of the seminal work of Townsend (1979) on poverty in the United Kingdom (see also A. Sen, 1983).

The above leads to a broader view of poverty and deprivation beyond the 'criterion of individual physical survival to satisfying a full social existence' (Bernstein, 1992, p. 16). One must be aware that the measurement and its inter-country comparisons are extremely difficult not least because of the subjectivity involved in the measurement of the component elements of participating in the everyday life of the society (World Bank, 1990, p. 27).

Chambers (1988) cautions against the bias to quantification of governments, aid agencies and professional researchers. This underscores the limit to which incidence of poverty can be meaningfully quantified. Based on Chambers (1988, pp. 8–9) the following five dimensions can be identified:

- Poverty proper – signifying lack of adequate income or assets or ability to generate income to sustain the basic consumption needs
- Physical weakness – resulting from under-nutrition, sickness or disability
- Isolation – physically or socially due to peripheral location, lack of or limited access to goods and services, ignorance and lack of literacy
- Vulnerability – to any kind of emergency and contingency and the risk of further poverty and dispossession (see also Alauddin and Tisdell, 1991, pp. 170–71).
- Lack of empowerment – within existing social, economic, political and cultural milieux.

Based on the above categorization Chambers (1988) further suggests the following priorities of the poor:

- Adequate income and consumption
- Security
- Independence and self-respect.

The first of the above is broadly consistent with the definitions that government policy makers and donor agencies employ. However, as Bernstein (1992, p. 18) rightly points out 'the virtually exclusive concentration of governments and development agencies on consumption and income based definition of poverty means that they exaggerate this aspect at the expense of others'. While the income or consumption-based definition of poverty seems useful, exclusive emphasis on it portrays a narrower definition of economic development as reflected in its quantitative dimension (growth) rather than the wider definition embodying both quantitative and qualitative dimensions (growth plus change). As Meier (1984, p. 6) rightly argues 'economic development is much more than the simple acquisition of industries. It may be defined as nothing less than the upward movement of the entire social system, or it may be interpreted as the attainment of a number of ideals of modernization, such as a rise in productivity social and economic equalization... that can remove the host of undesirable conditions in the social system that have perpetuated a state of underdevelopment.[1] This broader view of economic development is also echoed by Goulet (1971) and Todaro (1992).

Jodha (1988), based on a longitudinal study of socio-economic changes in the rural areas of the western Indian state of Rajasthan, argues against an exclusive reliance on quantification which can provide an inadequate and often misleading picture of the incidence of poverty. For the poor, achieving security, independence and self-respect (the qualitative dimension) is just as important as the income gains (the quantitative dimension). Jodha (1988) suggests a preference to trade off possible quantitative gains for qualitative indicators. As Jodha (1988, p. 2421) puts it: 'Households that have become poorer by conventional measurement of income in fact appear to be better off when seen through different qualitative indicators of their economic well-being. .... The study suggests the need for supplementing conventional measurements of income by qualitative indicators of change to arrive at a realistic understanding of rural socio-economic change'. Following Jodha (1988) the qualitative variables can be identified as follows (see also Bernstein, 1992, p. 18):

- Reduced dependence on the support, patronage or mercy of the well-to-do households in the village
- Freedom from debt trap
- Freedom from dependence and humiliation.

It is quite clear from the above that poverty is a complex and multi-dimensional process. Thus an analysis of poverty requires an investigation of complex realities rather than simple numbers or statistics (Chambers, 1988; see also Sen, 1995). The key dimensions of rural poverty can be identified as follows (see Bernstein, 1992, pp. 18–19; see also Chambers, 1998):

- Structural factors regarding access to land and non-land resources
- Structural factors determining socio-economic power and status
- Access to resources and employment that determine the ability of the household's livelihood strategies
- Social relations governing gender status.

The recent literature takes a broader view of poverty. In this context it is worth considering the views of Sen (2000):

> there is plenty of evidence from the positive experience of East and Southeast Asia that the removal of social deprivation can be very influential in stimulating economic growth and sharing the fruits of growth more evenly. If India went wrong, the fault lay not only in the suppression of market opportunities but also in the lack of attention to social poverty (for example, in the form of widespread

illiteracy). ... the country has paid dearly for leaving nearly half the people illiterate. Social poverty has helped perpetuate economic poverty as well.

11.3 THE BANGLADESH SCENARIO: BROAD PATTERN

According to the Fifth Five Year Plan of Bangladesh (BPC, 1998, p. 147) 'poverty refers to forms of economic, social and psychological deprivation occurring among people lacking sufficient ownership, control or access to resources for minimum required level of living'. Thus the Bangladesh Government recognizes poverty as a multi-dimensional problem involving income, consumption, nutrition, health, education, housing, and the capacity to cope with and manage crises. This recognition notwithstanding, with the exception of income/consumption measure, inadequacy of data poses serious difficulties in measuring trends over time in broader measures of poverty. The official documents in Bangladesh therefore focus primarily on the income dimension of poverty supplemented by available information on the other dimensions (BPC, 1998, p. 148).

The most commonly used measure of poverty is head-count ratio, which provides broad directionality of changes in the level of absolute poverty. A poverty line (expenditure level) is defined as per capita minimum calorie intake of 2122 calories. The head-count measure is the percentage of population with income below the minimum expenditure required to meet the daily calorie intake. Trends in poverty reduction can be summed up as follows:[2]

- Bangladesh achieved a modest improvement in poverty alleviation over a period of about a decade to 1991–92. The incidence of poverty on a head-count basis at the aggregate level declined from 52.3 per cent to 49.7 per cent. The incidence of poverty in urban areas declined from 40.9 per cent to 33.6 per cent. The corresponding figure for rural poverty registered a decline from 53.8 per cent to 52.9 per cent.
- The incidence of rural poverty stood at 48 per cent in 1995.

The evidence of a declining trend in head-count poverty in the early 1990s portrayed above is supported by an independent survey by the Bangladesh Institute of Development Studies (see BPC, 1998, p. 148).

Extreme poverty alleviation registered some improvement in recent years. The incidence of *hard-core* poverty[3] declined from 26 per cent to 23 per cent during 1987–94. Furthermore, during the 1990–95 period (BPC, 1998, p. 148) the proportion of rural households

- Living in extremely vulnerable housing fell from 9 per cent to 2 per cent

- Without minimum clothing (less than two sets) declined from 15 per cent to 4 per cent
- Without proper winter clothing also decreased from 22 per cent to 7 per cent.

Despite the above improvements, the pace of poverty reduction is quite slow. A recent report sheds some further light on this issue. For example, as Rahman (2000) argues 'in 1991–92, people under poverty constituted 49.7 per cent of the population, in 1995–96 the ratio came down to 47 per cent and in 1999 to 44.7 per cent. The striking conclusion which emerges here is the rate of poverty reduction throughout the 1990s has virtually remained stagnant at around 0.7 per cent per annum'.[4]

Let us now consider the extent to which some broader indicators of poverty have changed over time and how Bangladesh's performance compares with those of some other South Asian countries. These include *Human Development Index (HDI); Gender-related Development Index (GDI) Gender Empowerment Measure (GEM); Capability Poverty Measure (CPM) and Human Poverty Index (HPI– 1).*[5,6]

- *Human development index (HDI)* for Bangladesh increased from 0.318 in 1975 to 0.440 in 1997. Bangladesh is one of the lowest achievers in respect of this indicator. While there has been some improvement in its ranking it still ranks quite low. As of 1997 Bangladesh's rank is 150th out of a total of 174 countries (UNDP, 1999, p. 136) while its other South Asian neighbours rank comparatively higher (India ranks 132nd with an HDI score of 0.545, Pakistan 138th with an HDI score of 0.508, Sri Lanka ranks 90th with an HDI score of 0.721, and Nepal is 144th with an HDI score of 0.463).
- *Capability Poverty Measure (CPM)* scores available only for 1993 (UNDP, 1996, pp. 111–12) suggests that of the 101 countries listed Bangladesh has the second highest incidence of capability poor (76.9 per cent, rank =100) followed by India (61.5 per cent, rank = 89) and Pakistan (60.8 per cent, rank = 87). In this regard Bangladesh has only outperformed Nepal (77.3, rank = 101).
- *Human Poverty Index (HPI–1)* scores for 1997 (UNDP, 1999, pp. 146–7) suggest that of the ninety-two developing countries Bangladesh ranks 73rd with an HPI–1 score of 44.4 per cent (1994 score = 48.3 per cent). Among her South Asian neighbours, only Nepal ranks lower, 85th with an HPI–1 score of 51.9 per cent, while India ranks 58th with an HPI–1 score of 35.9 per cent (1994 score = 36.7 per cent) and Pakistan ranks 71st with an HPI–1 score of 44.9 per cent (1994 score = 46.8 per cent). Sri Lanka ranks relatively much higher, as 33rd with an HPI–1 score of 20.4 per cent (1994 score = 20.7 per cent) (UNDP, 1997, pp. 126–7).

The above suggests that there have been some improvements in human and social dimensions of development which have implications for broader dimensions of poverty reduction. In recent years, there have been discernible improvements in some social indicators (UNDP, 1991; 1997; 1999). For instance, as can be seen from the information contained in Table 11.1:

- Life expectancy at birth for Bangladesh has increased from 51.8 years in 1990 to 58.1 in 1997. But this is still the lowest among the major South Asian countries.
- While Bangladesh has made reasonable progress in respect of adult literacy, it is still at the bottom of all the major South Asian countries.
- Bangladesh has made significant progress in respect of under-5 mortality rate and infant mortality rate per '000 live births. Bangladesh's position is appreciably better than that of Pakistan and is not far behind that of India. However, Sri Lanka's performance is head and shoulders above the rest of South Asia on these two criteria.

Table 11.1 Trends in selected socio-economic indicators in Bangladesh and selected South Asian countries: 1990–97

Indicators	Country							
	Bangladesh		India		Pakistan		Sri Lanka	
	1990	1997	1990	1997	1990	1997	1990	1997
Life expectancy at birth (years)	51.8	58.1	59.1	62.6	57.7	64.0	70.9	73.1
Adult literacy rate (per cent)	32.0	38.9	44.0	53.5	31.0	40.9	86.0	90.7
Under 5 mortality rate per '000 live births	184	109	145	108	162	136	36	19
Infant mortality rate per '000 live births[a]	116	81	81	71	106	95	27	17

Note: a refers to 1989.

Sources: Adapted from UNDP (1991, pp. 123, 140–41; 1997, pp. 150–52; 1999, pp. 140–42).

While the above analysis suggests slow albeit steady improvements in some broader parameters of social poverty, one needs to look beyond these aggregate magnitudes. This is warranted because as Sen (1981, p. 152) puts it 'shocking disasters can lie deeply hidden in comforting aggregate magnitudes'. The remainder of this chapter provides a disaggregated picture focusing on gender and environmental dimensions of poverty.

11.4 WOMEN, DEVELOPMENT AND RURAL POVERTY

The last two decades have witnessed a prolific growth in the literature addressing gender issues in socio-economic development (see for example, Roy *et al.*, 1996). A substantial body of evidence suggests that women have consistently lost out in the development process (Pearson, 1992; Jahan and Alauddin, 1996a; Tisdell, 1996).

11.4.1 The Broad Picture

Some broader gender related indicators of development are set out in Tables 11.2 and 11.3 for the early and late 1990s for Bangladesh and selected South Asian countries. The information contained therein reveals that:

- All the countries in the sample including Bangladesh have experienced improvement in the gender development index (GDI). However, Bangladesh is at the bottom of the ladder. Furthermore, despite improvement in the absolute value of the index over time on an international scale, the relative positions of the South Asian countries in 1997 are on the decline compared to those in 1993.
- There exists gross inequality in the inter-gender distribution of earned incomes in all the countries under consideration during 1993 and 1994. The relevant female–male ratio in 1993 stood at 0.30 (0.30 in 1994), 0.33 (0.35 in 1994), 0.23 (0.26 in 1994) and 0.47 (0.53 in 1994) respectively for Bangladesh, India, Pakistan and Sri Lanka. While other South Asian countries experienced some improvement in the inter-gender distribution of earned income between 1993 and 1994, Bangladesh's position remained the same. However, Pakistan displays the highest level of inequality with the female share of earned income only a quarter that of the male. Relatively speaking, Sri Lanka seems to be the most egalitarian of the South Asian countries in this regard.
- In 1997, the female–male ratio of per capita GDP (purchasing power parity dollars) in absolute terms was highly unequal. However, of the four countries under consideration, Bangladesh with the lowest per capita income has the lowest degree of inequality (0.58) Sri Lanka with the highest per capita GDP displays the second lowest degree of inequality (0.41). There seems to be a significant difference between India and Pakistan in respect of this ratio even though there is very little difference between their per capita GDPs.

11.4.2 Some Micro–level Evidence[7]

An examination of micro-level indicators considered, *inter alia*, by Agarwal (1986; 1989), Ahooja-Patel (1996), Pearson (1992) and Roy *et al.* (1996)

clearly suggests that gender makes a difference in the share of benefits from the development process (see also Hamid, 1994). These include lower earnings of females relative to men, disparities in female–male literacy rates, representation of women in parliament and gender divisions of use of time. In each of these respects women compare unfavourably with men. This seems to have resulted from a failure to recognize the fact that 'development process or policy inevitably affects and is affected by the relation between genders in any society. All policies however technical or neutral they may appear to be, will have gender implications' (Pearson, 1992, p. 292). One needs to emphasize that in a broader context gender relations are social relations rather than biological or natural relations, which are essentially based on a stereotyped image of gender relations. It must be remembered though that 'social and economic discrimination in terms of gender, race, or similar characteristics is mutually reinforcing. These aspects together create a social and economic trap for them to escape by means of their individual efforts' (Roy *et al.*, 1996, p. 23).

Table 11.2 Trends in poverty/deprivation in Bangladesh and selected South Asian countries: gender-related indicators

Country	Gender development index (GDI)			Gender empowerment measure (GEM)		
	1993	1994	1997	1993	1994	1997
Bangladesh	0.336 (116)	0.339 (128)	0.428 (123)	0.291 (77)	0.303 (76)	0.304 (83)
India	0.410 (103)	0.419 (118)	0.525 (112)	0.235 (93)	0.228 (86)	0.240 (95)
Pakistan	0.383 (107)	0.392 (120)	0.472 (116)	0.165 (101)	0.189 (92)	0.176 (101)
Sri Lanka	0.679 (62)	0.694 (70)	0.712 (76)	0.306 (75)	0.307 (70)	0.321 (80)

Note: Figures in parentheses refer to rankings in the respective years.

Sources: UNDP (1996, pp. 138–43; 1997, pp. 150–54; 1999, pp. 140–44).

Given the predetermined division of labour accompanied by unequal access to and control over resources within the household, changes in rural policies and agricultural technology have not enhanced the status of rural women in Bangladesh. They are, as usual, subject to unequal treatment because of their gender, a prejudice deeply embedded in a culture of patriarchy and subjugation (Pearson, 1992). However, as a response to the challenge of the feminization of poverty, rural women are responding to their marginalization and acting significantly in grassroots initiatives for change.

Table 11.3   Ratio of female–male real per capita GDP in selected South Asian countries (PPP$)

Year	Country			
	Bangladesh	India	Pakistan	Sri Lanka
1993				
Male	77.2	75.2	81.4	66.9
Female	22.8	24.8	18.6	33.1
Female–male ratio	0.30	0.33	0.23	0.47
1994				
Male	76.9	74.3	79.2	65.5
Female	23.1	25.7	20.8	34.5
Female–male ratio	0.30	0.35	0.26	0.53
1997				
Male	1320	2389	2363	3545
Female	767	902	701	1452
Female–male ratio	0.58	0.38	0.30	0.41

Note: 1993 and 1994 figures refer to earned income shares for male and female.

Sources: Adapted from UNDP (1996, pp. 138–40; 1997, pp. 150–52; 1999, pp. 140–42).

Women in Bangladesh are allotted a lower socio-economic status than men. Socio-cultural norms, religious taboos and other barriers militate against an enhanced status of women in Bangladesh as is the case in many LDCs. In a pioneering study on female status in Bangladesh, Chaudhury and Ahmed (1980, p. 155) catalogue some factors for this lopsidedness in gender relations and discrimination against women. These, while not exhaustive, are important factors (see also Kabeer, 1989; 1991):

- Lower literacy rate among women compared to men
- In practice, marriage age of women on average being 8–10 years lower than men
- Greater liberty for men to divorce their wives even at simple pretexts with little or no opportunity for women to exercise that right
- Inheritance law discriminating women *vis-à-vis* men

- A society dominated by *purdah* restricting women's mobility and contact with the world outside
- Women lacking control over means of production.

Rural women are usually overworked. Jahan (1996) found that in rural Bangladesh women on average worked 10–20 per cent longer than men. This is consistent with the situation elsewhere in the developing world (see for example, Pearson, 1992, pp. 297–8). Despite women's involvement in household activity and in agricultural production, their contribution to the national economy largely remains unrecognized (Safilios-Rothschild and Mahmud, 1989). In fact, women make a substantial contribution to agricultural production and rural household activity. Since they usually do not own any land very little attention has been given to women's need for increasing their contribution to agricultural production. Hamid (1994, p. 1 and p. 38) in assessing the contribution of non-market work in national income estimates that women contributed more than 41 per cent to GDP in 1989–90 while their contribution to agriculture was about 37 per cent.

The Agricultural Sector Review of 1989 on women's roles in agriculture (Safilios-Rothschild and Mahmud, 1989) reported that women's participation in agriculture was no less than that of men. Economic participation of women includes income earning (marketing of livestock or of homestead horticultural produces) or contributing to value added (home-based crop processing, grain storage, and so on) activity. Even though women perform duties like transplanting, weeding, harvesting and irrigation on their family farm, social reluctance militates against their inclusion as being productive. Such work must confront social resistance.

Despite advancements in agricultural technology, women still remain at a disadvantage in their lives and their economic position. Agricultural modernization in the 1960s has had a negative impact on the economic position of women in land and other institutional support (Mahabub Hossain, 1988). Apart from unequal access to income-generating opportunities, women have hardly any control either through ownership or rights, over the means of production such as land, tools, animal, transport and other necessary resources for the production and distribution of agricultural products (Jahan and Alauddin, 1996a).

The emergence of structural and technological changes in many ways has provided limited avenues for rural female employment. Higher peak labour needs and time constraints for operations such as fertilizer application, weeding, harvesting and liberalization in agricultural input markets in fact increase the requirement of casual hired labour. Demand for casual labour has opened up the avenue for female workers (Khuda, 1982; Safilios-Rothschild and Mahmud, 1989). However, the rate and nature of participation of women in farm households varies with differential access to land. In female-headed households, women owning cultivable land area between 0.1 and 0.4 hectare are most likely to engage in on-field agriculture.

In the rural labour markets, wages are usually paid as a combination of cash and kind. Many women receive a part of their wages in the form of meals at work. According to Rahman (1991), in 86 per cent of the days of all employment, women's wage included food, either as the only payment or in combination with other components. Wage rates of unskilled rural wage workers are low. Women wage workers constitute the lowest paid group. In such a situation, a single breadwinner can hardly maintain a family of two or three above the poverty level. Female wage rates range between 45 and 60 per cent of their male counterparts (Jahan and Alauddin, 1996a). A survey undertaken by Jahan in two Bangladesh villages also reported similar female–male wage relativities. It appears that as women are hired for casual work, they lack bargaining power for higher wages. Furthermore, to continue in their work and earnings, women have to comply with any wages offered to them even though the wages they receive may not be commensurate with the rise in price level. This picture is no different from that in the non-agricultural sector (Majumder and Zohir, 1994).[8]

Rahman and Hossain (1995) report that females have a nutritional intake of only 88 per cent that of males and typically earn 46 per cent of the male wage (see also Rahman, 1995). Recent surveys and available evidence from Bangladesh suggest that women have shared a disproportionately higher burden of poverty and suffered chronic deficits in food intake, both in absolute terms and in relation to men (Jahan, 1998; Pearson, 1992). In Bangladesh around 50 per cent of the rural poor live below the poverty line (a daily intake of less than 1850 kilocalories). The incidence of poverty is higher for women compared to men. Employing farm-level evidence from two Bangladesh villages and various measures of poverty (head-count index, Foster–Greer–Thorbecke poverty gap and distributionally sensitive measure) Jahan (1996, p. 91 and p. 105) reveals that the burden of poverty is disproportionately borne by women. On further interpretation of Jahan's findings (Jahan, 1996, p. 105) it is clear that by every measure of poverty female–male relativities were higher than unity and ranged between 1.13 and 2.17. The findings of Alauddin and Tisdell (1998) who reported a significant intra-household disparity between male and female members in rural Bangladesh support this. Similar evidence was found in some West Bengal villages (Roy and Tisdell, 1993). This is also consistent with Rahman (1986) who found overwhelming evidence of unequal sharing of food within the family – with female members getting a much lower share than male members both in terms of food quality and quantity.

Furthermore, a chronic shortage in fuel due to deforestation affects women's cooking arrangements: the nutritional quality of meals suffers when women use less fuel and are able to cook fewer items. Thus while in general their diets are *a priori* less varied, less nutritious and more dreary (see also Alauddin and Tisdell, 1991), given the intra-household inequality against women they are more likely to bear the brunt of this decline in dietary quality (Jahan, 1996). The survey undertaken in two rural areas of Bangladesh supports the view that women bear a higher burden of nutritional disadvantage in intra-household food consumption (see also Jahan and Hossain, 1998).

Thus on the whole women seem to be over-represented in the ranks of the poor throughout the developing world. Bangladesh is no exception. In particular, families headed by single females experience a more acute level of poverty. Given the magnitude of poverty, the sharp rise in the incidence in female-headed households may have contributed to a *feminization* of poverty (Jahan, 1998). This also indicates the importance of distinguishing between households headed by women and those headed by men. Overall the process of development is far from gender neutral.

The 'female marginalization thesis' explains women's worsening position in terms of reduced access to and control over the means and rewards of productive activity in the developing world (Beneria and Sen, 1982). The thesis identifies the changing role of women and men with social modernization. With the inception of large units of production, women are effectively prohibited from gaining access to the new forms of economic activity, thus reducing their ability to contribute to household income (Beneria and Sen, 1982).

11.5 ENVIRONMENTAL DEGRADATION AND RURAL POVERTY

As discussed in detail in Chapter 9, the present environmental degradation which has resulted from the process of economic growth raises concerns about its sustainability. Voicing this concern the Rio Declaration (UNCED, 1993) strongly refuses to allow the concept of *sustainable development* to be simply turned into an *economic notion*, restricted to new technologies and subordinated to the latest market products. The reason is that these perpetuate *structural poverty* and wealth arising from the dominant discourse of development whose validity has been seriously called into question (see, for example, Lele, 1996, p. 28).

In general, large populations and poverty are blamed for environmental destruction such as over-exploitation of land, deforestation and unplanned use of natural resources. However, over-population, poverty, underdevelopment and environmental deterioration are critically linked with one another. The link between poverty and the environment still remains a subject of considerable controversy or at best is much more complicated than a simplistic cause and effect portrayal (see, for example, Alauddin and Tisdell, 1998; Lele, 1991; Bifani, 1992). Thus one should exercise caution against such a simplistic generalization. While poverty is viewed as a major cause and an effect of global environmental problems, it is essential to realize that it is futile to attempt to deal with the environment–poverty nexus without a broader perspective that encompasses the factors underlying poverty and inequality (Jahan and Alauddin, 1999).

In rural Bangladesh resource use patterns and practices in the main may have led to environmental degradation. The relationship between poverty and unsustainable agricultural practices is also cited in many recent publications (see for example, Alauddin and Tisdell, 1998). Imprudent use of the agricultural resource base irreversibly reduces the capacity for generating sustainable production and hence perpetuates poverty.

The pressure by the increasingly marginalized rural poor on common lands is identified as an important link between socio-economic development and environmental degradation. It can be argued, however, that such a view ignores the dominant causes of the environmental crisis, namely industrial toxic wastes and over-consumption by the affluent people (Bifani, 1992).

Therefore environmental degradation cannot be attributable solely to the rural poor, especially when a very small number of farmers own about 80 per cent of the land and other resources of the country (see, for example, Alauddin and Tisdell, 1991). It is true that lack of conservation practices, inadequate technology and increasing intensive production practices have contributed to accelerated degradation and consequently to increases in rural poverty which in turn can act to the detriment of the environment. Against this background it is now widely recognized that women play a critical role in bringing about social, economic and environmental change and in turn can be affected by these changes. The linkages are complex and can be captured somewhat in terms of the conceptual model set out in Figure 11.1.

The income of the rural poor, composed of landless and near landless households, consists of two important components: exchange income (primarily wage income) and non-exchange income (Alauddin and Tisdell, 1991, p. 161). Market forces largely determine exchange income while non-exchange income is determined primarily by institutional arrangements and rural sociology, including property rights, and is usually obtained directly from nature without exchange. The basic ingredients that constitute the non-exchange source of income include, *inter alia*, wild fruits, wild animals, firewood, building and thatching materials, water from tanks, streams and ponds for growing vegetables and fruit mainly for home consumption, free ranging of poultry and some limited grazing or fodder for livestock. These sources of non-exchange income depend to some extent on common access or low-cost access to natural resources. The poor survive on common resources or what are known as 'ecological reserves'. According to Sobhan (1998a, p. 106) in Bangladesh 'about 40 per cent of the current consumption of the poorest section of the population now derives from the country's ecological reserves'. With rapid population growth, depletion of the natural resource base and greater penetration of technological and market forces, the cushioning effect of access to natural resources in adverse circumstances on the rural poor has become increasingly limited. The process has undermined their income security (Alauddin and Tisdell, 1991; Alauddin *et al.*, 1995). As Sobhan (1998a, p. 106) rightly argues 'unfortunately, there is no policy or institutional arrangements to take cognisance of this reality'. Furthermore, there has been very little understanding of the relationship encompassing the environment, women and poverty. Such a relationship is portrayed in Figure 11.2.

11.6 CONCLUDING OBSERVATIONS

This chapter takes a broader view of poverty and the poor than the conventional approach. Social poverty has a broader connotation and accords with a wider view of development (growth plus change) than growth only. While successive development plans have focused on poverty alleviation, nearly half the population remains below the poverty line although the percentage of population below the extreme poverty line has fallen somewhat. Available evidence indicates that Bangladesh has made little progress in respect of either the capability poverty measure or the human poverty index.

Bangladesh has made slow but steady progress in some socio-economic indicators of development. These include, *inter alia*, adult literacy rate, life expectancy at birth and infant mortality rate. Nevertheless, Bangladesh languishes toward the bottom of the ranks in a global context. Her performance compares less than favourably with that of the South Asian region as a whole.

Women in Bangladesh in general and rural areas in particular are over-represented in the ranks of the disadvantaged, the vulnerable and the poor. Women earn much less than men. Both in terms of gender-related development measure and gender empowerment measure Bangladesh performs poorly in the context of the developing world, let alone in the world as a whole. Women's contribution to development has not been given due recognition. The dominant discourse of development embodies and epitomizes a process of virtual exclusion and alienation of women who constitute half the total population.

In the conventional literature, poverty is portrayed as the cause of environmental degradation. This study cautions against such a simplistic generalization and argues that the poverty–environment nexus is more complex and needs to be discussed taking cognizance of the underlying complexities of the process. The causation is not uni-directional, running from poverty to environmental degradation, but could be bi-directional. In Bangladesh as elsewhere in the developing world this reality does not seem to have been fully appreciated. Furthermore, the role of women as managers and carers of the environment has not been given due recognition. 'Gender inequality aids to pervade poverty and worsens the environment poverty situation' (Abed, 1998, p. 99). Protection of the environment can be directly linked to the process of economic development, which can have significant employment-generating as well as poverty-reducing implications (Islam, 1998, p. 84).

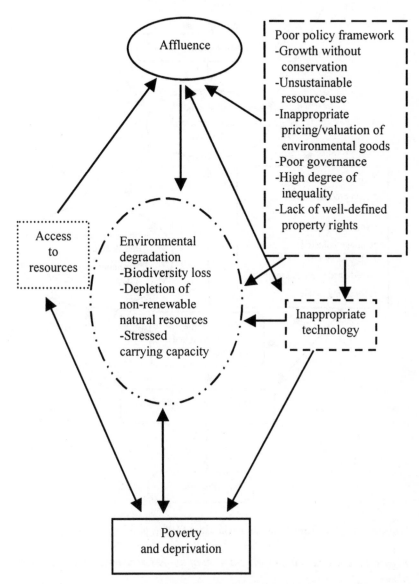

Figure 11.1 A schematic representation of the environment– poverty nexus

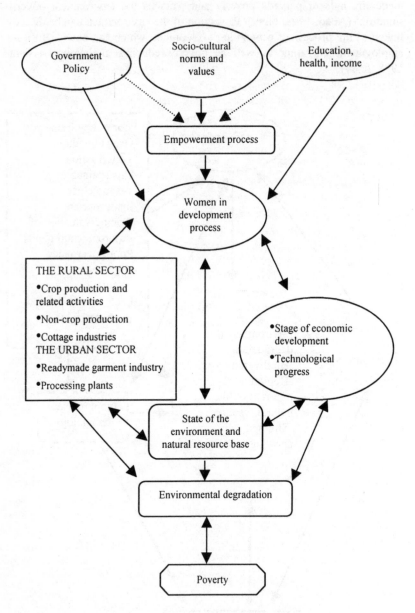

Source: Adapted from Jahan and Alauddin (1999, p. 306).

Figure 11.2 A schematic representation of the environment–gender–poverty nexus

NOTES

1 For details see Myrdal (1968, p. 869) and Black (1966, pp. 55–60).
2 Based on information from *Household Expenditure Surveys* of the Bangladesh Bureau of Statistics contained in BPC (1998, p. 148).
3 Corresponding to less than 80 per cent of the daily calorie requirement.
4 This is much slower than the record of East and Southeast Asian countries (BPC, 1998, p. 148).
5 Based on UNDP (1999, pp. 159–63) these can be considered as follows:
   * *Human Development Index (HDI)* based on three indicators: longevity proxied by life expectancy at birth, educational attainment as measured by a combination of adult literacy and combined primary, secondary and tertiary enrolment rates, and standard of living measured by real GDP per capita (in terms of purchasing power parity dollars).
   * *Gender-related Development Index (GDI)* based on the same indicators as HDI but adjusted by the average achievement of each country in life expectancy, educational attainment and income in accordance with the disparity in achievement between male and female.
   * *Gender Empowerment Measure (GEM)* based on indicators to measure the relative empowerment of men and women in political and economic spheres: parliamentary representation; managerial and administrative positions; professional and technical positions; shares of males and females in economically active population; income shares.
   * *Capability Poverty Measure (CPM)* composed of three indicators: living a healthy and well-nourished life; having the capability of safe and healthy reproduction; and being literate and knowledgeable. The CPM focuses on people's lack of capabilities rather than on average level of capabilities as measured by the HDI.
   * *Human Poverty Index (HPI– 1)* for developing countries concentrates on the three essential dimensions of human life already reflected in the HDI – longevity, knowledge and a decent standard of living. The first deprivation relates to survival – vulnerability to death at a relatively early age. The second deprivation relates to knowledge – being excluded from the world of reading and communication. The third relates to a decent standard of living in terms of overall economic provisioning.
6 The technical merits of these measures and their comparability intertemporally or cross-sectionally are matters of debate among professionals, policy makers and practitioners of development (see, for example, McGillvray, 1991; Alauddin and Tisdell, 1998; Sengupta, 1998). These have, however, unequivocally established the primacy of human and social development as an objective of development policy (see also Sen, 1999).
7 This and the following section draw heavily on materials in Jahan and Alauddin (1999, pp. 301–8).
8 A study by Majumder and Zohir (1994) relating primarily to the urban context found significant socio-economic changes have occurred in the women's living conditions with garment workers experiencing the greatest change. However, the beneficial effects of socio-economic transformation brought about by the wage employment in the garment industry is considerably neutralized by some negative implications such as exploitation in terms of low wage, irregular wage employment, job insecurity, gender discrimination in earnings and so on. Poor occupational health and safety standards are also matters of grave concern. Outbreaks of factory fires and resulting casualties including deaths of women workers are a regular phenomenon and clearly indicate occupational hazards in garment factories.

12. Conclusions, Challenges and Prospects

12.1 INTRODUCTION

The present study has investigated the relationship embracing poverty, gender issues and the environment in the process of agricultural growth in Bangladesh taking particular note of the process of a changing policy environment over a period of five decades. In examining the process of growth, socio-economic and environmental changes, the study has employed a blend of secondary and farm-level evidence.

It is argued that past development processes have failed fully to appreciate the inextricable linkage between agricultural development and the environment. Most of the issues that arise in Bangladesh in the context of the poverty–gender–environment nexus are not unique to it nor are they exhaustive. Parallels abound elsewhere in the developing world especially other South Asian countries. Furthermore, they are fairly representative of those that confront South Asia in general and Bangladesh in particular.

This chapter summarizes the major findings from this study, identifies major challenges that confront Bangladesh agriculture and assesses its prospects.

12.2 SUMMARY OF CONCLUSIONS

The study yields several important conclusions. These are presented in the thematic sequence and chapter references employed in the study.

12.2.1 The Physical Environment of Bangladesh Agriculture

Topography and soils, water and land resources critically influence the complex physical environment surrounding Bangladesh agriculture. The existing cropping patterns have been developed over decades or even longer, and are based on the complex ecosystem. Intensification of agriculture and other factors, some of which are transboundary in nature, have put these resources under considerable strain (Alauddin and Tisdell, 1998; Jahan, 1998). Some of these have manifested themselves in the form of a dwindling supply of arable land. With urbanization likely to increase much beyond the current level (Alauddin and Tisdell, 1998) and land required for human settlement, the land area available for crop production can only decline. Increased intensification far beyond the current level seems to be the only recourse to increase an effective supply of land. This is likely to expose the fragility of the physical environment even further.

12.2.2 Growth and Change in the Crop Sector

Bangladesh agriculture has experienced massive transformation over a period of nearly five decades, the most important manifestation of this process being its intensification. While the process of change has been a continuous phenomenon over the years, the most important episode is the introduction of the green revolution technologies in the late 1960s. Significant output growth has resulted from technological change. The output of food-grains in the 1990s is two and a half times that of the 1950s. Since the late 1960s overall food-grain output has increased by more than 60 per cent due to a moderate rise in rice output and spectacular growth in wheat output. However, the Bangladesh crop sector remains a virtual rice monoculture. The period under consideration has witnessed a trend away from non-cereals with no noticeable increase in the output of non-cereal crops as a whole. If anything, outputs of some of these crops might have remained static or in some cases may have fallen. In terms of growth in total factor productivity, the process exhibits a phenomenon of a slow down, if not retrogression. This implies that greater use of modern input, such as chemical fertilizers and pesticides, has underpinned crop output growth in Bangladesh. However, in the late 1990s Bangladesh agriculture has regained some momentum and the annual growth rate in agriculture has consistently topped 5 per cent.

The above process of crop output growth has significant implications for the balance between food supply and demand. Furthermore, the process has engendered spillover effects, which have ramifications for the environment and the sustainability of the livelihoods of the rural masses. Subsequent chapters discuss these issues in greater depth.

12.2.3 Overall Food Supply and Food Self-sufficiency

Although overall food-grain output has increased markedly in absolute terms, it has not necessarily resulted in an overall qualitative improvement in dietary balance. It is also clearly evident that despite some decline in the import intensity of food-grains, import of non-cereals such as edible oils, chillies and lentils has strained Bangladesh's balance of payments. Thus, the supply of most non-cereal food items has not kept pace with rising aggregate demand because of population growth and to a much lesser extent growth in per capita income. Successive development plans since the 1950s have aimed to achieve food self-sufficiency, defined simply as making available a per capita annual quantity of 165–70 kg of food-grains. The most recent available evidence seems to indicate that Bangladesh has achieved food-grain self-sufficiency for the first time in its history (*Daily Independent*, 1 June 2000).

However, the real significance of the technological change in Bangladesh agriculture lies not so much in raising the living standards of the average Bangladeshi, but in preventing mass starvation.

12.2.4 The Non-crop Sectors within Bangladesh Agriculture

The non-crop sector comprising livestock, fisheries and forestry in Bangladesh agriculture as a whole has remained neglected relative to the crop sector over the years. Despite this, the value added of non-crop agriculture has grown at a faster rate than the crop sector over the 1972–97 period.

Livestock
The livestock sector has undergone significant changes over the years. In the 1990s, the growth has been faster, due primarily to significant increases in the number of poultry and goats. However, the rate of growth of the cattle population has remained sluggish. Given the pivotal importance of cattle in the Bangladesh livestock sector, the slow growth in the cattle population has arrested its overall growth rate.

Per capita supply of food products from the livestock sector has remained stagnant and falls far short of requirements. Furthermore, Bangladesh suffers from an acute shortage of draught power with significant variations across regions within Bangladesh. This has resulted from slow cattle growth, an inadequate artificial insemination programme and a poor disease control and vaccination programme. Natural disasters have also claimed a large number of livestock animals on a regular basis, especially the devastating cyclones of 1970 and 1991, and the floods of 1974, 1988 and 1998.

The growth of the livestock sector has had a significant favourable impact on dietary conditions and rural poverty alleviation. The Small Farmers Livestock Development Project introduced in 1993 by the Department of Livestock Services, in collaboration with three NGOs, has brought a significant and positive impact on the poultry population, disease control and mortality. Further ramifications have manifested themselves in employment and income generation and poverty reduction especially for women in rural Bangladesh (Alam, 1997, p. 259). Given the limited employment potential of the crop sector (Alauddin and Tisdell, 1995), this achievement is significant.

Fisheries

Decline, recovery and growth characterize the Bangladesh fisheries sector. Fish production declined up to the late 1970s, then remained more or less stagnant until the mid-1980s. Since then, it gradually recovered to regain the early 1970s level by the end of the 1980s. In the 1990s, fish production increased quite significantly. A combination of man-made and natural factors contributed to this process. These include, among other things, the destruction of habitats, over-exploitation, favourable policy, and changes in cultural practices, institutional arrangements and high private profitability. Both governmental and non-governmental organizations have played an important role.

Open water capture fishery in respect of riverine and estuarine fishery has suffered significantly since the 1970s. The increased catch of floodplain fisheries has compensated this decline. The most remarkable feature of inland fishery is the prolific growth in pond culture and coastal aquaculture. The environmental impact of the former is benign (Smith, 1973) while that of the latter is adverse (Alauddin and Hamid, 1999).

Shrimp-producing countries of the developing world engage in shrimp farming primarily to cater for the export markets of the high-income countries of Western Europe, North America and Japan. Other emerging markets are Singapore, Hong Kong and Malaysia. The exporting countries have to adhere to the rules and regulations of the importing countries. These include, *inter alia*, various non-tariff barriers including health and environmental standards, labour laws and so on. The consumers, and hence importers, are highly sensitive to the quality of the products that they are importing.

While there are encouraging signs of development in the fisheries sub-sector, there is very little room for complacency. The physical environment, which is already badly damaged, has been stressed to the limit especially in the case of shrimp culture. A viable fisheries industry needs to be based on sound government policy embracing incentives, technology, marketing and value adding. Of critical importance is the need to address environmental issues resulting from the process of growth of the fisheries sub-sector.

Forestry

Like other components of the non-crop sector of Bangladesh agriculture, the forestry sub-sector is a very neglected area. This sector has experienced a progressive decline over the last few decades.

Increasing pressure on land for crop production and human settlement, lack of public policy focus on conservation of forestry resources, rapid deforestation, poor management and cultural practices underlie this decline. Several unprecedented floods and other natural hazards of severe intensity and magnitude during the last three decades have exacerbated the process of destruction of forestry resources.

The alarming rate of deforestation and depletion and degradation of forestry resources has, among other things, led to:

- Declining supplies of main forest products such as timber, fuel wood and bamboo and subsidiary forest products such as fish, *golpata* and honey, which constitute a direct economic loss.
- Degradation of forestry resources leading to loss of biodiversity and loss of ecological balances (Alauddin and Tisdell, 1998).
- Loss or depletion of livelihoods of the people who live in rural and hill areas (Alauddin *et al.*, 1995; Vyas, 1995; Gain, 1998).
- Decrease in water holding capacity, increased soil erosion.

Estimated loss due to adverse environmental impacts following or accompanying deforestation could lead to a loss of 1 per cent of GDP in 1990 (BBS, 1999a, p. 17; World Bank, 1997).

The government and non-governmental organizations have taken a number of initiatives to create awareness and strengthen institutional capacity to handle multi-dimensional environmental problems. The problem is complex and one should not expect any simple or simplistic solutions. The concept of social/homestead forestry is very sound but faces some formidable constraints.

The major constraint on homestead forestry is the lack of available land. The small landowners are unable to expand because of the lack of homestead land. The very poor face insecurity of tenure, as at least 10 per cent of rural homesteaders do not own the land on which they live. Furthermore, the cost of transporting seedlings from central nurseries to homesteads is a burden to farmers, many of whom depend on natural regeneration as their source of seedling supply. There are local influential people who are destroying the forests for their own benefits. The settlement of migrants in forest areas has caused great harm as fallow periods are shortened due to land pressures. Uncontrolled grazing in both public and private forests hampers tree regeneration. There is also inadequate training and extension support services. Finally, the complete lack of awareness of ecological and environmental problems inhibits forestry development.

In social forestry, there is poor coordination between the local people and the Forest Department. The strip plantation programme implemented both by government and NGOs needed hired supervisors/guards for protecting the trees. This is because the local people use the strips for various other purposes. The cattle owners use the strips for grazing animals; in low-lying areas, the road embankments are used for shelter during flood periods and trees often viewed as a hindrance. The farmers who worked the land adjacent to the strip often objected that trees would shade their crops and impede their access to the agricultural land near the strips.

Property rights have a significant bearing on resource use and environmental management (Perrings, 1995, p. 106). Property rights are not well defined and management responsibilities frequently devolve on several departments, which often work in a piecemeal fashion rather than in any rationally coordinated way (Alauddin and Tisdell, 1998).

12.2.5 Agrarian Relations and Property Rights

Land is of central importance to the social, political and economic life of rural Bangladesh. The process of growing landlessness and near-landlessness has not only marginalized the rural peasantry but also made the poor increasingly dependent on wage employment for their subsistence. While landlessness per se may not necessarily be a major problem if adequate income–generating opportunities for the landless are provided, the crux of the problem is that economic growth in Bangladesh, especially in the agricultural sector, has not been high enough gainfully to absorb the bulk of the landless population (Rahman, 1998).

Previous land reform policies have failed or have been only partially successful, because they have just taken a view of the land policy debate where it has primarily emphasized the redistributive aspects. Little attention was paid to the myriad of problems including, *inter alia*, major flaws in land record keeping, registration procedures, court processes and land administration. It is argued that an effective national land policy for Bangladesh must embrace productivity, equity land administration and environmental and ecological issues. Taken as a whole these will have an ameliorating effect both on the rural environment and on rural poverty.

12.2.6 Agrarian Change, Sustainable Resource Use and the Rural Environment

Bangladesh's environmental resources, more specifically land and water, are under considerable strain from the intensification and extension of agriculture to marginal areas, deforestation and loss of natural vegetation cover. Agricultural development processes primarily emphasizing increased grain production have not paid adequate attention to spillovers or opportunity costs.

Unsustainable extraction of groundwater, indiscriminate use of pesticides and unbalanced use of chemical fertilizers led to degradation of the environment and the ecosystem. There has been a significant decline in soil quality across all agro-ecological zones.

Given that Bangladesh has very little or no scope for expanding agricultural production through extensive cultivation, agricultural intensification must take into account the adverse environmental effects. The pollution and resource degradation will affect the survival of the next generation. Alternative ways should be developed to stop the indiscriminate use of agro-chemicals. Issues of environmental management warrant serious consideration, as the physical environment could become a limiting factor in sustaining future agricultural production. The signs are already in evidence (see for example, Pagiola, 1995; Asaduzzaman and Toufique, 1997; Alauddin, 1999c).

12.2.7 Agricultural Research and Extension

While both the research system and extension services have made significant contributions to agricultural development they suffer from vital weaknesses that emanate from lack of resources, lack of coordination and above all appropriate focus. These manifest themselves in duplication and the fragmented nature of research and extension services.

Increased investment on spending on agricultural research is critically important. Bangladesh needs to enhance its research capability to generate technologies consistent with socio-cultural endowments and agro-ecological conditions. The government needs to weigh up the relative merits of subsidies involved in fertilizer marketing, agricultural output marketing and agricultural research spending. Despite being dependent on agriculture Bangladesh suffers from an inadequate human-resource base in agricultural research and needs to invest more in researching and building up an expertise base (Reaz Ahmed, 2000; Alauddin, 2000).

Due to poor and inadequate linkages between research, extension and education, Bangladesh has not been able to derive the full benefits from strong international linkages. These have led to inefficiency in research resource allocation and transmission of research results both within Bangladesh and from international sources.

Bangladesh needs to switch from commodity-based research to farming systems-based research. Agricultural extension services and education need to be revamped accordingly. Farming systems research is an important factor in a country like Bangladesh. There are wide variations in the physical, social and economic factors that influence the way a farm is run. Farming system research is an approach to the new generation of agricultural technology for the family farms with resource limits. For this a thorough understanding of the environment which includes the biological, social, cultural, economic and institutional environment in which the farming system would operate needs to be set up. There should be a smooth interaction among the crop produced, animal and household subsystems. Then again there should be the right interaction of those subsystems with economic, social and institutional environments. The proper interactions among all the subsystems will result in the increase of overall productivity of the farming system, which in turn would take care of the welfare of individual farming families.

12.2.8 Agricultural Growth and Rural Poverty

This study takes a broader view of poverty and the poor than the conventional approach. Social poverty has a broader connotation than is consistent with a wider view of the development. Successive development plans of Bangladesh have focused on poverty alleviation. This notwithstanding, today nearly half the population live below the poverty line even though the percentage of population below the extreme poverty line has fallen somewhat. Available evidence indicates that Bangladesh has made little progress in respect of either capability poverty measure or the human poverty index. Since the mid-1980s, however, Bangladesh has made slow but steady progress in some socio-economic indicators of development such as adult literacy rates, life expectancy at birth and the infant mortality rate. Nevertheless, Bangladesh languishes toward the bottom of the ranks in a global context as well as in the South Asian context (Alauddin, 1999b).

Women in Bangladesh in general and rural areas in particular are over-represented in the ranks of the disadvantaged, the vulnerable and the poor. Women earn much less than men. Both in terms of the gender-related development measure and the gender empowerment measure Bangladesh performs poorly in the context of the developing world. Thus women's contribution in development has not been given due recognition.

In the conventional literature, poverty is portrayed as a cause of environmental degradation. The present study cautions against such a simplistic generalization and argues that the poverty-environment nexus is more complex and needs to be discussed taking cognizance of the underlying complexities of the process. The causation is not uni-directional running from poverty to environmental degradation but could be bi-directional. In Bangladesh, as elsewhere in the developing world this reality does not seem to have been fully appreciated. Furthermore, the role of women as managers and carers of the environment has not been given due recognition. Protection of the environment can be directly linked to the process of economic development, which can have significant employment-generating as well as poverty-reducing implications.

12.3 CHALLENGES AND PROSPECTS

Bangladesh faces formidable challenges in sustaining agricultural production to feed a growing population and extricating itself from a low-level equilibrium trap. The process of agricultural development to date has focused on maximizing output from land. It initially extended cultivation to marginal areas and, upon exhaustion of the possibility of the extensive margin, more than three decades ago Bangladesh resorted to the process of agricultural intensification. This entailed deforestation and reclaiming wastelands, through unbalanced and indiscriminate application of chemical fertilizers and other agro-chemicals. On the whole, therefore, Bangladesh's agricultural development to date has left a legacy of environmental degradation if not a significant destruction. Thus high environment intensity epitomizes the agricultural production process in Bangladesh.

It is well known that innovation in processes leads to an upward shift of the production function or a downward movement of the production isoquant (Koutsoyannis, 1979, p. 85). This implies that the same level of output can be produced from a smaller quantity of factor inputs or the same quantity of factor inputs can generate a higher amount of output. Following Hicks (1932) one could term all techniques designed to facilitate the substitution of the other inputs for labour as *labour-saving* and the ones designed to facilitate the substitution of other inputs for land as *land-saving* (Hayami and Ruttan, 1985, p. 75). In agriculture two kinds of technology generally correspond to this taxonomy. Mechanical technology is generally identified as being *labour-saving* while biological and chemical technology is identified as being *land-saving*. This is similar to the distinction between *labouresque* and *landesque* capital employed by Sen (1960, pp. 91–6; see also Hayami and Ruttan, 1985, p. 75 and p. 200). Assume a production process that treats environmental capital as a factor of production while all other inputs including man-made capital and labour including human capital is treated as a composite input (composite capital). Following Sen (1960) environmental capital-saving innovations can be termed as *environmentalesque*. In the absence of process innovation in *environmentalesque*-type *ceteris paribus* is likely to lead to deterioration in the quality of the physical environment. This in turn is likely to lead to a downward shift of the production function and an upward movement of the production isoquant. This implies that greater quantities of inputs are needed to maintain the level of output or from the same input quantity a smaller volume of output is likely to result.

This point can be pursued further. Hayami and Ruttan (1985, pp. 309–11) introduce the concept of 'internal land augmentation' and 'external land augmentation'. The former refers to a situation where qualitative improvement in land input takes place, for instance through irrigation, while the latter refers to a situation where cultivation is based on extensive margin. With abundant land resources, the frontier can be extended with little or no addition to the marginal cost. But beyond a certain point where the cultivation frontier is extended to marginal areas, cost of production at the margin can rise quite rapidly and the marginal cost curve is likely to become very steep. In the case of internal land augmentation, initial investment of, say, irrigation could be quite high so that the marginal cost curve in such a situation is likely to lie above the one for the external augmentation scenario. In the long run, because of qualitative improvements in land input marginal cost will fall.

It seems quite clear that there is an emerging factor proportions problem in Bangladesh somewhat analogous to the factor proportions problems in underdeveloped areas as analyzed by Eckaus (1955; see also Thirlwall 1994). Figure 12.1 depicts a hypothetical representation of the current and desirable patterns of environmental capital intensity of agricultural production in Bangladesh. The horizontal axis measures the environmental capital while man-made capital and human labour including human capital as a composite input is measured along the vertical axis. The flatter ray OD typically represents the current Bangladesh scenario as production is more environment-intensive given the high propensity to treat environment as a non-scarce or abundant factor or worse still as a 'free gift' of nature. The steeper ray OC on the other hand depicts a hypothetical desirable environment-intensity of agricultural production. Given the fragility of the physical environment, environmental resources in Bangladesh need to be valued more highly than at present.

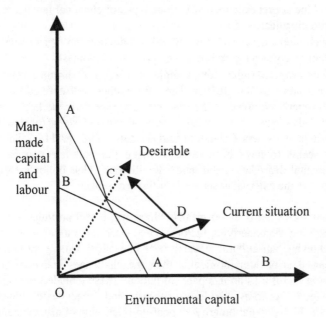

Figure 12.1   A hypothetical scenario portraying current and desirable environmental capital intensity in agricultural production in the context of Bangladesh

The failure to treat environment as an important element in the process of production stems from several directions: policy failure, property rights issues and market failure. These can be summed up as follows:

- Inappropriate technology policy – 'cereals only' for most of the last four decades even though there has been some technological change in non-cereal crops.
- Inadequate emphasis on agricultural R&D despite demonstrated high returns to R&D. Mass emigration of highly trained and experienced agricultural scientists (many with PhDs and with 10–20 years' research experience) to Australia and New Zealand has caused serious skill shortages.
- Inadequate input pricing policy, for example underground water remains an unpriced input leading to wasteful use. The owners of STWs and DTWs extract significant rent from the sale of underground water in order to irrigate lands of those who do not own the irrigation machinery. Thus a communal resource is to a significant extent being used for private gain.
- Inadequate support service for awareness building and sensitization regarding the appropriate mix of various types of chemical fertilizers and other agro-chemicals.
- Too much dependence of agricultural production on agro-chemicals rather than on conserving and re-using agricultural biomass.
- Inadequate property rights, for example in relation to shrimp farming in the coastal areas of Bangladesh. They are neither well defined nor can they be properly enforced as the *gher* owners, especially the larger ones, take full advantage of the weaker socio-economic status of the less organized land owners (Alauddin and Tisdell, 1998, p. 110). To date nothing seems to have been done to make the polluters pay for the environmental degradation and land rehabilitation. Thus policy measures to internalize the external costs are manifestly absent.

While the above list is by no means exhaustive, it still provides a useful aid to identifying the underlying factors. Bangladesh faces a daunting uphill task of achieving agricultural development consistent with a sustainable environment. It is no less formidable than the challenges that confronted Bangladesh at its birth as an independent nation. These included, *inter alia,* a war-ravaged economy, badly damaged and inadequate physical infrastructure, high population growth, pent-up frustration of historic neglect and prolonged economic deprivation of the masses of population, mass illiteracy, abject poverty, and poor health and sanitation. Bangladesh currently faces a highly degraded and depleted physical environment, population pressure on arable twice as high as in the late 1960s and environmental issues exacerbated by the arsenic crisis.

However, one needs to note among other things the following positive achievements:

- Several decades ago Bangladesh had very little experience in terms of skilled manpower, managerial skills or flexible political institutions to support massive and ambitious development programmes. While this problem still remains, the lessons of experience seem clear.

- Increase in adult literacy rate and female literacy rate
- Significant reduction in infant mortality rate
- Limited but steady empowerment of women through a combined effort of governmental and non-governmental organizations.
- The resilience of the people of Bangladesh to survive against seemingly insurmountable odds. Bangladesh seems to have transformed its food policies to free itself from the constant threat of famine (Raisuddin Ahmed, 2000). Bangladesh has come of age in managing natural disasters, for instance the 1998 flood, the most devastating in living memory.
- Network of roads and highways throughout the length and breadth of the country.

In the light of the above, Bangladesh is walking a tightrope as it strives for development with a view to raising the living standards of the masses of population. The environment–development nexus is at the crossroads. It is clear that the development process to date has stressed the ecology and environment to the limit. An agricultural development strategy compatible with a sustainable environment must, among other things, embrace the following:

- Greater investment in agricultural R&D especially on non-cereal crops – fruits, vegetables, pulses, oilseeds and spices
- Greater linkage between education, extension and research
- Topmost priority on developing highly skilled scientific manpower for agricultural research
- Greater emphasis on farming systems research than on individual commodities or crops
- Research on agricultural development on the basis of broad topography and soil types or agro-ecological zones
- Initiate research so that in the medium to long-term it is possible gradually to switch away from rice as a staple food to greater dependence than at present on fruits and vegetables which are generally less environment-intensive especially less water-consuming than rice
- Significant change in agricultural policy direction to switch away from concentration on crops at the expense of the non-crop component of the agricultural sector
- Increased resource allocation for awareness building and sensitization regarding use of agrochemicals *vis-à-vis* biomass conservation and use in agricultural production

- A pricing policy for use of underground water for irrigation and other environmental resources
- Introduce system of 'polluters pay' for environmental amelioration especially in coastal Bangladesh
- Emphasis on broad-based rural development including promotion of agro-based industries including cottage industries and handicrafts. This will create an environment for integrated rural development and employment opportunities and will put a brake on the exodus to the cities whose environment and infrastructure are bursting at the seams.
- Active marketing and promotion of cottage industries and handicrafts in foreign markets
- Create economic opportunities for the landless and the dispossessed in the rural areas. The recent government initiatives such as 'Ashrayan' (The Shelter) to build clusters of settlements with integrated farming arrangements and 'Ghare Fera' (homecoming) with micro-credit as the core element to encourage return migration from urban to rural areas are steps in the right direction, the magnitude of the problem notwithstanding
- Environmental accounting needs to be given serious consideration in order to be able quantitatively to assess the damage inflicted on the environment and to identify the divergence between conventional GDP measures and environment-adjusted GDP measures
- The issue of environmental management is of critical importance. Where there is evidence of market failure and government failure (Asaduzzaman, 1998) a communitarian solution in which the community becomes the agent for managing and ensuring the equity and sustainability of the common resources (Sobhan, 1998) is called for.

Bibliography

Abdullah, A.A. (1976), 'Land Reform and Agrarian Change in Bangladesh', *Bangladesh Development Studies*, **4** (1), 67–114.

Abdullah, A.A. (1978), 'Formulating a Viable Land Policy for Bangladesh – What Do We Need to Know?', *Bangladesh Development Studies*, **6** (4), 355–86.

Abdullah, A.A. and Shahabuddin, Q. (1997), 'Recent Developments in Bangladesh Agriculture: Crop Sector', in R. Sobhan (ed.), *Growth or Stagnation? A Review of Bangladesh's Development 1996*, Dhaka: Centre for Policy Dialogue and University Press Ltd., pp. 221–52.

Abdullah, A.A., Hasanullah, M. and Shahabuddin, Q. (1996), 'Bangladesh Agriculture in the Nineties: Some Selected Issues', in R. Sobhan (ed.), *Experiences with Economic Reform: A Review of Bangladesh's Development 1995*, Dhaka: Centre for Policy Dialogue and University Press Ltd., pp. 127–79.

Abdullah, A.A., Hossain, Mosharaff and Nations, R. (1976), 'Agrarian Structure and the IRDP – Preliminary Considerations', *Bangladesh Development Studies*, **4** (2), 209–66.

Abed, F.H. (1998), 'Empowering the Poor of South Asia', in A.A. Ahmed et al. (eds), *Environment and Poverty: Key Linkages for Global Sustainable Development*, Dhaka: University Press Ltd., pp. 98–9.

ACO (1962), *Pakistan Census of Agriculture 1969: Final Report – East Pakistan*, vol. I, part I, Karachi: Agricultural Census of Organisation, Ministry of Food and Agriculture, Government of Pakistan.

ADB/NACA (1996), *Aquaculture Sustainability Action Plan, Regional Study and Workshop on Aquaculture Sustainability and the Environment (RETA 5534)*, Asian Development Bank and the Network of Aquaculture Centres in Asia-Pacific, Bangkok, Thailand: Network of Aquaculture Centres in Asia-Pacific.

Agarwal, B. (1986), 'Women, Poverty and Agricultural Growth in India', *Journal of Peasant Studies*, **13** (4), 165–220.

Agarwal, B. (1989), 'Rural Women, Poverty and Natural Resources: Sustenance, Sustainability and Struggle for Change', *Economic and Political Weekly*, **24** (3), ws46–ws65.

Ahmad, Q.K. and Hasanuzzaman, S.M. (1998), 'Agricultural Growth and Environment', in R. Faruqee (ed.), *Bangladesh Agriculture in the 21st Century*, Dhaka: University Press Ltd., pp. 81–108.

Ahmed, M. (1988) *Bangladesh Agriculture: Towards Self-Sufficiency*, Dhaka: Winrock International.

Ahmed, Raisuddin (1998), 'Assessing Past Agricultural Policies', in R. Faruqee (ed.), *Bangladesh Agriculture in the 21st Century*, Dhaka: University Press Ltd. 49–66.

Ahmed, Raisuddin (2000), *Out of the Shadow of Famine: Evolving Food Markets and Food Policy in Bangladesh*, Washington, DC: International Food Policy Research Institute.

Ahmed, Reaz (2000) 'Agri-Research Ignored', *Daily Star*, 23 June.

Ahooja-Patel, K. (1996), 'Emerging Gender Inequalities within Asia', in J. Lele and W. Tettey (eds), *Who Pays for Development: Women, Environment and Popular Movement*, Aldershot, UK: Dartmouth, pp. 124–50.

Alagarswami, K. (1995), 'India', Country Paper, in FAO/NACA, Regional Study and Workshop on the Environmental Assessment and Management of Aquaculture Development (TCP/RAS/2253), *NACA Environment and Aquaculture Development Series*, No. 1 Bangkok, Thailand: Network of Aquaculture Centres in Asia-Pacific, pp. 141–86.

Alam, J. (1997), 'Recent Developments in Bangladesh Agriculture: Non-Crop Sector', in R. Sobhan (ed.), *Growth or Stagnation? A Review of Bangladesh's Development 1996*, Dhaka: Centre for Policy Dialogue and University Press Ltd., pp. 253–86.

Alauddin, M. (1981), 'Agricultural Research Organization and Policy in Bangladesh', *Bangladesh Journal of Agricultural Economics,* 4(2), 1–24.

Alauddin, M. (1982), 'Inputs and Returns to Agricultural Research in Bangladesh', *Journal of Management, Business and Economics*, 8 (2), 130–147.

Alauddin, M. (1997), 'Readymade Garment Industry of Bangladesh and Changing Structure of Foreign Trade', in K.C. Roy, H.C. Blomqvist, and I. Hossain (eds), *Development That Lasts*, New Delhi: New Age International, pp. 99–113.

Alauddin, M. (1999a), 'Trade Among South Asian Nations: Complementarities and Competitiveness', in M. Alauddin and S. Hasan (eds), *Development, Governance and the Environment in South Asia: A Focus on Bangladesh*, London: Macmillan, pp. 125–39.

Alauddin, M. (1999b), 'South Asia's Experiences, Challenges and Prospects in Global Context', in M. Alauddin and S. Hasan (eds), *Development, Governance and the Environment in South Asia: A Focus on Bangladesh*, London: Macmillan, pp. 315–31.

Alauddin, M. (1999c), 'Environmentalising Economic Development in South Asia: Achievements and Prospects', A Paper presented at the Conference on Second Generation Reforms in India organized by the Australia South Asia Research Centre, Australian National University, Canberra and Madras School of Economics, Chennai, India, December 8–10.

Alauddin, M. (2000), 'Land Productivity and Environmental Issues', Note prepared for Roundtable Discussion with Mr Shah A.M.S. Kibria, Finance Minister, the Government of Bangladesh on Eco-friendly Budget organized by *Poribesh Rokkha Sapath* (Porosh), Bangladesh Institute of Development Studies (BIDS), Coalition of Environmental NGOs (CEN), Bangladesh Centre for Advanced Studies (BCAS), and *Prothom Alo*, Dhaka, 26 April 2000.

Alauddin, M. and Hamid, M.A. (1996), 'Economic, Social and Environmental Implications of Shrimp Farming in Bangladesh: An Overview of Issues and Agenda for Research', in M. Alauddin, and S. Hasan (eds), *Bangladesh: Economy, People, and the Environment*, Economics Conference Monograph Series 1, Brisbane, Australia: Department of Economics, The University of Queensland, pp. 278–99.

Alauddin, M. and Hamid, M.A. (1999) 'Coastal Aquaculture in South Asia: Experiences and Lessons', in M. Alauddin and S. Hasan (eds), *Development, Governance and the Environment in South Asia: A Focus on Bangladesh*, London: Macmillan, pp. 289–99.

Alauddin, M. and Tisdell, C.A. (1986), 'Bangladeshi and International Agricultural Research: Administrative and Economic Issues', *Agricultural Administration*, **21** (1), 1–20.

Alauddin, M. and Tisdell, C.A. (1991), *The Green Revolution and Economic Development: The Process and Its Impact in Bangladesh*, London: Macmillan.

Alauddin, M. and Tisdell, C.A. (1995), 'Labour Absorption and Agricultural Development in Bangladesh: Prospects and Predicaments', *World Development*, **23** (2), 281–97.

Alauddin, M. and Tisdell, C.A. (1998), *The Environment and Economic Development in South Asia: An Overview Concentrating on Bangladesh*, London: Macmillan.

Alauddin, M., Mujeri, M.K. and Tisdell, C.A. (1995), 'Technology–Employment–Environment Linkages and the Rural Poor of Bangladesh: Insights From Farm-Level Data', in I. Ahmed and J. A. Doeleman (eds), *Beyond Rio: The Environmental Crisis and Sustainable Livelihoods in the Third World*, London: Macmillan, pp. 221–55.

Ali, M.O. (1994), 'Trees and Environment', in A.A. Rahman, R. Haider, S. Huq, and E.G. Jansen (eds), *Environment and Development*, Vol. 2, Dhaka: University Press Ltd., pp. 217–39.

Ali, M.Y. (1991), *Towards Sustainable Development: Fisheries Resources of Bangladesh*, Dhaka: Bangladesh Ministry of Environment and Forest and National Conservation Strategy Secretariat.

Arndt, T.M., Dalrymple, D.G. and Ruttan, V.W. (eds) (1977), *Resource Allocation and Productivity in National and International Agricultural Research*, Minneapolis: University of Minnesota Press.

Asaduzzaman, M. (1998), 'When Both Market and the State Fail: The Crisis of Solid Waste Management in Urban Bangladesh', in R. Sobhan (ed.), *Crisis in Governance: A Review of Bangladesh's Development 1997*, Dhaka: Centre for Policy Dialogue and University Press Ltd., pp. 383–400.

Asaduzzaman, M. and Toufique, K.A. (1997), 'Rice and Fish: Environmental Dilemmas of Development in Bangladesh', in R. Sobhan (ed.), *Growth or Stagnation? A Review of Bangladesh's Development 1996*, Dhaka: Centre for Policy Dialogue and University Press Ltd., pp. 447–94.

ASCC (1995), *Asian Shrimp News*, Third Quarter, Issue No. 23, Bangkok: Asian Shrimp Culture Council.

Banik, A. (1990), 'Changes in the Agrarian Structure in Bangladesh: 1960–84', *Bangladesh Development Studies*, **18** (4), 55–64.

Bardhan, P.K. (1984), *Land, Labor and Rural Poverty: Essays in Development Economics*, New Delhi: Oxford University Press.

BBS (1972), *Master Survey of Agriculture in Bangladesh*, (7th Round, 2nd Phase), Dacca: Bangladesh Bureau of Statistics.

BBS (1975), *Statistical Digest of Bangladesh 1973*, Dacca: Bangladesh Bureau of Statistics.

BBS (1976), *Agricultural Production Levels of Bangladesh 1947–72*, Dacca: Bangladesh Bureau of Statistics.

BBS (1979), *1979 Statistical Yearbook of Bangladesh*, Dacca: Bangladesh Bureau of Statistics.

BBS (1980), *Yearbook of Agricultural Statistics of Bangladesh*, Dacca: Bangladesh Bureau of Statistics.

BBS (1981a), *1980 Statistical Yearbook of Bangladesh*, Dacca: Bangladesh Bureau of Statistics.

BBS (1981b), *Report on the Agricultural Census of Bangladesh 1977 (National Volume)*, Dacca: Bangladesh Bureau of Statistics.

BBS (1982), *1982 Statistical Yearbook of Bangladesh*, Dhaka: Bangladesh Bureau of Statistics.

BBS (1984a), *Monthly Statistical Bulletin of Bangladesh*, Dhaka: Bangladesh Bureau of Statistics, March.

BBS (1984b), *1983–84 Statistical Yearbook of Bangladesh*, Dhaka: Bangladesh Bureau of Statistics.

BBS (1985a), *1983–84 Yearbook of Agricultural Statistics of Bangladesh*, Dhaka: Bangladesh Bureau of Statistics.

BBS (1985b), *1984–85 Statistical Yearbook of Bangladesh*, Dhaka: Bangladesh Bureau of Statistics.

BBS (1985c), *1984–85 Yearbook of Agricultural Statistics of Bangladesh*, Dhaka: Bangladesh Bureau of Statistics.

BBS (1986a), *Monthly Statistical Bulletin of Bangladesh*, Dhaka: Bangladesh Bureau of Statistics, May.

BBS (1986b), *The Bangladesh Census of Agriculture and Livestock: 1983–84, Volume I, Structure of Agricultural Holdings and Livestock Population*, Dhaka: Bangladesh Bureau of Statistics.

BBS (1986c), *The Bangladesh Census of Agriculture and Livestock: 1983–84, Volume II, Cropping Patterns*, Dhaka: Bangladesh Bureau of Statistics.

BBS (1986d), *Monthly Statistical Bulletin of Bangladesh*, Dhaka: Bangladesh Bureau of Statistics, November.

BBS (1988a), *1987 Yearbook of Agricultural Statistics of Bangladesh*, Dhaka: Bangladesh Bureau of Statistics.

BBS (1988b), *Report of the Bangladesh Household Expenditure Survey 1985–86*, Dhaka: Bangladesh Bureau of Statistics.

BBS (1991), *Report of the Household Expenditure Survey 1988–89*, Dhaka: Bangladesh Bureau of Statistics.

BBS (1993a), *1992 Yearbook of Agricultural Statistics of Bangladesh*, Dhaka: Bangladesh Bureau of Statistics

BBS (1993b), *Twenty Years of National Accounting of Bangladesh*, Dhaka: Bangladesh Bureau of Statistics.

BBS (1996), *1995 Statistical Yearbook of Bangladesh*, Dhaka: Bangladesh Bureau of Statistics.

BBS (1997a), *Preliminary Report – Agriculture Census 1996*, Dhaka: Bangladesh Bureau of Statistics.

BBS (1997b), *1995 Yearbook of Agricultural Statistics of Bangladesh*, Dhaka: Bangladesh Bureau of Statistics.

BBS (1997c), *Summary Report of the Household Expenditure Survey 1995–96*, Dhaka: Bangladesh Bureau of Statistics.

BBS (1998a), *Household Expenditure Survey 1995–96*, Dhaka: Bangladesh Bureau of Statistics.

BBS (1998b), *1997 Statistical Yearbook of Bangladesh*, Dhaka: Bangladesh Bureau of Statistics.

BBS (1999a), *Bangladesh Compendium of Environment Statistics 1997*, Dhaka: Bangladesh Bureau of Statistics.

BBS (1999b), *Monthly Statistical Bulletin of Bangladesh*, Dhaka: Bangladesh Bureau of Statistics, April.

Beneria, L. and Sen, G. (1982), 'Class and Gender Inequalities and Women's Role in Economic Development: Theoretical and Practical Implications', *Feminist Studies*, **8** (1), 157–76.

Bernstein, H. (1992), 'Poverty and the Poor', in Bernstein, H., Crow, B. and

Johnson, H. (eds), *Rural Livelihoods: Crises and Responses*, London: Oxford University Press, pp. 13–26.

BFFEA (Bangladesh Frozen Foods Exporters Association) (1995), Leaflet, Dhaka: BFFEA.

Bifani, P. (1992), 'Environmental Degradation in Rural Areas', in A.S. Bhalla (ed.), *Environment, Employment and Development*, Geneva: International Labour Office, pp. 99–120.

Biggs, S.D. and Clay, E.J. (1981), 'Sources of Innovation in Agricultural Technology', *World Development*, 9 (4), 321–36.

Black, C.E. (1966), *The Dynamics of Modernization: A Study in Comparative History*, New York: Harper and Row.

Bose, S.R (1970), 'East–West Contrast in Pakistan's Agriculture', E.A.G. Robinson, and M. Kidron (eds), *Economic Development in South Asia*, London: Macmillan, pp. 127–46.

Bowonder, B., Prasad, S.S.R. and Unni, N.V.M. (1988), 'Dynamics of Fuel Prices in India: Policy Implications', *World Development*, 16 (10), 1213–29.

Boyce, J.K. (1987), *Agrarian Impasse in Bengal: Institutional Constraints to Technological Change*, Oxford: Oxford University Press.

BPC (1973), *The First Five Year Plan 1973–78*, Dhaka: Bangladesh Planning Commission.

BPC (1978), *The Two Year Plan 1978–80*, Dhaka: Bangladesh Planning Commission.

BPC (1980), *The Second Five Year Plan 1973–78*, Dhaka: Bangladesh Planning Commission.

BPC (1985), *The Third Five Year Plan 1985–90*, Dhaka: Bangladesh Planning Commission.

BPC (1991), *The Fourth Five Year Plan 1990–95*, Dhaka: Bangladesh Planning Commission.

BPC (1998), *The Fifth Five Year Plan 1997–2002*, Dhaka: Bangladesh Planning Commission.

Bramer, H. (1997), *Agricultural Development Possibilities in Bangladesh*, Dhaka: University Press Ltd.

Brandon, C. (1998), 'Environmental Degradation and Agricultural Growth', in R. Faruqee (ed.), *Bangladesh Agriculture in the 21st Century*, Dhaka: University Press Ltd., pp. 109–18.

Cain, M. (1983), 'Landlessness in India and Bangladesh: A Critical Review of National Data Sources', *Economic Development and Cultural Change*, 32 (1), 149–68.

CGIAR (1981), *Second Review of the CGIAR*, Washington, DC: Consultative Group on International Agricultural Research.

Chakraborty, D. (1995), 'Arsenic in Drinking Water in West Bengal *vis-a–vis* Bangladesh', a paper presented in a conference held in NIPSOM,

Dhaka, August.

Chakravarty, S. (1990), 'Development Strategies for Growth with Equity: The South Asian Experience', *Asian Development Review*, **8** (1), 133–59.

Chambers, R. and Leach, M. (1989), 'Trees as Savings and Security for the Rural Poor', *World Development*, **17** (3), 329–42.

Chambers, R.G. (1987) 'Sustainable Livelihoods, Environment and Development: Putting Poor Rural People First', I.D.S. Discussion Paper No. 240, University of Sussex, Brighton.

Chambers, R.G. (1988), *Poverty in India: Concepts, Research and Reality*, Discussion Paper 241, Institute of Development Studies, University of Sussex, Brighton.

Chambers, R.G. (1998), 'Poverty and Livelihoods: Whose Reality Counts? An Overview', in A.A. Ahmed et al. (eds), *Environment and Poverty: Key Linkages for Global Sustainable Development*, Dhaka: University Press Ltd., p. 85.

Chaudhury, R.H. and Ahmed, N.R. (1980), *Female Status in Bangladesh*, Dhaka: Bangladesh Institute of Development Studies.

Christensen, L.R. and Jorgenson, D.W. (1969), 'The Measurement of US Capital Input, 1929–1967', *Review of Income and Wealth*, **15** (4), 293–320.

Christensen, L.R. and Jorgenson, D.W. (1970), 'The Measurement of US Real Product and Real Factor Input, 1929–1967', *Review of Income and Wealth*, **16** (1), 19–50.

Crow, B. (1992), 'Understanding Famine and Hunger' in T. Allen and A. Thomas (eds), *Poverty and Development in the 1990s*, London: Oxford University Press, pp. 15–33.

Crow, B., Lindquist, A. and Wilson, D. (1995), *Sharing the Ganges: The Politics and Technology of River Development*, Dhaka: University Press Ltd.

Daily Independent (2000) 'Rice Production Achieves Target Ahead of Schedule', 1 June.

Dantwala, M.L. (1973), 'From Stagnation to Growth: Relative Roles of Technology and Economic Policy and Agrarian Institutions', in R.T. Shand (ed.), *Technical Change in Asian Agriculture*, Canberra: Australian National University Press, pp. 259–81.

David, W.P. (1993), *Environmental Impacts of Declining Groundwater Levels*, Dhaka: Ministry of Agriculture/UNDP/FAO.

Dey, M.M. and Evenson, R.E. (1991), *The Economic Impact of Rice Research in Bangladesh*, Economic Growth Center Discussion Paper, Yale University, New Haven, CT.

Dey, M.M., Miah, M.N.I, Mustafi, B.A.A. and Hossain, Mahabub (1996), 'Rice Research Constraints in Bangladesh: Implications for Further Research Priorities', in R. Evenson, R.W. Herdt and Mahabub Hossain (eds), *Rice Research in Asia: Progress and Priorities*, Oxford, UK: CAB International, pp. 179–91.

Eckaus, R.S. (1955), 'The Factor Proportions Problem in Underdeveloped Areas', *American Economic Review*, **45** (4), 539–65.

EPBB (1995), *Exports from Bangladesh 1972–73 to 1993–94*, Dhaka: Export Promotion Bureau of Bangladesh.

EPBS (1969), *Statistical Digest of East Pakistan*, no.6, Dacca: East Pakistan Bureau of Statistics.

ESCAP (1988), *Coastal Environmental Management Plan for Bangladesh*, Volume II: Final Report, Bangkok: United Nations Economic and Social Commission for Asia and the Pacific.

Evenson, R..E. and Pray, C.E. (eds) (1991), *Research and Productivity in Asian Agriculture*, Ithaca and London: Cornell University Press.

Faaland, J. and Parkinson, J.R. (1976), *Bangladesh: The Test Case of Development*, London: C. Hurst and Co.

FAO (1978) 'Agricultural Research in Developing Countries', Vol. 1, Research Institutions, Rome: Food and Agricultural Organization.

FAO (1994a), 'Aquaculture Production 1986–1992', FAO Fisheries Circular No. 815, Rev.6, Rome: Food and Agriculture Organisation.

FAO (1994b), 'Mangrove Forest Management Guidelines', FAO Forestry Paper No. 117, Rome: Food and Agriculture Organisation.

FAO (1995), 'Review of the State of World Fishery Resources: Aquaculture', FAO Fisheries Circular No. 886, Rome: Food and Agriculture Organisation.

FAO/NACA (1995), 'Survey, and Analysis of Aquaculture Development Research Priorities and Capacities in Asia', FAO Fisheries Circular No. 930, Rome: Food and Agriculture Organisation.

Farmer, B.H (ed.) (1977), *Green Revolution? Technology and Change in Rice Growing Areas of Tamil Nadu and Sri Lanka*, London: Macmillan.

Feld, S.A. (1995), *Environmental Impacts of Accelerated Transformation to Minor Irrigated Agriculture in Bangladesh*, Ministry of Agriculture/ United Nations Development Programme/Food and Agriculture Organization of the United Nations.

Gain, P. (ed.) (1998), *Bangladesh: Land, Forest and Forest People*, Dhaka: Society of Environment and Human Development.

GB (1940) *Report of the Land Revenue Commission* (Sir Francis Flood Chairman), in six volumes, Alipore: Bengal Government Press, Government of Bengal.

Gill, G.J. (1981), 'Operational Funding Constraints on Agricultural Research in Bangladesh', BARC Agricultural Economics and Rural Science Papers No. 9, Dhaka; Bangladesh Agricultural Research Council.

Gill, G.J. (1983), 'Agricultural Research in Bangladesh: Costs and Returns', Dhaka; Bangladesh Agricultural Research Council.

GOB (1998) *Bangladesh: Economic Review 1998*, Dhaka: Finance Division, Ministry of Finance, Government of the People's Republic of Bangladesh.

GOI (1998) *Agricultural Statistics at a Glance*, New Delhi: Directorate of Economics and Statistics, Department of Agriculture and Co-operation, Ministry of Agriculture, Government of India.

Goldburg, R.J. (1996), 'Benefits and Risks of a Growing Aquaculture Industry', http://www.edf.org/pubs/EDF–Letter/1996Jan/1_aquacult.html

GOP (1951), *Pakistan Census of Population 1951, Vol.2, East Pakistan*, Karachi: Government of Pakistan.

Goulet, D. (1971), *The Cruel Choice: A New Concept in the Theory of Development*, New York: Atheneum.

Gujarati, D. (1995), *Basic Econometrics*, New York: McGraw-Hill.

Hambrey, J. (1999), 'The Mangrove Questions', http://www.shrimpfarming/org/mangrove/mangrove_quest.htm.

Hamid, M.A. and Alauddin, M. (1996), 'The Shrimp Industry and Employment Generation in Bangladesh', in M. Alauddin and S. Hasan (eds), *Bangladesh: Economy, People and the Environment*, Economics Conference Monograph Series 1, Brisbane, Australia: Department of Economics, The University of Queensland, pp. 301–321.

Hamid, M.A. and Alauddin, M. (1998), 'Coming out of Their Homesteads? Employment for Rural Women in Shrimp Aquaculture in Coastal Bangladesh', *International Journal of Social Economics*, 25 (2–4), 314–37.

Hamid, S. (1994), 'Non-Market Work and National Income: The case of Bangladesh', *Bangladesh Development Studies*, 22 (2–3), 1–48.

Haq, M. (1963), *The Strategy of Economic Planning*, Karachi: Oxford University Press.

Hayami, Y. and Ruttan, V.W. (1985) *Agricultural Development: An International Perspective*, Baltimore, MD: Johns Hopkins University Press.

Hicks, J.R. (1932), *The Theory of Wages*, London: Macmillan.

Hossain, M. Ismail., Rahman, M.A. and Rahman, M. (1997), 'Current External Sector Performance and Emerging Issues', in R. Sobhan (ed.), *Growth or Stagnation? A Review of Bangladesh's Development 1996*, Dhaka: Centre for Policy Dialogue and University Press Ltd., pp. 161–220.

Hossain, Mahabub (1984), 'Agricultural Development in Bangladesh: A Historical Perspective', *Bangladesh Development Studies*, 12 (4), 30–57.

Hossain, Mahabub (1986), 'A Note on the Trend of Landlessness in Bangladesh', *Bangladesh Development Studies*, 14 (2), 93–100.

Hossain, Mahabub (1988), *Credit for Alleviation of Rural Poverty: The Grameen Bank in Bangladesh*, Washington DC: International Food Policy Research Institute, Research Report No. 65.

Hossain, Mosharaff (1991), *Agriculture in Bangladesh: Performance, Problems and Prospects*, Dhaka: University Press Ltd.

Hossain, Mosharaff (1994) 'Self-sufficiency in Food: Myth or Reality?' *Holiday*, May 6.

Hossain, Mosharaff, Islam, A.T.M and Saha, S.K. (1987), *Floods in Bangladesh: Natural Disasters and People's Survival*, Dhaka: Universities Research Institute.

Hussain, M.Z. (1990), *Sustainable Development of Forest Resources of Bangladesh*, An output of NRIC under IUCN/NORAD Support, Dhaka: Multi-disciplinary Action Research Centre.

Hussain, S.T (1989), 'Economic Development with and without Land Reform in Bangladesh', *Bangladesh Development Studies*, **17** (3), 119–47.

Ishaque, H.S.M. (1946), *Agricultural Statistics by Plot-to-Plot Enumeration in Bengal, 1944–45, Part I*, Alipore: Bengal Government Press, Government of Bengal.

Islam, A. (1993), *Soil Resources and Irrigated Agriculture in Bangladesh*, Dhaka: Ministry of Agriculture/ United Nations Development Programme/ Food and Agricultural Organisation of the United Nations.

Islam, M.M. (1978), *Bengal Agriculture 1920–1946: A Quantitative Study*, Cambridge: Cambridge University Press.

Islam, N. (1974), 'The State and Prospects of the Bangladesh Economy', in E.A.G. Robinson and K.B. Griffin (eds), *The Economic Development of Bangladesh within a Socialist Framework*, London: Macmillan, pp. 1–15.

Islam, R. (1998), 'Linkages between Environment, Poverty and Employment: A Developing Country Perspective', in A.A. Ahmed et al. (eds), *Environment and Poverty: Key Linkages for Global Sustainable Development*, Dhaka: University Press Ltd., p.84.

Jahan, K. and Hossain, Mosharaff (1998), *Nature and Extent of Malnutrition in Bangladesh: Bangladesh National Nutrition Survey, 1995–96*, Dhaka, University of Dhaka: Institute of Nutrition and Food Science (*Part I* and *Part II*).

Jahan, N. (1996), 'Agrarian Change and Rural Poverty in Bangladesh', in M. Alauddin and S. Hasan (eds), *Bangladesh: Economy, People and the Environment*, Economics Conference Monograph Series 1, Brisbane, Australia: Department of Economics, The University of Queensland, pp. 83–106.

Jahan, N. (1998), *Changing Agricultural Productivity in Bangladesh: Its Nature and Implications for Poverty, Women, Off-Farm Employment and the Environment*, PhD thesis, Brisbane, Australia: Department of Economics, The University of Queensland.

Jahan, N. and Alauddin, M. (1996a), 'Have Women Lost Out in the Development Process? Some Evidence from Rural Bangladesh', *International Journal of Social Economics*, **23** (4–6), 370–90.

Jahan, N. and Alauddin, M. (1996b), 'Total Factor Productivity Growth in Bangladesh Agriculture: An Analysis of the Crop Sector', Discussion Paper No.187, Brisbane: Department of Economics, University of Queensland.

Jahan, N. and Alauddin, M. (1999), ''Women and the Environment with Special Reference to Rural Bangladesh', in M. Alauddin and S. Hasan (eds), *Development, Governance and the Environment in South Asia: A Focus on Bangladesh*, London: Macmillan, pp. 301-13.

Jahan, N., Alauddin, M. and Tisdell, C.A. (1999), 'Structural Reforms in Bangladesh: Their Impact on Efficiency in Resource Use, Equity and Environment' in R.T. Shand (ed.), *Economic Liberalisation in South Asia*, New Delhi: Macmillan, pp. 436–64.

Jahan, R. (1972), *Pakistan: Failure in National Integration*, New York: Columbia University Press.

Jayasinghe, J.M.P.K. (1995), 'Sri Lanka', Country Paper, in FAO/NACA (1995b), pp. 357-76.

Jodha, N.S. (1988), 'Poverty Debate in India: A Minority View', *Economic and Political Weekly*, **23** (45–47), 2421–28.

Jones, S. (1984), 'Agrarian Structure and Agricultural Innovation in Bangladesh: Panimara Village, Dhaka District', in T.P. Bayliss-Smith and S. Wanmali (eds), *Understanding Green Revolutions: Agrarian Change and Development Planning in South Asia*, Cambridge: Cambridge University Press, pp. 194–211.

JU (1994), 'Arsenic in Ground Water in Six Districts of West Bengal, India: The Biggest Arsenic Calamity in the World', Calcutta: Jadavpur University, School of Environmental Studies.

Kabeer, N. (1989), 'Monitoring Poverty as if Gender Mattered', Discussion Paper 255, Institute of Development Studies, University of Sussex, Brighton.

Kabeer, N. (1991), 'Gender Dimensions of Rural Poverty: Analysis from Bangladesh', *Journal of Peasant Studies*, **18** (2), 241–62.

Karim, Z. and Iqbal, A. (1997), 'Climate Change: Implications on Bangladesh Agriculture and Food Security', *Journal of Remote Sensing and Environment*, **1**, 71–83.

Karmel, P.H. and Polasek, M. (1970), *Applied Statistics for Economists*, Melbourne: Sir Issac Pitman (Aust.), Pty. Ltd.

Kashem, A. (1996), '*Chingri Chashe Biplabattak Utpadan ebong Raptani Aye* [Revolutionary production in shrimp farming and export income]', *The Daily Ittefaq*, 25 February (*in Bangla*).

Khan, A. R. (1972), *The Economy of Bangladesh*, London: Macmillan.

Khan, Q.M. (1985), 'A Model of Endowment-Constrained Demand for Food in an Agricultural Economy with Empirical Applications to Bangladesh', *World Development*, **13** (9), 1055–65.

Khuda, B. (1982), *The Use of Time and Underemployment in Rural Bangladesh*, Dhaka: University of Dhaka.

Koutsoyannis, A. (1979), *Modern Microeconomics*, London: Macmillan.

Lele, J. (1996), 'Introduction: Searching for Development Alternatives: Class, Gender and Environment in Asian Economic Growth' in J. Lele and W. Tettey (eds), *Asia – Who Pays for Growth: Women, Environment and Popular Movement*, Aldershot, UK: Darmouth, pp.1–37.

Lele, S. (1991) 'Sustainable Development: A Critical Review', *World Development*, **19** (3), 607–21.

Lewis, W.A. (1966), *Development Planning: The Essentials of Economic Policy*, London: Allen and Unwin.

Lockwood, G.S. (1997), 'World Shrimp Production with Environmental and Social Accountability: A Perspective and a Proposal', *World Aquaculture*, **28** (3), 52–55.

Lucien-Brun, H. (1997), 'Evolution of World Shrimp Production: Fisheries and Aquaculture', *World Aquaculture*, **28** (4), 21–33.

Mahmood, N. (1986), *Effects of Shrimp Farming and Other Impacts on Mangrove of Bangladesh*, Bangkok: IPFC Workshop.

Mahtab, F. and Karim, Z. (1992), 'Population and Agricultural Land Use: Towards a Sustainable Food Production System in Bangladesh', *Ambio*, **20** (1), 50–55.

Majumder, P.P. and Zohir, S.C. (1994), 'Dynamics of Wage Employment: A Case of Employment in the Garment Industry', *Bangladesh Development Studies*, **22** (3), 179–216.

Market Asia (1995), 'U.S. Market for Frozen Shrimp Grows Rapidly', **2** (2), http://www.milcom.com/rap/v22/shrimp.html.

Mazid, M.A. (1995), 'Bangladesh', Country Paper, in FAO/NACA, Regional Study and Workshop on the Environmental Assessment and Management of Aquaculture Development (TCP/RAS/2253), *NACA Environment and Aquaculture Development Series*, No. 1 Bangkok, Thailand: Network of Aquaculture Centres in Asia-Pacific, pp. 61–82.

McGillvray, M. (1991), 'The Human Development Index: Yet Another Composite Development Indicator?', *World Development*, **19** (10), 1461–8.

Meier, G.M. (ed.) (1984), *Leading Issues in Economic Development*, New York: Oxford University Press.

Mellor, J.W. (1994) 'Review of *The "Green Revolution" and Economic Development: The Process and Its Impact in Bangladesh*, London: Macmillan 1991, xxi + 322pp.', *Economic Development and Cultural Change*, **42** (3), 683–8.

Menasveta, P. (1997), 'Mangrove Destruction and Shrimp Culture Systems', *World Aquaculture*, **28** (4), 36–42.

Mosemann, A. H. *et al.* (1980), *Bangladesh Agricultural Research System*, Dhaka: Bangladesh Agricultural Research Council.

MPO (1986), *Final Report (Vols. I–III)*, Dhaka: Master Plan Organisation.

Myrdal, G. (1968), *Asian Drama: An Inquiry into Poverty of Nations*, London: Penguin.

NFB (1999), 'Depletion of 13 wildlives harming bio-diversity', News From Bangladesh, http//:www.bangladesh–web.com/news, November 9. org/mangrove/mangrove_quest.htm

Ostrom, E. (1990), *Governing the Commons: The Evolution of Institutions for Common Actions*, Cambridge: Cambridge University Press.

Pagiola, S. (1995), *Environmental and Natural Resource Degradation in Intensive Agriculture in Bangladesh*, Land, Water and Natural Habitats Division, Washington, DC: World Bank.

Papanek, G.F. (1967) *Pakistan's Development: Social Goals and Private Incentives*, Cambridge, MA: Harvard University Press.

Pearson, R. (1992), 'Gender Matters in Development', in T. Allen and A. Thomas (eds), *Poverty and Development in the 1990s*, London: Oxford University Press, pp. 291–312.

Perrings, C. (1995), 'Incentives for Sustainable Development in Sub-Saharan Africa', in I. Ahmed and J. A. Doeleman (eds), *Beyond Rio: Environmental Crisis and Sustainable Livelihoods in the Third World*, London: Macmillan, pp. 95–132.

PPC (1970), *Report of the Panel of Economists for the Fourth Five-Year Plan*, Islamabad: Pakistan Planning Commission.

Pray, C.E. and Ahmed, Z. (1991), 'Research and Agricultural Productivity Growth in Bangladesh', in R.E. Evenson, and C.E. Pray (eds), *Research and Productivity in Asian Agriculture*, Ithaca and London: Cornell University Press, pp. 113–32.

Pray, C.E. and Anderson, J.R. (1985), *Bangladesh and the CGIAR Centers: A Study of their Collaboration in Agricultural Research*, CGIAR Study Paper No. 8, Washington, DC: World Bank.

Quasem, M.A. (1986), 'The Impact of Privatisation on Entrepreneurial Development in Bangladesh Agriculture', *Bangladesh Development Studies*, **14** (2), 1–20.

Rahman, A. (1986) 'Poverty Alleviation and the Most Disadvantaged Groups in Bangladesh Agriculture', *Bangladesh Development Studies*, **14**(1), 29-58.

Rahman, A. (1994), 'The Impact of Shrimp Culture on the Coastal Environment', in A.A. Rahman, R. Haider, S. Huq and E.G. Jansen (eds), *Environment and Development*, Vol. 1, Dhaka: University Press Ltd., pp. 499–524.

Rahman, A., Islam, M.A. Azad, L. and Islam, K.S. (1995), *Shrimp Culture and Environment in the Coastal Region*, Dhaka: Bangladesh Institute of Development Studies.

Rahman, A.K.A. (1993) 'Socio-economic Issues in Coastal Fisheries Management of Bangladesh', Paper presented at the IPFC Symposium, 23–26 November 1993, Indo-pacific Fisheries Commission, FAO, Bangkok.

Rahman, H.Z. (1995), 'Conclusions' in H.Z. Rahman and Mahabub Hossain (eds), *Rethinking Rural Poverty: Bangladesh as a Case Study*, Dhaka; Bangladesh Institute of Development Studies, pp. 283–98.

Rahman, H.Z. (1998), 'Rethinking Land Reform' in R. Faruqee (ed.), *Bangladesh Agriculture in the 21st Century*, Dhaka: University Press Ltd., pp. 67–79.

Rahman, H.Z. (2000), 'A Report Card on Mr Kibria', *Daily Star*, 23 June.

Rahman, R. I. (1991), *An Analysis of Employment and Earnings of Poor Women in Rural Bangladesh*, unpublished Ph.D. thesis, Canberra: Australian National University.

Rahman, H.Z. and Mahabub Hossain (1995), *Rethinking Rural Poverty: Bangladesh as a Case Study*, Dhaka: Bangladesh Institute of Development Studies.

Rashid, H. (1977), *Geography of Bangladesh*, Dhaka: University Press Ltd.

Ray, B. (1998), 'Farakka Treaty – Expectations may not be Fulfilled', *Statesman*, January 16 and 17 (Calcutta).

Redclift, M. (1984), *Sustainable Development: Exploring the Contradictions*, London: Methuen.

Repetto, R., Magrath, W., Wells, M., Beer, C. and Rossini, F. (1989), *Wasting Resources: Natural Resource in National Income Accounts*, Washington, DC: World Resources Institute.

Robinson, E.A.G. (1973), *Economic Prospects for Bangladesh*, London: Overseas Development Institute.

Rosenberry, B. (1995), *World Shrimp Farming 1995: Annual Report*, San Diego: Shrimp News International.

Roy, K.C. and Tisdell, C.A. (1993), 'Poverty among Females in Rural India: Gender-based Deprivation and Technological Change', *Economic Studies*, **31** (4), 257–79.

Roy, K.C., Tisdell, C.A. and Blomqvist, H.C. (1996), 'Economic Development and Women: An Overview of Issues', in K.C. Roy, C.A. Tisdell, and H.C. Blomqvist (eds), *Economic Development and Women in the World Community*, West Point, CT.: Praeger, pp. 97–124.

Roy, M.K. (1987), *Forestry Sector and Development in Bangladesh*, Master of Forestry Thesis, Australian National University, Canberra.

Safilios-Rothschild, C. and Mahmud, S. (1989), *Women's Roles in Agriculture – Present Trends and Potential for Growth*, Monograph for Agriculture Sector Review, Dhaka: UNDP and UNIFEM.

Samuelson, P.A. (1948), *Foundations of Economic Analysis*, Cambridge, MA: Harvard University Press.

Sawant, S.D. (1983), 'Investigation of the Hypothesis of Deceleration in Indian Agriculture', *Indian Journal of Agricultural Economics*, **38** (4), 475–96.

Sen, A. (1960), *Choice of Techniques: An Aspect of Planned Economic Development*, Oxford: Clarendon Press.

Sen, A. (1981), *Poverty and Famines: An Essay on Entitlement and Deprivation*, Oxford: Clarendon Press.

Sen, A. (1983), 'Poor – Relatively Speaking', *Oxford Economic Papers*, **35**, 153–69.

Sen, A. (1999), 'Assessing Human Development' in UNDP, *Human Development Report*, New York: Oxford University Press, p.2.

Sen, A. (2000), 'Will There be Any Hope for the Poor?', *Time Europe*, **155**(21), 24-25.

Sen, B. (1995), 'Rural Poverty Trends, 1963–64 to 1989–90', in H.Z. Rahman and Mahabub Hossain (eds), *Rethinking Rural Poverty: Bangladesh as a Case Study*, Dhaka; Bangladesh Institute of Development Studies, pp. 39–54.

Sengupta, A. (1998), 'Growth with Equity: Humanising Development Economics', *AMITECH, News from Bangladesh*, http://Bangladesh-web.com/news, 7 August.

Shahabuddin, Q. and Rahman, R.I. (1998), *Agricultural Growth and Stagnation in Bangladesh*, Dhaka: Centre on Integrated Rural Development for Asia and the Pacific.

Shand, R.T. (1996), 'Foreword', in M. Alauddin, and S. Hasan (eds), *Bangladesh: Economy, People, and the Environment*, Economics Conference Monograph Series 1, Brisbane, Australia: Department of Economics, The University of Queensland, pp.ix-x.

Shand, R.T. (1999a), 'South Asia in Reform Mode: Experiences, Obstacles and Prospects', in M. Alauddin and S. Hasan (eds), *Development, Governance and the Environment in South Asia: A Focus on Bangladesh*, London: Macmillan, pp. 35–67.

Shand, R.T. (ed.) (1999b), *Economic Liberalisation in South Asia*, New Delhi: Macmillan.

Shand, R.T. and Alauddin, M. (1997), *Economic Profiles in South Asia: Bangladesh*, Canberra, Australia: South Asia Research Centre, The Australian National University.

Siddiqui, A.K.M.T. (1998), 'Issues in Agricultural Extension', in R. Faruqee (ed.), *Bangladesh Agriculture in the 21st Century*, Dhaka: University Press Ltd., pp. 255–66.

Smith, D.V. (1973) 'Opportunity for Village Development: The Tanks of Bangladesh', *Bangladesh Economic Review*, **1** (3), 298–308.

Sobhan, R. (1968), *Basic Democracies Works Programme and Rural Development in East Pakistan*, Dacca: Bureau of Economic Research, University of Dacca.

Sobhan, R. (1993), *Bangladesh: Problems of Governance*, Dhaka: University Press Limited.

Sobhan, R. (1998), 'Structural Adjustment, Macro-Policies and Poverty', in A.A. Ahmed *et al.* (eds), *Environment and Poverty: Key Linkages for Global Sustainable Development*, Dhaka: University Press Ltd., pp. 105–106.

SRDI (1995), *Reconnaissance Soil Survey*, Dhaka: Soil Resources Development Institute.

Staub, W.J. and Blasé, M.G. (1974), 'Induced Technical Change in Developing Agricultures: Implication for Income Distribution and Development', *Journal of Developing Areas*, **8**(4), 581–95.

Task Force Report (1991), *Report of the Task Forces on Bangladesh Development Strategies for the 1990s, Environment Policy, Vol. 4*, Dhaka: University Press Ltd.

Thirlwall, A.P. (1994), *Growth and Development with Special Reference to Developing Countries*, London: Macmillan.

Tisdell, C.A. (1972), *Microeconomics: The Theory of Economic Allocation*, Sydney: John Wiley and Sons.

Tisdell, C.A. (1996) 'Discrimination and Changes in the Status of Women with Economic Development: General Views and Theories', in K.C. Roy, C.A. Tisdell, and H. C. Blomqvist (eds), *Economic Development and Women in the World Community*, West Point, Conn.: Praeger, pp. 25–36.

Tisdell, C.A. (1999), 'Socio-Economic Policy and Change in South Asia: A Review Concentrating on Bangladesh', in M. Alauddin and S. Hasan (eds), *Development, Governance and the Environment in South Asia: A Focus on Bangladesh*, London: Macmillan, pp. 17–33.

Tisdell, C.A. and Alauddin, M. (1997), 'The Environment and Development in South Asia', in K.C. Roy, H.C. Blomqvist, and I. Hossain, (eds), *Development That Lasts*, New Delhi: New Age International, pp. 139–50.

Tisdell, C.A. and Dragun, A.K. (1999), 'Agricultural Sustainability: The Impact of Trade Liberalisation', in A.K. Dragun and C.A. Tisdell (eds), *Sustainable Agriculture and Environment: Globalisation and the Impact of Trade Liberalisation*, Cheltenham, UK and Northampton, MA, USA: Edward Elgar, pp. 1–6.

Todaro, M.P (1992), *Economics for a Developing World*, New York: Longman.

Townsend, P. (1979), *Poverty in the United Kingdom*, Harmondsworth: Penguin.

UNCED (1993) *Agenda 21: Programme of Action for Sustainable Development: Rio Declaration of Environment and Development*, New York: United Nations Committee on Environment and Development.

UNDP (1991), *Human Development Report 1991*, New York: Oxford University Press.

UNDP (1996), *Human Development Report 1996*, New York: Oxford University Press.

UNDP (1997), *Human Development Report 1997*, New York: Oxford University Press.

UNDP (1998), *Human Development Report 1998*, New York: Oxford University Press.

UNDP (1999), *Human Development Report 1999*, New York: Oxford University Press.

Vyas, V.S. (1995), 'The Agrarian Structure and Sustainable Livelihoods of the Tribal People in Indian Forestry', in I. Ahmed and J. A. Doeleman (eds), *Beyond Rio: Environmental Crisis and Sustainable Livelihoods in the Third World*, London: Macmillan, pp. 289–316.

World Bank (1982), 'Bangladesh: Foodgrain Self-Sufficiency and Crop Diversification (Annexes and Statistical Appendix)', Report no. 3953-BD, Washington, DC: World Bank.

World Bank (1990), *World Development Report 1990*, New York: Oxford University Press.

World Bank (1996), *Environment Matters*, Fall.

World Bank (1997), *World Development Report 1997*, Washington, DC: World Bank.

WRI and CIDE (1990) 'Bangladesh: Environment and Natural Resource Assessment', Final Report, Prepared for US Agency for International Development (USAID), Washington, DC: World Resources Institute and Center for International Development and Environment.

WRI, UNEP and UNDP (1994), 'World Resources 1994–95', New York: Oxford University Press published for World Resources Institute, United Nations Environmental Program and United Nations Development Program.

WRI, UNEP, UNDP and World Bank (1997), *World Resources 1996–97*, New York: Oxford University Press published for World Resources Institute, United Nations Environmental Program, United Nations Development Program and the World Bank.

Index

Abdullah, A.A., 6, 78, 162, 176, 178
Abed, F.H., 239
Adaptive Research, 212
Agarwal, B., 231
Agro-ecological zones (AEZs), 5, 188, 199
Ahmad, Q.K., 4, 188
Ahmed, M., 100
Ahmed, N.R., 233
Ahmed, Raisuddin, 4, 253
Ahmed, Reaz, 215, 222, 248
Ahmed, Z, 216
Ahooga-Patel, K, . 231
Alagarswami, K., 125
Alam, J., 6, 75, 88, 89, 95-8, 112, 117, 120-2, 136, 139, 140, 151, 244
Alauddin., M., 1, 4-7, 34-7, 39, 41, 49, 52, 55, 57-8, 61, 64, 67, 72, 98, 122-9, 146, 155-6, 181, 210-2, 214-6, 222, 224, 226, 231, 235-8, 240-9, 252
Ali, M.O., 155
Anderson, J.R., 39
Applied Research, 212
Arndt, T.M., 224
Asaduzzaman, M., 4, 125, 182, 209, 210, 248, 254
Ashrayan (the Shelter), 254

Bangladesh Agricultural Research Council, 214
Bangladesh Agricultural Research Institute, 211

Bangladesh Rice Research Institute, 211
Bangladesh Sugar Cane Institute, 211
Banik, A., 157
Bardhan, P.K., 165
Basic Democracy, 161, 178
Basic Research, 212
Beneria, L, 236
Bernstein, H.,7, 225, 227
Bifani, P., 236, 237
Black, C.E., 241
Blasé, M.G. 57
Bose, S.R., 1
Bowonder, B., 155
Boyce, J.K., 178
Bramer, H., 6, 10, 11, 12, 15, 24
Brandon, C., 3,

Cain, M., 157
Capability poverty measure, 229, 241
Capacity Transfer, 39
Chakraborty, D.,181, 205
Chakravarty, S., 3
Chambers, R.G., 226
Chaudhury, R.H., 233
Christensen, L.R., 49
Crow, B., 210

Dalrymple, D.G., 224
Dantwala, M. L., 122
Deforestation, 6
Demographic transition, 3
Design Transfer, 38